Exam Ref 70-413 Designing and Implementing a Server Infrastructure, Second Edition

Paul Ferrill
Tim Ferrill

PUBLISHED BY
Microsoft Press
A Division of Microsoft Corporation
One Microsoft Way
Redmond, Washington 98052-6399

Library of Congress Control Number: 2014935079
ISBN: 978-0-7356-8540-6

Printed and bound in the United States of America.

First Printing

Microsoft Press books are available through booksellers and distributors worldwide. If you need support related to this book, email Microsoft Press Book Support at mspinput@microsoft.com. Please tell us what you think of this book at http://www.microsoft.com/learning/booksurvey.

Acquisitions Editor: Anne Hamilton
Developmental Editor: Karen Szall
Editorial Production: Box Twelve Communications
Technical Reviewer: Brian Svidergol
Cover: Twist Creative • Seattle

Contents

What do you think of this book? We want to hear from you!

Microsoft is interested in hearing your feedback so we can continually improve our
books and learning resources for you. To participate in a brief online survey, please visit:

www.microsoft.com/learning/booksurvey/

Chapter 4   Design and implement an Active Directory infrastructure (logical)   193

Chapter 5 Design and implement an Active Directory infrastructure (physical) 259

What do you think of this book? We want to hear from you!

Microsoft is interested in hearing your feedback so we can continually improve our
books and learning resources for you. To participate in a brief online survey, please visit:

www.microsoft.com/learning/booksurvey/

Introduction

This book is written for IT professionals who want to earn the MCSE: Server Infrastructure certification for Windows Server 2012 R2. This certification requires that you've passed the following three exams, which have already earned you the MCSA: Windows Server 2012 certification:

- **70-410** Installing and Configuring Windows Server 2012
- **70-411** Administering Windows Server 2012
- **70-412** Configuring Advanced Windows Server 2012 Services

Alternatively if you hold one of the qualifying certifications from the Windows Server 2008 certification track, you can take the following exam in order to upgrade your existing certification to the MCSA: Windows Server 2012:

- **70-417** Upgrading Your Skills to MCSA Windows Server 2012

The 70-417 exam is basically a consolidation of the three exams required for the MCSA certification, primarily focused on changes and new features. Once you've achieved the MCSA: Windows Server 2012 certification, two additional exams must be passed in order to gain the MCSE: Server Infrastructure certification:

- **70-413** Designing and Implementing a Server Infrastructure
- **70-414** Implementing an Advanced Server Infrastructure

This book is primarily focused on the 70-413 exam, which indicates a couple of things. You can safely assume that the knowledge tested in the first three exams contain some prerequisite information for the 70-413 exams. In fact much of the content in this book (and the 70-413 exam) will draw directly upon the information you've already learned, but will require you to utilize this knowledge specifically from a design perspective. One thing you should pay special attention to throughout this book are requirements, as they will often drive what you can and can't do in certain situations.

As you are probably aware, the Windows Server 2012 R2 release introduced several major features, as well as updates and changes to existing features in Windows Server 2012. Both Windows Server 2012 and Windows Server 2012 R2 will be tested in the 70-413 exam, and you should be ready to answer questions asking which version is required to enable a certain feature.

The 70-413 exam tests your understanding of five domains and 20 objectives, encompassing critical services and features that form the basis of an enterprise server infrastructure.

For the purpose of this book, the focus is primarily on new features and capabilities in both Windows Server 2012 and Windows Server 2012 R2, though many of the core features and services have existed in previous versions of Windows Server. Because the 70-413 exam is focused on the design phase of building an enterprise infrastructure, this book emphasizes the theory behind effective design—not the step-by-step or hands-on knowledge you'll likely find in the other exams.

While we've made every effort to cover all of the information being tested in the 70-413 exam, only the Microsoft exam team has access to the exam questions. This makes it impossible to cover each question or exam topic individually. Additionally, Microsoft commonly adds new questions to the exam, and some of the technologies covered here (such as those pertaining to Microsoft Azure or Windows PowerShell) are receiving updates at an ever-increasing frequency. For up-to-date information on these fast-moving technologies, both real-world and for the exam, use the resources provided by Microsoft at MSDN and TechNet.

This book is not a replacement for real-world experience; you will want to get your hands dirty and work with some of the services and tools covered in this book in order to fully understand how they function. If you don't have a lab environment available for your use, TechNet offers virtual labs, which can be an indispensable tool for getting hands-on time with the roles and features.

Microsoft certifications

Microsoft certifications distinguish you by proving your command of a broad set of skills and experience with current Microsoft products and technologies. The exams and corresponding certifications are developed to validate your mastery of critical competencies as you design and develop, or implement and support, solutions with Microsoft products and technologies both on-premises and in the cloud. Certification brings a variety of benefits to the individual and to employers and organizations.

> **MORE INFO** **ALL MICROSOFT CERTIFICATIONS**
>
> For information about Microsoft certifications, including a full list of available certifications, go to *http://www.microsoft.com/learning/en/us/certification/cert-default.aspx*.

Acknowledgments

Paul Ferrill   To my wife, Sandy, for your tireless support of me and of our family. I could not have done this without you. You truly are a precious gift. To our children, not the least of which is my co-author Tim. It has been a joy to get to work together with my son on this project and I appreciate his taking on the bulk of the writing.

Thanks to the Microsoft Press team for the quality support and consistent professional approach to a tough process. Writing a book is hard work and this book would not have been completed without the efforts of Karen Szall, Anne Hamilton, and the project management of Jeff Riley. Brian Svidergol's technical expertise made a tremendous difference in the communication of a multitude of topics.

Tim Ferrill   This book would never have been possible without the frequent and consistent assistance from the Microsoft Press team. The clarity, professionalism, and attention to detail made this process much smoother than it could have been. Thanks to Anne Hamilton for her assistance in getting everything rolling and answering any questions along the way. To Karen Szall for her patience, and for her communication skills and tact when she had to pass along the news that we had more work to do. To Jeff Riley for his willingness to help a beginner along, and his constant support when I started to become overwhelmed. A special thanks to Brian Svidergol, whose knowledge and experience with Windows Server and the enterprise is twice what I could ever hope to obtain.

I'd also like to thank my parents, Paul and Sandy Ferrill. Dad shared his love of technology with me, the passion to try new things, and the propensity to push buttons to see what happens. Mom was my teacher. This book is due, in part, to the English papers that came back bloodied and bruised from her crrection (sic) pen.

Finally, this book could never have happened without my beautiful wife, Jodi, being the ultimate example of patience. Not only did she give up her own time with me, she provided time to write while she was corralling five kids and going through a pregnancy. Jodi is my hero.

Errata, updates, & book support

We've made every effort to ensure the accuracy of this book and its companion content. You can access updates to this book—in the form of a list of submitted errata and their related corrections—at:

> http://aka.ms/ER413R2

If you discover an error that is not already listed, please submit it to us at the same page.

If you need additional support, email Microsoft Press Book Support at mspinput@microsoft.com.

Please note that product support for Microsoft software and hardware is not offered through the previous addresses. For help with Microsoft software or hardware, go to http://support.microsoft.com.

We want to hear from you

At Microsoft Press, your satisfaction is our top priority and your feedback is our most valuable asset. Please tell us what you think of this book at:

http://aka.ms/tellpress

The survey is short, and we read every one of your comments and ideas. Thanks in advance for your input!

Stay in touch

Let's keep the conversation going! We're on Twitter: *http://twitter.com/MicrosoftPress*.

Preparing for the exam

Microsoft certification exams are a great way to build your resume and let the world know about your level of expertise. Certification exams validate your on-the-job experience and product knowledge. While there is no substitution for on-the-job experience, preparation through study and hands-on practice can help you prepare for the exam. We recommend that you round out your exam preparation plan by using a combination of available study materials and courses. For example, you might use the Exam Ref and another study guide for your "at home" preparation and take a Microsoft Official Curriculum course for the classroom experience. Choose the combination that you think works best for you.

CHAPTER 1

Plan and deploy a server infrastructure

The first step or phase in the process of any major project is planning. Building a comprehensive plan takes time and input from all parties with a vested interest in the project. Planning for a new server deployment requires knowledge of the existing environment and a good understanding of the overall IT goals and objectives. After you have the information you need, it is just a matter of putting the right pieces into place. With Windows Server 2012 R2, you can deploy both physical and virtual servers. System Center 2012 R2 Virtual Machine Manager (VMM) is the tool for deploying and managing all pieces of a virtualization infrastructure. File and storage services must also have a part in the overall plan to ensure that adequate resources are available and that new capabilities in Windows Server 2012 R2, such as storage tiering, are evaluated for possible incorporation.

> **IMPORTANT**
>
> ***Have you read page xiv?***
>
> It contains valuable information regarding the skills you need to pass the exam.

Objectives in this chapter:

- Objective 1.1: Design and plan for an automated server installation strategy
- Objective 1.2: Implement a server deployment infrastructure
- Objective 1.3: Plan and implement server upgrade and migration
- Objective 1.4: Plan and deploy Virtual Machine Manager services
- Objective 1.5: Plan and implement file and storage services

Objective 1.1: Design and plan for an automated server installation strategy

Automation is a vital part of keeping any IT infrastructure running smoothly. Microsoft provides a variety of tools to help the IT administrator automate almost every task required to get the job done. Specific tools for deploying server images include the Deployment Image Servicing and Management (DISM) utility, the Windows Assessment and Deployment Kit (ADK) and Windows Deployment Services (WDS).

Building the right deployment strategy depends a great deal on the number of systems to be deployed and their location. Installing a full blown deployment infrastructure would not be appropriate for small organizations with a limited number of servers. All automated deployment strategies require the use of a baseline image containing the necessary drivers for the target hardware or, in the case of virtual images, a base operating system image. Understanding how to create these baseline images will be important to the success of any deployment.

Other key parts of a server deployment strategy include the use of staging servers and proper network configuration to support the transfer of everything necessary to get a system up and running regardless of location.

This objective covers how to:

- Understand design considerations for deployment images
- Design a server implementation using Windows Assessment and Deployment Kit (ADK)
- Design a virtual server deployment
- Plan for deploying servers to Microsoft Azure IaaS
- Plan for deploying servers using App Controller and Windows PowerShell
- Plan for multicast deployment
- Plan for Windows Deployment Services (WDS)

Understanding design considerations for deployment images

Before you get started with building images, it's important to understand the most common scenarios for deploying them, including deciding whether to use thin or thick images, deciding how much automation to use (zero touch, light touch, and so on), how many images you need for a given scenario, and the best way to design the deployment infrastructure based on a given scenario. You can then move on to actually building images to meet the specific scenarios necessary for your implementation.

One of the key aspects of crafting a plan for an automated server deployment capability is to build a baseline or reference image to use as a part of the installation process. Bare metal deployments require one baseline image from which to boot and one for the actual installation. In this sense, a bare metal machine has no operating system installed or has its existing operating system totally replaced. For virtual deployment scenarios, it is possible to create a baseline virtual machine without going through the entire installation process because the underlying hardware doesn't change. Other pieces of the deployment puzzle include automated answer files and a networking infrastructure that supports Preboot eXecution Environment (PXE).

Figure 1-1 shows the process of designing a Windows image as outlined in the help file that accompanies the Windows Assessment and Deployment Kit (ADK). Physical images require more planning and a good understanding of the target environment. Any non-standard driver requirements need to be identified first to ensure a successful deployment.

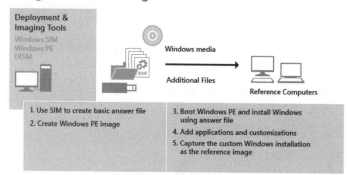

First, install and customize a Windows image. Then add branding, drivers, and other customizations to Windows. This step produces a *reference image* that represents all of the basic customizations that are used on the computers you create.

FIGURE 1-1 The help file from the Windows ADK Quick Start guide

Creating images

Several steps are required when creating images for use in operating system deployment. A typical deployment scenario uses two types of images: boot and install. Boot images typically use Windows PE to initialize the hardware prior to installing an operating system. Install images contain everything necessary to install the operating system.

One of the primary tools used to create and manipulate images is Deployment Image Servicing and Management (DISM). DISM comes with every version of Windows since Windows 7 and Windows Server 2008. Use DISM to perform the following tasks:

- Capture an image and save it as a WIM file
- List all images within a WIM, VHD, or VHDX file
- Manage several images in a single WIM file by appending, removing, or enumerating the images
- Prepare a Windows PE image
- List information about a Windows PE image
- Mount a Windows image
- List specific information about an image mounted from a WIM, VHD, or VHDX file, including where it is mounted, the mount status, and the index of each image in a WIM file

- List all drivers in an image or information about a specific driver
- Add out-of-box or boot-critical drivers to support new hardware
- Add operating-system updates such as hotfixes and Windows features
- Add or remove a language pack and configure international settings
- List all international settings and languages in an image
- Troubleshoot imaging problems using the integrated status and logging
- Manage multiple image versions
- List all features in a package or specific information about a Windows feature
- Check the applicability of a Windows Installer MSP file
- Update multiple Windows editions by updating a single image
- Upgrade to a later edition of Windows
- List all the Windows editions to which an image can be upgraded
- Apply settings using an Unattend.xml answer file
- Split a large WIM file into several smaller files to fit on selected media

Windows PE is a small operating system used as the basis of a boot image to install, deploy, and repair Windows. Tools for building Windows PE–based images come as part of the Windows ADK and should be downloaded and installed on a system running Windows 8, Windows 8.1, Windows Server 2012, or Windows Server 2012 R2. A boot.wim file uses Windows PE as the operating system and typically includes a setup executable and a WDS client.

The basic version of boot.wim can be found on either a Windows installation DVD or inside an ISO file of the Windows installation media. (You find boot.wim in the sources folder of either source.) This base boot.wim file can be used to create customized boot images for use by WDS. These customized boot images can be created using either the capture or discover method. A capture image is typically taken after the operating system and all roles, features, and applications have been installed.

The System Preparation (Sysprep) tool must be run on the target system prior to booting with the capture image. Sysprep converts a generalized system into a specialized state and back again. The resulting image can be deployed to any computer. Using Sysprep on an installed physical or virtual machine removes any information such as a security identifier (SID), making it possible to use a customized installation as a base image for other systems. Using the capture image on a physical system works particularly well when you have many installations to accomplish on the same type of hardware.

It is possible to convert WIM files directly to a virtual hard disk (VHD) with Windows PowerShell using a free tool. The latest version of this tool as of this writing is 6.3 and is available for download from the Microsoft Script Center site (*http://technet.microsoft.com/ en-us/scriptcenter/bb410849.aspx*) under the name Convert-WindowsImage.ps1. Microsoft

Consulting Services currently maintains the script, providing updates and bug fixes when necessary. Use the following command to launch a UI option and complete steps 1 through 4 in the dialog box to configure the VHD.

```
.\Convert-WindowsImage.ps1 -ShowUI
```

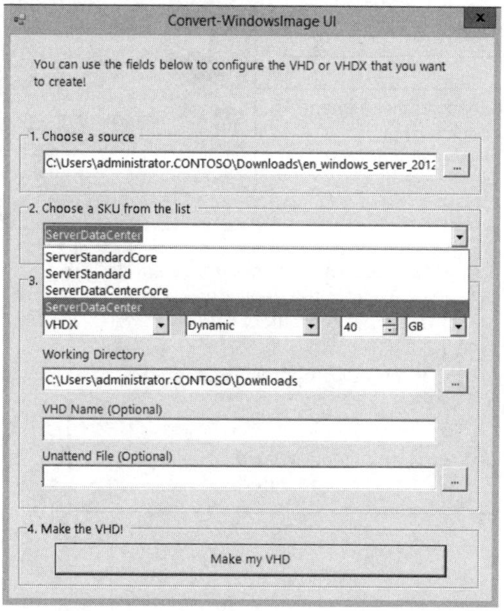

FIGURE 1-2 The Convert-WindowsImage PowerShell script

After you choose a source file in step 1, step 2 gives you the option to select from a list of versions (refer to Figure 1-2) for the stock-keeping unit (SKU) or type of image you want to create. Options include Windows Server 2012 R2 Standard with GUI or Core and Windows Server 2012 R2 Datacenter with GUI or Core. In step 3, you also have the option to choose to create a VHD or VHDX file. At the time of this writing, you must select VHD if you plan to push the virtual machine (VM) to Azure. With step 4, you apply your selections and create the VHD.

Microsoft Deployment Toolkit

Another free tool for automating the deployment process is the Microsoft Deployment Toolkit (MDT). MDT works in conjunction with the Windows ADK and requires it to be installed for some operations. Figure 1-3 shows an image from the MDT help file that describes the deployment process quite well. The MDT help file has a wealth of information about each of the steps outlined in the diagram.

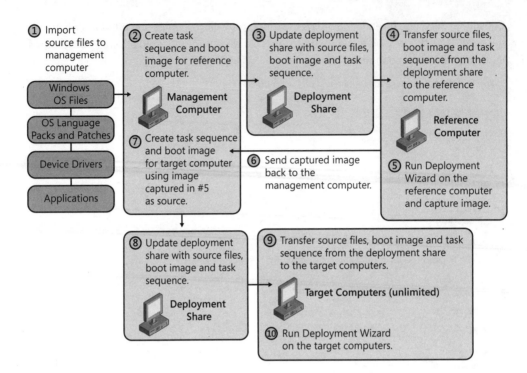

FIGURE 1-3 The ten steps to prepare for deployment

After the MDT is installed, you have access to the Deployment Workbench application with a list of capabilities and features. Figure 1-4 shows what the basic Deployment Workbench application looks like. If you look closely, you see a download operation in progress for the Windows Automated Installation Kit (x64). The Deployment Workbench requires a number of additional tools that must be installed in order to perform certain tasks. For convenience the Deployment Workbench makes it possible to download and install these additional pieces directly from the main Components window.

The Windows Automated Installation Kit (WAIK), which is required for performing some operations, can be downloaded and installed from the Deployment Workbench. Many of the role migrations require a deployment share to use for moving files between source and target systems. The Deployment Workbench configures a new share with appropriate permissions for you by using a wizard to prompt for all required information.

To launch the New Deployment Share Wizard, right-click Deployment in the console tree and choose New Deployment Share. Individual pages prompt for a path, file share, and de-scriptive name. The Options page (see Figure 1-5) allows you to configure default options for processes such as entering a product key and prompting for a local Administrator password. Click Next to see a Summary page and then a Progress page as a new share is created and all files are copied to the share.

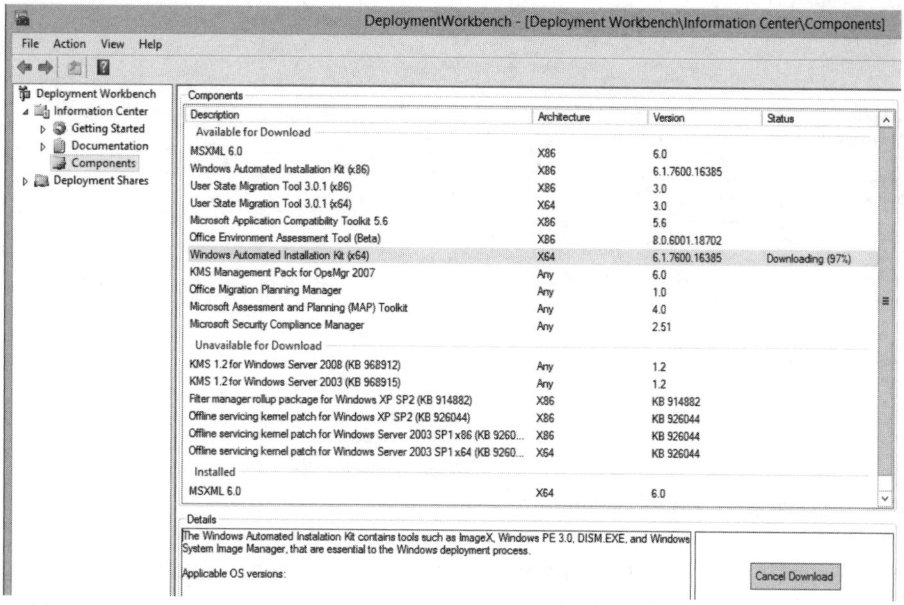

FIGURE 1-4 The Deployment Workbench

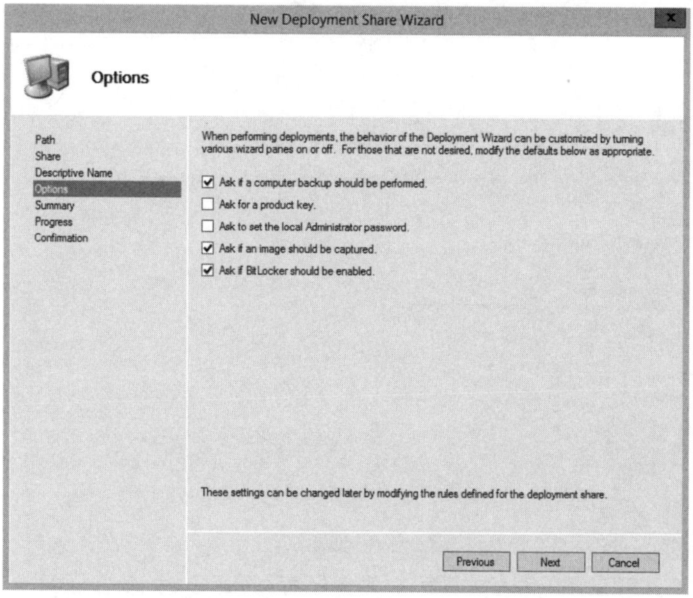

FIGURE 1-5 The Options page of the New Deployment Share Wizard

After the wizard completes, you should see a number of directories and files listed in the DeploymentShare, as shown in Figure 1-6.

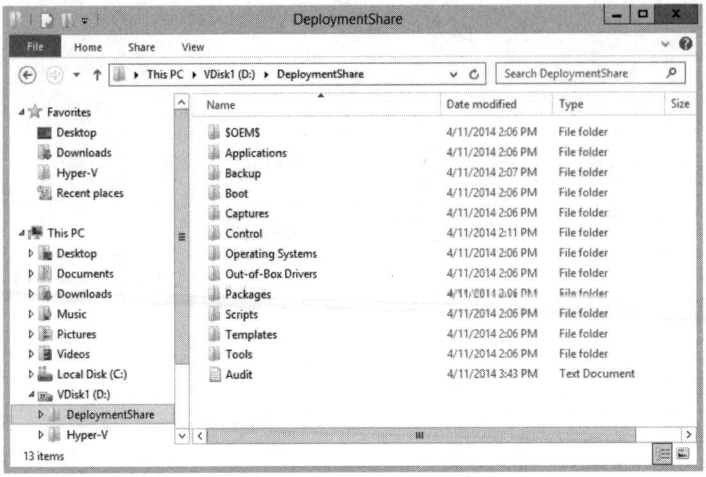

FIGURE 1-6 The DeploymentShare directory

The last thing you might want to do is import an operating system image for use in later steps. Figure 1-7 shows the initial page of the Import Operating System Wizard. You can see the available options are a full set of source files, a custom image, or a WDS image.

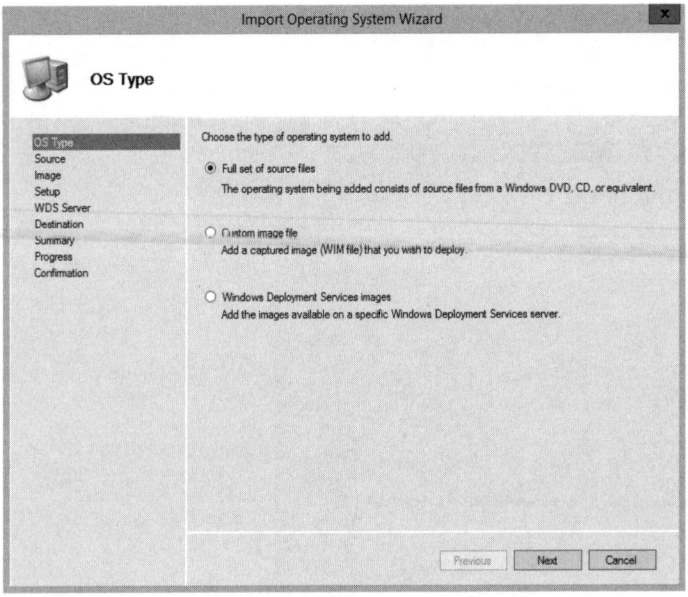

FIGURE 1-7 The Import Operating System Wizard

This wizard steps you through the process of importing an existing operating system from either a physical DVD or a mounted ISO file.

Using the Windows Assessment and Deployment Kit

The latest Microsoft release of the Windows ADK was published in October of 2013 and includes a number of useful tools. The tools of most interest for the purposes of this book include the Deployment Tools and Windows PE. You can use the assessment tool to look for any potential issues with hardware and drivers.

> *MORE INFO* **WINDOWS PE**
>
> For more detailed information on Windows PE, visit *http://technet.microsoft.com/en-us/library/hh825110.aspx*. For a complete technical reference on all the Windows Deployment Tools, see *http://technet.microsoft.com/en-us/library/hh825039.aspx*.

Understanding how to use the different tools in the Windows ADK is an important part of a successful deployment and crucial for passing the certification exam.

EXAM TIP

The Windows ADK is used to create customized images and knowledge of it is a skill you must demonstrate for the test. Specifically, you should know how to use the Windows System Image Manager (SIM) to create answer files and Windows PE images.

The process of installing a Windows operating system involves answering a series of questions that would typically be answered in an interactive fashion. Creating an answer file provides a way to respond to the questions in an automated fashion for an unattended installation.

Windows SIM is a free tool from Microsoft that simplifies the process of creating an answer file. To use Windows SIM, you need an image file (WIM). It also requires a catalog file that will be created if not found. After the initial steps have completed, you should see a dialog box similar to the one in Figure 1-8.

Note that the output of the Windows SIM tool is an XML file. If you use an answer file to specify information such as passwords, they will be stored in the clear unless you do something to obfuscate them. The latest version of Windows SIM has Hide Sensitive Data selected by default on the Tools menu.

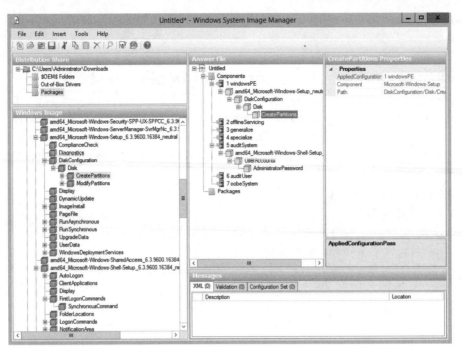

FIGURE 1-8 The Windows SIM tool

Creating a new answer file consists of picking specific components from the Windows image you want to customize. Figure 1-8 shows two customizations added at this point in the process: one for creating a partition and the second to specify an Administrator password. Other possibilities include adding drivers that might not be in the standard distribution or adding custom logon instructions. After the customization is complete, choose File and then Save to save the XML file and validate the answers in the process. Any errors are displayed in the Validation tab.

Planning for deploying servers to Microsoft Azure IaaS

Microsoft Azure represents an ideal target for moving specific workloads up to the cloud. Infrastructure as a Service (IaaS) is a cloud computing service model in which a service provider owns and maintains hardware and equipment that you can use, usually paying on a per-use basis.

The two primary Microsoft services available on Azure as of this writing include Microsoft Active Directory and SQL Database. VMs make it possible to deploy any workload in addition to these services. A custom application can be deployed to Azure as a VM instance connecting to a SQL Server database and using Azure Active Directory for all authentication. This use case represents Azure taking advantage of the capability to scale individual VMs to meet demand as necessary.

Azure provides a number of preconfigured Windows Server images in the Image Gallery available for use as part of your deployment. You can also upload your own images as long as they are in the VHD format. Creating a new VM from the gallery uses the Azure management portal New function (see Figure 1-9). Sign in to the management portal, click on the New tab and then choose Compute, Virtual Machine, and then From Gallery to start the wizard.

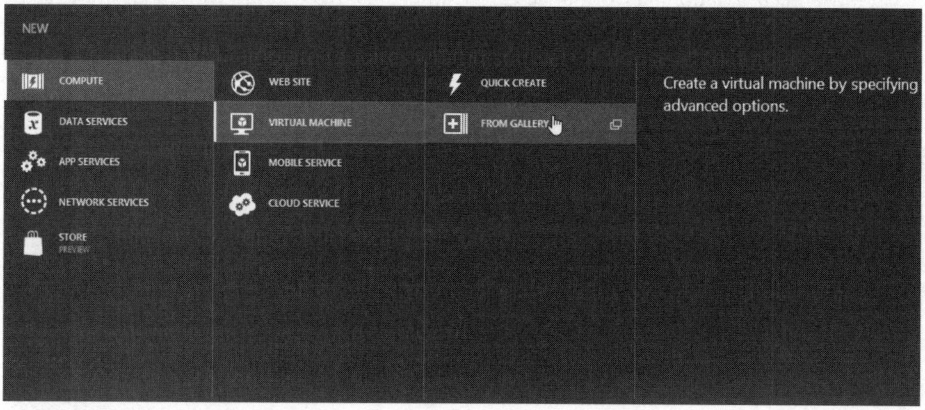

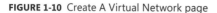

FIGURE 1-9 Creating a new VM

An Azure virtual network includes the capability to create a private network resident exclusively within Azure or connected to an on-premises network using a site-to-site virtual private network (VPN). A new network on Azure can be created by using either the management portal or with Microsoft Azure PowerShell. In the management portal, click the New tab, choose Networks, Virtual Network, and then Custom Create to start the configuration wizard. Figure 1-10 shows the Virtual Network Details page for creating a new virtual network.

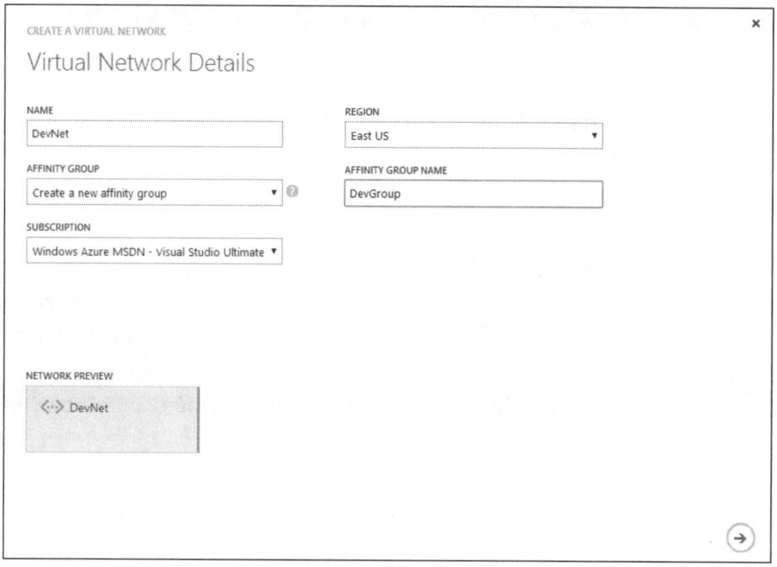

FIGURE 1-10 Create A Virtual Network page

Two additional pages let you specify a custom Domain Name System (DNS) provider and finally the range of IP addresses for the network. After a network is defined, you can provision VMs connected exclusively to that network. Another Azure configuration point concerns selecting a specific datacenter or region for VMs and websites. Azure has a construct called an *affinity group* that provides a mechanism to group services together and restrict them to a specific geographical location. Performance can be improved by locating workloads in the same datacenter or near the greatest number of users. An affinity group can be set by using either the management portal or Windows PowerShell. Figure 1-11 shows the management portal and the Settings page.

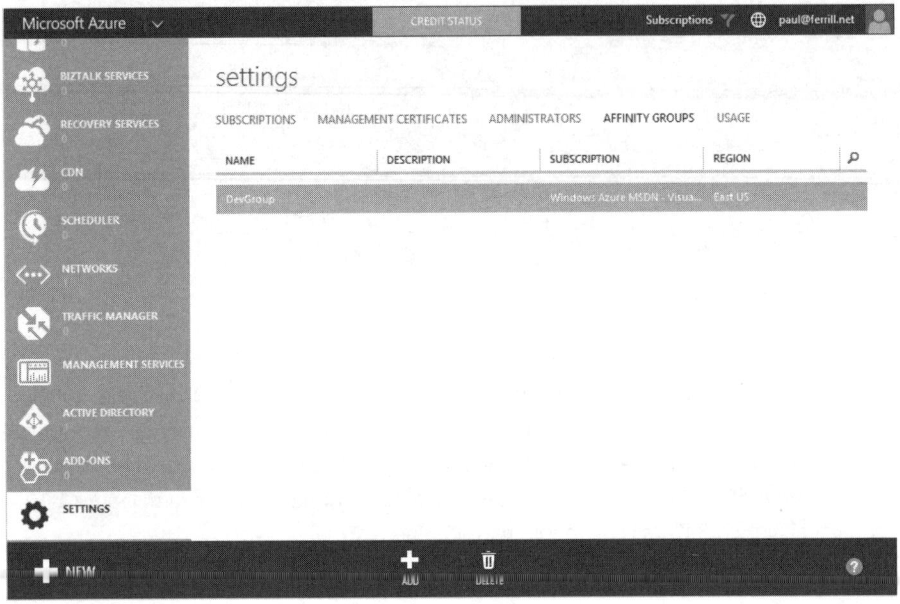

FIGURE 1-11 The Settings page for Affinity Groups

The Settings page includes the Affinity Groups item for creating new named groupings. A number of networking issues should be addressed during the deployment planning stages. These issues include the need for a site-to-site VPN connection and IP address issues to include name resolution. Azure networking includes support for any private address ranges to include 10.0.0.0/8, 172.16.0.0/12, and 192.168.0.0/16.

Choosing where to source your DNS servers depends on your overall network topology. For a hybrid on-premises and off-premises solution, you want to provide redundancy on both sides of the firewall. The Azure UI provides a convenient way to configure the main information such as the DNS server name and address and the IP address space. Figure 1-12 shows an example of this page.

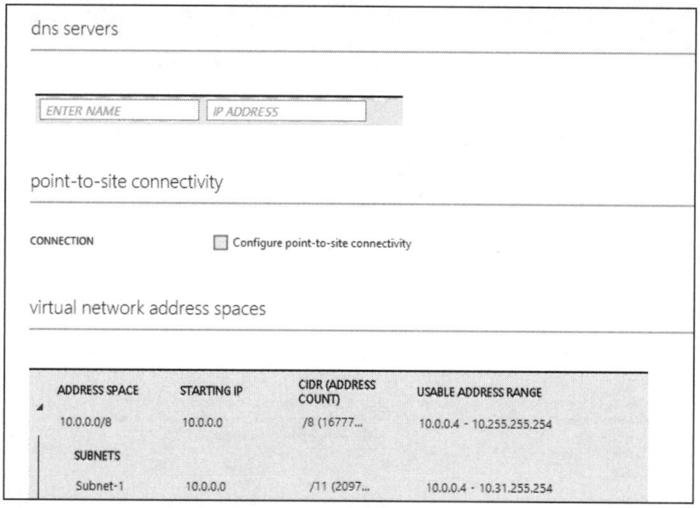

FIGURE 1-12 The Azure network Settings page

Planning for deploying servers using System Center App Controller and Windows PowerShell

With System Center 2012, Microsoft introduced App Controller, which is a tool to help configure, deploy, and manage VMs on-premises or in the cloud. App Controller provides a number of automation capabilities for deployment not found in any other Microsoft product. If you plan to use this tool, you need a number of supporting pieces, not the least of which is Microsoft System Center 2012 R2 VMM. You also need an Azure account to establish a connection between App Controller and the cloud.

App Controller is meant to be used by application or service owners as well as system administrators, so it depends on a VMM administrator to configure networks or create the various profiles used to create new VM instances. Figure 1-13 shows the web-based interface that is available after the App Controller installation is finished.

If you don't have a private cloud defined in VMM, you have to do that before you proceed. App Controller is the link between a private and public cloud and deals with entities only at the cloud level.

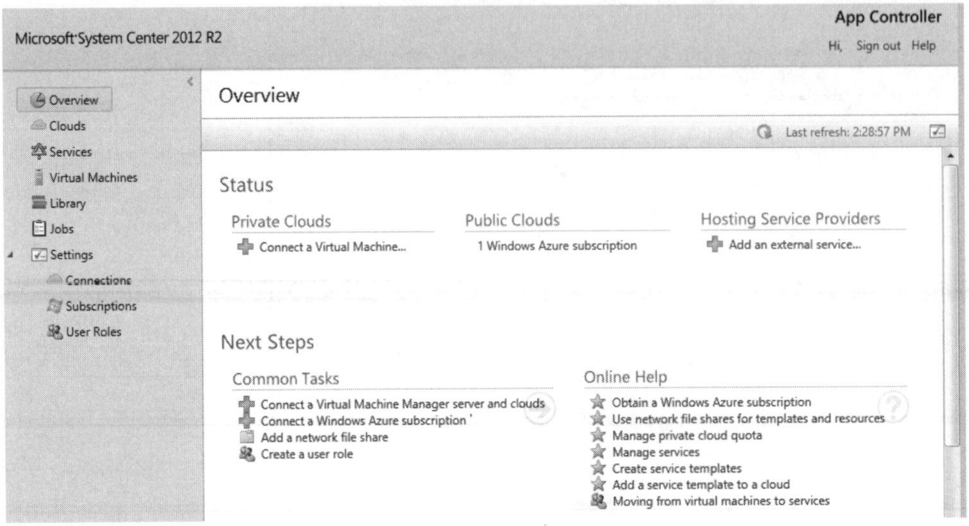

FIGURE 1-13 The Overview page in the App Controller user interface

Azure first steps

The best way to learn about any subject is to practice as much as possible. Microsoft makes that easy with trial Azure subscriptions. A link on the Azure website lets anyone sign up for a one-month trial. Azure uses certificates to secure the connection between a specific subscription and a management platform such as System Center. A certificate for Internet Information Services (IIS) should be created during the installation of App Controller and is visible from the IIS Manager Server Certificates page (see Figure 1-14).

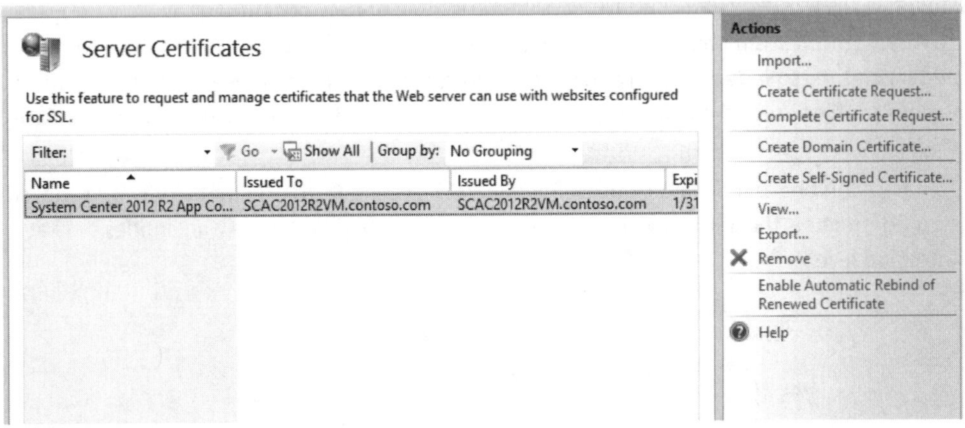

FIGURE 1-14 The IIS Manager is used to create self-signed certificates

You need to export this certificate in two different formats to connect App Controller to an Azure subscription. This step requires launching the Microsoft Management Console (MMC)

and loading the certificates snap-in. To launch MMC, type **MMC** at a command prompt or in the Run dialog box (launch using Windows+R). From MMC, add the Certificates snap-in with either Control+M or the Add/Remove snap-in from the File menu. Make sure to choose Computer Account when prompted to choose which certificate store to manage.

To export the key, select the System Center App Controller certificate from the Personal store and then choose More Actions, All Tasks, Export to launch the Certificate Export Wizard as shown in Figure 1-15. For the local certificate, you must choose to export the private key and provide a password, which creates a PFX file to be used in App Controller. Launch the Certificate Export Wizard a second time to create the second file without the private key. This action creates a CER file that must be uploaded to Azure.

FIGURE 1-15 The Certificate Export Wizard is used to export keys

The Azure management console includes a Settings section with a Management Certificates page that has a button labeled Upload. Clicking this button prompts you to browse for the CER file previously exported. When the upload process completes, you should see the new certificate listed along with a subscription ID. This number is needed in the next step, in which you add the subscription to App Controller.

From the System Center App Controller UI, click Add Azure Subscription to connect to your Azure account using the PFX file previously generated. Figure 1-16 shows the dialog box with the text boxes completed.

When this connection is established, you have full access to all VMs and virtual disks associated with the account.

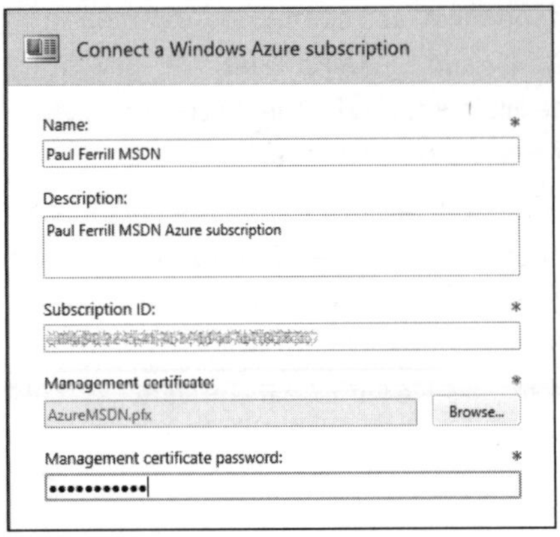

FIGURE 1-16 Connecting to an Azure subscription using a subscription ID

Microsoft Azure PowerShell

Microsoft offers a PowerShell module specifically for working with Azure on the Azure website (*http://www.windowsazure.com/en-us/downloads/*). When installed, this module provides a number of new cmdlets for managing VM instances on Azure. Installation requires the Microsoft Web Platform Installer that can be downloaded from the Azure website. Launching this link displays a dialog box that has a link near the bottom that displays a list of everything to be installed (see Figure 1-17).

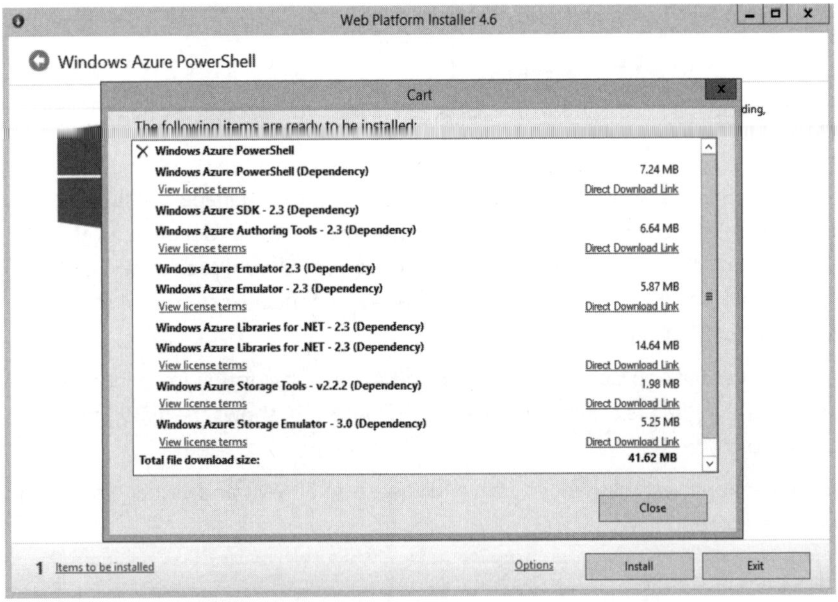

FIGURE 1-17 The Web Platform Installer

Clicking Install launches the installation process that begins downloading the necessary items. After the download completes, each item is installed. Upon completion, the Azure PowerShell cmdlets are available from either the PowerShell command line or the PowerShell Integrated Scripting Environment (ISE).

A total of 29 cmdlets specific to App Controller make it possible to completely automate the process of creating, copying, and moving VMs and virtual disks between a local or on-premises system and Azure. You need to connect to your Azure subscription prior to actually deploying any files. Two PowerShell commands help facilitate the establishment of credentials:

```
Get-AzurePublishSettingsFile
```

```
Import-AzurePublishSettingsFile
```

The first command opens a webpage and allows you to retrieve the .publishsettings file. After this file is retrieved, use the Import-AzurePublishSettingsFile cmdlet to import the credentials into your local environment.

Azure command-line interface

A final option for deploying servers is the Azure command-line interface, which is different from the PowerShell option and includes downloadable installers for Windows, Mac, and Linux (see Figure 1-18). The Azure command-line interface is a cross-platform tool written in JavaScript and uses Node.js, which provides a consistent set of commands across the three client operating systems. With this tool, you can manage all aspects of your Azure account to include creating and copying VMs. It is also possible to take advantage of underlying operating system commands that you're familiar with to further automate the process.

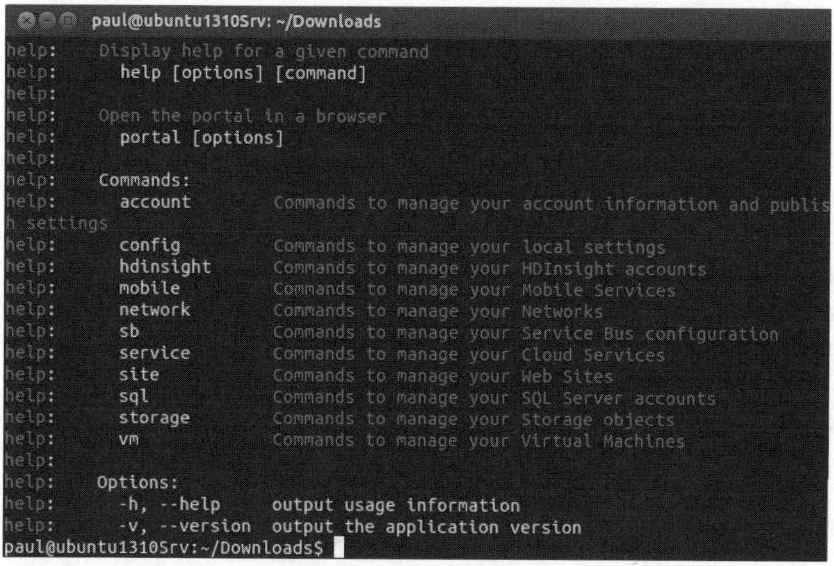

FIGURE 1-18 The Azure command-line interface

Planning for multicast deployment

WDS uses either multicast or unicast protocol as a part of the process of deploying a new server instance. The difference between multicast and unicast is implied in the name: *multicast* is sent to multiple computers; *unicast* is sent to a specific computer. All configurations of multicast deployments use the WDS MMC snap-in that should have been installed along with the WDS role. Multicast transmissions are configured using the WDS management console. Figure 1-19 shows the Create Multicast Transmission Wizard.

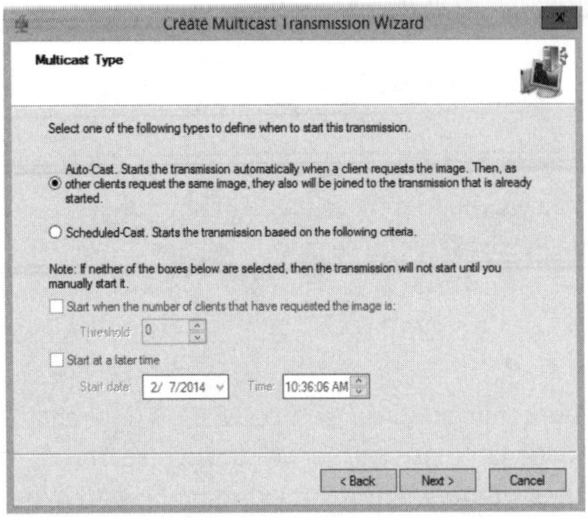

FIGURE 1-19 Providing a Multicast Type in the Create Multicast Transmission Wizard

Choosing Auto-Cast configures the WDS server to monitor boot requests and automatically use multicast when additional clients request the same image.

Planning for Windows Deployment Services

WDS is the primary tool for enabling the distribution and deployment of Windows operating systems over the network. WDS makes it possible to fully automate the installation process of a new Windows-based machine over the network with no human intervention required. It supports deployment of the latest versions of the Windows operating system as well as legacy versions back to Windows 7 and Windows Server 2003.

To use WDS requires the Windows Deployment Services role to be installed by using either Server Manager or PowerShell. Two role services are installed along with WDS by default: Deployment Server and Transport Server. Both of these role services require a working DHCP server and DNS somewhere on the network, plus an NTFS volume to store installation images.

A Transport Server is required for environments without Active Directory Domain Services (AD DS), DNS, or DHCP. For Transport Server–only installs, you must use a public share with no authentication required to store the boot and install images. Both from an authentication and a practical perspective, WDS works best in an Active Directory–enabled environment.

Another AD DS advantage comes in the capability to use prestaged clients to speed up and secure deployment.

> **NOTE DEPLOYMENT AND TRANSPORT ROLE CONFIGURATION**
>
> You must configure the Deployment and Transport roles at the time of installation. If you need to change the location for the image store or the type of server (Standalone or Active Directory Integrated), you have to remove and reinstall the role.

WDS uses a file system directory to store all boot and install images, PXE boot files, and management tools. Requirements for this directory include the following:

- Must reside on an NTFS partition
- Must not be the system partition
- Must have enough room to contain all images

Figure 1-20 shows the WDS console and the menu presented when you right-click a boot image. A capture boot image is created from an existing boot image and contains the tools necessary to create an install image from a physical or VM. After the image is created, you can boot any system connected to the same network as the WDS server from that image and then proceed with the capture process.

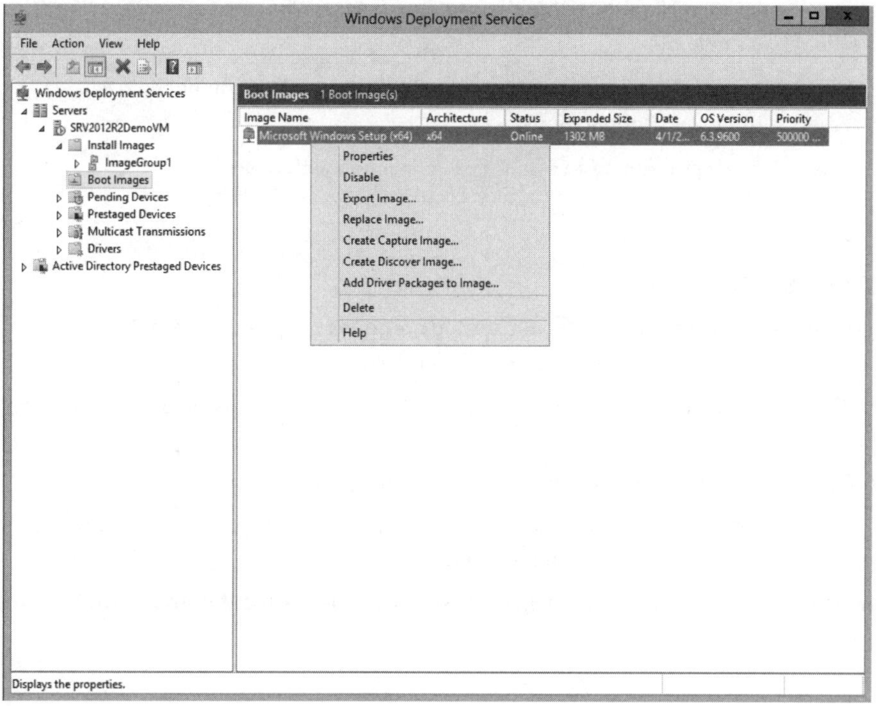

FIGURE 1-20 The WDS console displaying a menu of options for boot images

Creating a baseline virtual image is not difficult if you have the right files. With an ISO file of the Windows Server 2012 R2 media, create a new VM using Hyper-V Manager with appropriate memory and processor settings. Site-specific configuration information must be entered when the installation process completes. The final result is a VHD file that can be used to create new VMs directly or can be exported for use by using the import function.

> **MORE INFO**   **WINDOWS DEPLOYMENT SERVICES (WDS)**
>
> For more detailed information on the deployment process and WDS, visit *http://technet. microsoft.com/en-us/library/hh831764.aspx*.

Thought experiment
Prepare a boot and install image

In this thought experiment, apply what you've learned about this objective. You can find answers to these questions in the "Answers" section at the end of this chapter.

Before you undertake a server deployment, you must prepare several images to use as a part of the process.

1. Describe the steps required to build a boot image for a Windows Server 2012 R2 rollout to a single site.

2. Describe the steps needed to create an install image for a large number of Dell servers with similar configurations.

3. Describe the steps required to establish a connection with Azure.

Objective summary

- Designing an automated deployment strategy requires the use of several Microsoft-provided tools to include the Windows ADK and WDS.
- Use the Windows ADK and related tools such as DISM to build custom images for deployment.
- Boot and install images are required for bare metal deployment.
- Azure provides a new target for the deployment of VMs, and the process is fully integrated into System Center and Windows PowerShell.
- Understanding network requirements for distributed deployment is important for a successful design.

Objective review

Answer the following questions to test your knowledge of the information in this objective. You can find the answers to these questions and explanations of why each answer choice is correct or incorrect in the "Answers" section at the end of this chapter.

1. Several recommended methods for creating images are available to use for deployment. Which of the following would be suitable solutions? (Choose all that apply.)

   A. Installation images are available on the Windows Server 2012 installation media.

   B. Images can be downloaded from the Microsoft Download Center.

   C. Images can be captured using the WDS tools.

   D. Images can be extracted from a running VM.

2. The Windows SIM is used for what purpose?

   A. To create an image for installing an operating system to a new system

   B. To build an answer file for use in an automated operating system installation

   C. To modify an existing system image to add customized drivers and software

   D. For installing a system image on a new computer

3. What tools come with WDS? (Choose all that apply.)

   A. Windows PE

   B. Windows SIM

   C. Windows Deployment Toolkit

   D. Windows Migration Toolkit

Objective 1.2: Implement a server deployment infrastructure

When you have a plan in place that meets the requirements of your organization, you should be ready to take the next step and start the implementation. It is important to stick to the plan. If you do encounter issues along the way, you should revisit the original plan and make adjustments as necessary. This iterative process helps to ensure that you accurately document the process and identify any deviations discovered during execution.

> **This objective covers how to:**
> - Configure multicast deployment
> - Configure multisite topology and distribution points
> - Configure a multiserver topology
> - Configure autonomous and replica WDS servers

Configuring multisite topology and transport servers

Deployment over a distributed, multisite network requires a phased approach to implement because some pieces must be up and running before others are. Configuration of multisite deployments includes additional pieces to handle the file replication. For Windows Server 2012 R2, the primary tool for replicating files is the Distributed File System (DFS).

The name of the DFS service used in the context of server deployment is DFS Replication, or DFSR. Windows Server 2012 R2 adds a number of updates and new features to DFSR to keep up with requirements from other tools such as WDS, including initial cloning capability and improvements in both performance and scalability. For large distribution directories, it can take time and bandwidth to accomplish the initial synchronization.

One way to improve the initial setup and configuration of DFSR is to prestage files (this is especially true for large files such as deployment images or ISO files). Some types of external media must be used to accomplish a preseed such as a USB disk device. An initial copy of the directory to be replicated is made on an external device and then used at the target site to populate the replica directory. All changes after that point occur by using differencing technology and bits transfer.

Prestaging of clients involves assigning them to use either a local server or the nearest WDS server to obtain the installation images. The WDS management console provides a wizard to complete the process of configuring a prestaged device. To launch this wizard, right-click Active Directory Prestaged Devices in the left pane and choose Add Device, as shown in Figure 1-21.

FIGURE 1-21 Adding a prestaged client from Active Directory

The first dialog box in the wizard prompts for Name, Device ID, Device Group, and OU (see Figure 1-22). For the Device ID, enter either a GUID, UUID, or Mac address so that the WDS server can identify the client when it queries for a deployment server.

This dialog box requires you to have previously added a computer object in Active Directory and that the information you need to complete the dialog box is available. A Mac address can be used instead of a system GUID.

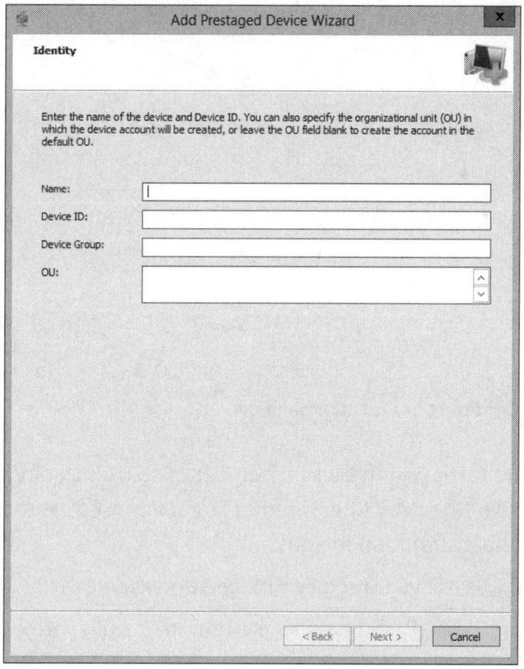

FIGURE 1-22 The Add Prestaged Device Wizard requires a unique identifier for each device

Configuring a multiserver topology

All configuration for WDS happens using the WDS management console. For large installations, it makes sense to use a redundant server topology to increase efficiency and provide additional reliability. A multiserver scenario can also use prestaged clients (as discussed in the previous section).

Keep in mind that WDS is not cluster-aware, so each server effectively operates independently to service specific clients. Management of all servers happens with the WDS console or with any of the 33 new cmdlets in Windows PowerShell.

WDS requires a number of configuration steps before it is ready to actually deploy anything. This process involves using the WDS MMC snap-in to configure the server for either AD DS integrated or stand-alone mode. You must also configure whether and how each server responds to client requests.

For servers configured with both Deployment and Transport Server roles, you can add images as part of running the configuration wizard. This launches an additional wizard and requires access to distribution media.

If you haven't previously configured WDS, you must accomplish this task before moving on. To start the configuration process, right-click the server in the left pane of the MMC console, as shown in Figure 1-23.

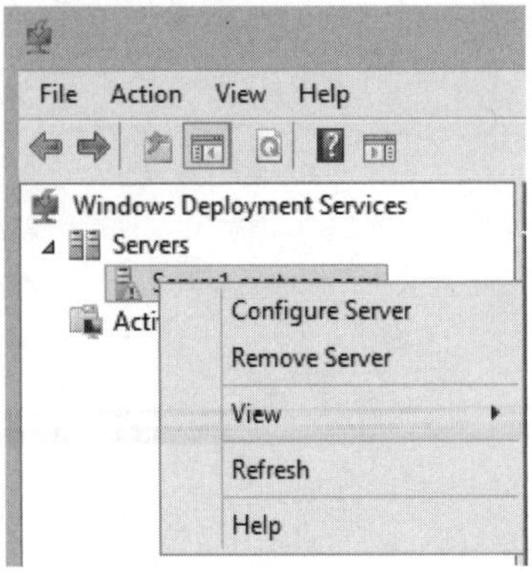

FIGURE 1-23 The Windows Deployment Services Configure Server command

This launches the configuration wizard and takes you through a number of steps including one point where you must choose either Active Directory Integrated or Standalone. You must also designate a directory in which to store the distribution images.

- **Install Options**   Choose Integrated with Active Directory or Standalone server.

- **Remote Installation Folder Location**   Specify the path to the remote installation folder. It defaults to C:\RemoteInstall.

- **Proxy DHCP Server**   There are two check boxes available. Your choice depends on whether DHCP is running on the WDS server or if a non-Microsoft DHCP server is on the network:

  - Do Not Listen On DHCP And DHCPv6 Ports

  - Configure DHCP Options For Proxy DHCP

- **PXE Server Initial Settings**   There are three options:

  - Do Not Respond To Any Client Computers (Default)

  - Respond Only To Known Client Computers

  - Respond To All Client Computers (Known And Unknown). This option includes an option that allows you to require administrator approval for unknown computers.

If you choose the system disk, you'll see a message like the one shown in Figure 1-24.

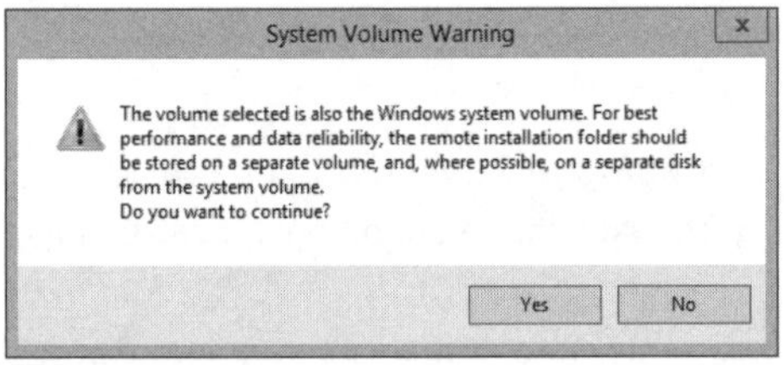

FIGURE 1-24 System Volume Warning message

The next page asks what types of clients you want to service. Options here include None, Only Known, or Any Client with a request. If you plan to use prestaged clients, you should choose known clients. After this question has been answered, the wizard proceeds to initialize the WDS server.

EXAM TIP

WDSUTIL is a command-line utility that allows you to script everything you would normally do using the WDS console. For the exam, you should know what this tool can do and how to use it.

Most of the settings in WDS can be modified using the Properties page available by right-clicking the server name in the WDS MMC snap-in. The most important thing is to ensure that settings match between different servers.

Deploying servers to Azure IaaS

Azure provides a number of different methods for deploying servers. The simplest method is to pick an instance from the VM gallery and then customize it to meet your needs. Figure 1-25 shows some of the options available in the gallery.

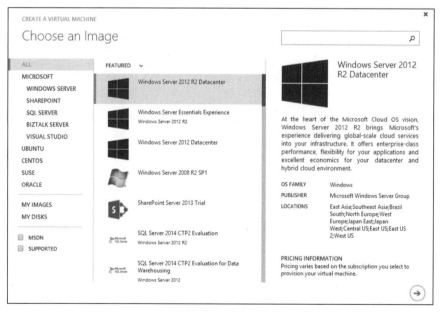

FIGURE 1-25 The management portal with the Windows Server 2012 R2 Datacenter image selected

NOTE   AZURE SUPPORTS VHD FILES ONLY

At the time of this writing, Azure supports only VHD files for VMs.

Another option is to upload a VHD file containing a server image to Azure. This image must have been properly prepared before to include running Sysprep to generalize the image. When it is accomplished, you can use Windows PowerShell to actually upload the image to Azure.

Deploying servers to public and private cloud by using App Controller and Windows PowerShell

Using either App Controller or Windows PowerShell is the easiest part of the entire deployment process. All that is left after the image preparation step is to deploy to either a target host machine or to Azure. You must connect App Controller to an Azure account and a local VMM instance to move VMs between the two.

After you have a local App Controller instance connected to an Azure account, you can drag between the two. Both services use the concept of a cloud to which you deploy things such as a VM. Using App Controller, the IT administrator decides whether the VM resides in the private cloud (on-premises) or in the public Azure cloud.

The Azure service offers a number of baseline platform images ready for deployment into the cloud. To retrieve an image named BaselineImage to a local cloud with PowerShell, use the following:

```
Get-AzureVMImage | Select "BaselineImage"
```

And to copy an image to the cloud and provision it, use these commands:

```
$image - "BaselineImage"
$newvm = New-AzureVMConfig -Name "TestVM" -InstanceSize "Small" -Image $image
$pwd = "P@ssW0rd"
$un = "pferrill"
$vm1 | Add-AzureProvisioningConfig -Windows -AdminUserName $un -Password $pwd
$vm1 | New-AzureVM -ServiceName "clcTestSvc1" -Location "East US"
```

Thought experiment
Microsoft Azure PowerShell scripting

In this thought experiment, apply what you've learned about this objective. You can find answers to these questions in the "Answers" section at the end of this chapter.

Automation is the key to implementing a smooth-running server deployment strategy, and Windows PowerShell is the best tool for the job.

Building a proof-of-concept automated deployment script requires good planning and programming practices.

1. List several reasons for using Microsoft Azure PowerShell instead of other tools.

2. How can you find out what PowerShell cmdlets apply to Azure without using a search engine?

3. List the steps required to actually deploy a VM to Azure using only PowerShell commands.

Microsoft Azure PowerShell is a powerful tool, and it benefits you to learn how to use it in the long run. Microsoft has a wide range of resources if you want to learn more.

Objective summary

- After you have a plan of attack for implementation, you have to execute the plan.
- Although a multisite topology might seem difficult to configure, it takes only a few steps.
- Azure provides the perfect target for deploying servers to the cloud.
- App Controller is a part of the Microsoft System Center family and provides a friendly UI for managing both public and private cloud assets.
- Using Windows PowerShell with the Azure cmdlets is another way to manage public and private cloud assets.

Objective review

Answer the following questions to test your knowledge of the information in this objective. You can find the answers to these questions and explanations of why each answer choice is correct or incorrect in the "Answers" section at the end of this chapter.

1. What is the purpose of prestaging client images? (Choose all that apply.)

    A. To provide images on a local network in a multisite topology to speed up the process

    B. To make custom prepared images available to any client

    C. To control the deployment process

    D. To prevent overuse of a wide area network (WAN) with image traffic

2. What tool should you use to create a multicast server to handle large numbers of deployment images?

    A. Server Manager in Windows Server 2012 R2

    B. Network control tool in Control Panel

    C. WDS MMC snap-in

    D. Windows PowerShell

3. What are methods for deploying a VM to Azure? (Choose all that apply.)

    A. Use System Center App Controller to move an existing private cloud VM to Azure.

    B. Use Microsoft Azure PowerShell to copy a local VM up to the cloud.

    C. Use the Azure command line from a Linux machine to copy VMs to and from the cloud.

    D. Use a command window and the xcopy command.

Objective 1.3: Plan and implement server upgrade and migration

One of the most common tasks facing any system administrator with the introduction of a new version of an operating system is to migrate specific roles or upgrade from an older version. The steps required to perform a migration vary depending on what operating system is running on the system to be migrated.

Planning for role migration

The first step in any significant migration effort is to come up with a plan. In the case of a server operating system migration, many factors must be taken into consideration before you think about the actual migrations. This is especially important if the migration includes server consolidation because application architecture must be evaluated to ensure no interruption to operations.

If you don't have a good understanding of your infrastructure and the applications running in your production environment, you should use some type of inventory tool to create a complete map. The Windows Server Migration Tools (WSMT) provide a comprehensive set of PowerShell-based tools to help facilitate the job of migrating server roles, features, and operating system settings along with data and shares from Windows Server 2003, Windows Server 2008, and Windows Server 2008 R2 to Windows Server 2012.

To install the WSMT using PowerShell, type the following in a PowerShell window with elevated privileges:

```
Install-WindowsFeature Migration -ComputerName <computer_name>
```

When this operation completes, you have access to new cmdlets that make migrating the different roles much easier.

> **MORE INFO**   **WINDOWS SERVER MIGRATION TOOLS (WSMT)**
>
> For more detailed information on the WSMT, visit *http://technet.microsoft.com/en-us/ library/jj134202.aspx.*

The first tool you should run is the Get-SmigServerFeature cmdlet to list the features the target server has installed. Figure 1-26 shows the output of this command.

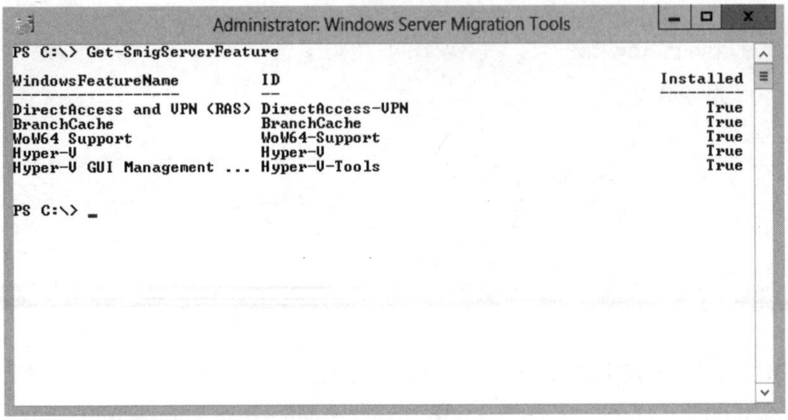

FIGURE 1-26 The PowerShell window showing results of running the Get-SmigServerFeature cmdlet

After you have a list of roles needing migration, gather the information necessary to accomplish the process, including the following:

- Source and destination server names and IP addresses
- Specific hardware requirements such as number of network ports or amount of available memory
- Location of a file share accessible by both source and destination machines for storing migration files

There are several steps to populate the deployment share prior to actually starting the migration. The actual files depend on what operating system the source machine currently runs. To create these files, use the smigdeploy.exe tool. The easiest way to create these files is to first change the directory to the location of the tool, which is C:\Windows\System32\ServerMigrationTools by default. Then type the following:

```
SmigDeploy.exe /package /architecture X86 /os WS08 /path <deployshare>
```

This code creates the necessary files needed to migrate from a system running a 32-bit version of Windows Server 2008. To accomplish the same task for a system running a 64-bit version of Windows Server 2008 R2, type this:

```
SmigDeploy.exe /package /architecture amd64 /os WS08R2 /path <deployshare>
```

With this step accomplished, you must register the migration tools on the source system by typing **SMIGDEPLOY.EXE** in the folder in which the migration files were created. You then see an item on the Start menu for the WSMT, as shown in Figure 1-27.

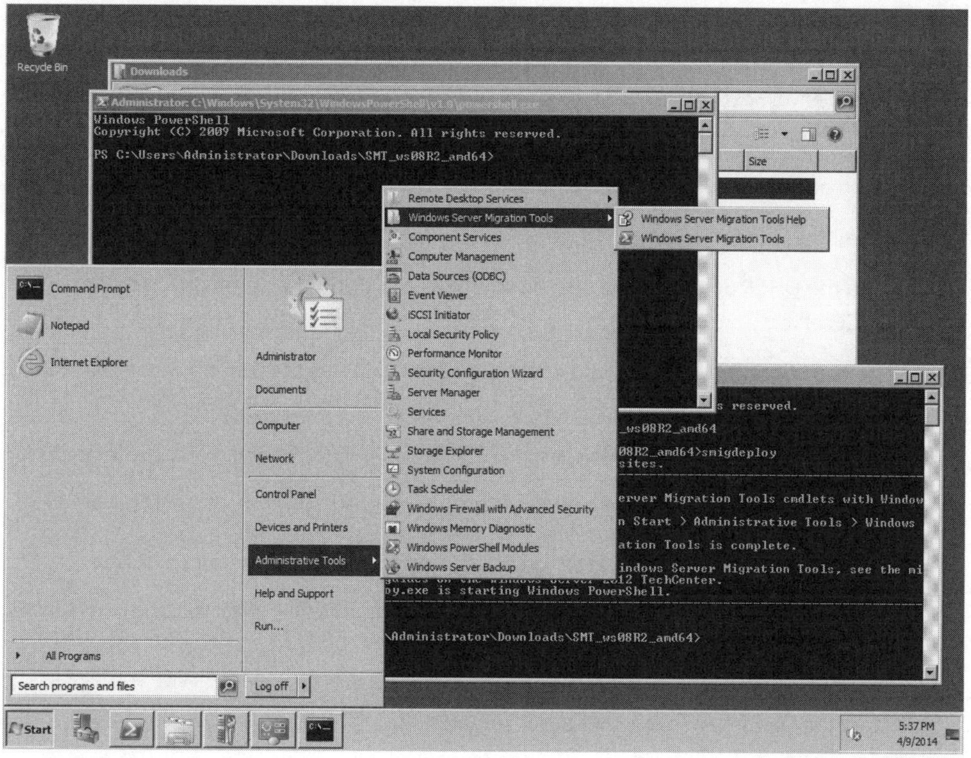

FIGURE 1-27 The Windows Server 2008 R2 Start menu showing Windows Server Migration Tools

Migrating server roles

The actual migration process can happen in a number of different ways, depending on the criticality of the specific role. If a server is functioning in a role that needs to continue uninterrupted, perform a live migration if possible. If the role is running on a VM, the live migration process is relatively painless.

Microsoft provides guidance for migrating specific roles, including AD DS and DNS, DHCP, file and print services, and IIS.

DHCP migration

Migrating a DHCP server can be a tricky process unless you follow the Microsoft-prescribed procedure. The process requires the installation of the WSMT on both the source and destination servers. You should also ensure that the destination server has the same number of (or more) network adapters as the source server.

Two Windows PowerShell cmdlets, Export-SmigServerSetting and Import-SmigServerSetting, accomplish the key step of moving the DHCP server settings from one machine to the other. You might consider using the WSMT to move your IP configuration to ensure that those settings move from one machine to the next. The command to export the IP configuration on the source machine in PowerShell is the following:

```
Export-SmigServerSetting -IPConfig -Path <SharedFolderPath> -Verbose
```

This code should be run from a PowerShell session from the Start menu by launching the WSMT as an administrator. The steps to accomplish the migration are as follows:

1. Install the DHCP role on the target server.

2. Stop the DHCP Server service on the source server using the command Stop-Service DHCPserver.

3. Use the Migration Tool cmdlet Export-SmigServerSetting to collect data on the source server.

4. Delete the DHCP authorization on the source server with the following command:

   ```
   Netsh DHCP delete server <FQDN of source server> <IP address of source server>
   ```

5. Run the Import-SmigServerSetting cmdlet on the destination server as follows:

   ```
   Import-SmigServerSetting -featureID DHCP -User All -Group -Ipconfig <All | Global
   | NIC> -SourcePhysicalAddress <IP address of source server> -TargetPhysicalAddress
   -Force -path <path to file>
   ```

6. Start the DHCP service on the target server:

   ```
   Start-Service DHCPServer
   ```

7. Authorize the target server (command is case sensitive) with the following command:

   ```
   netsh DHCP add server <FQDN of target server> <IP address of target server>
   ```

Hyper-V migration

Many benefits come with migrating your Hyper-V platform to Windows Server 2012 R2, especially if it is running on anything older than Windows Server 2012. Hyper-V 3.0 has many features that make it significantly more capable than previous versions. New features in Windows Server 2012 R2 Hyper-V should make the effort required to migrate worthwhile.

Although the actual migration is relatively simple, you should accomplish a number of steps on the source system prior to starting the migration, including deleting any snapshots taken of running VMs because they are not supported for migration. You'll also want to set the MAC address option in the settings of each VM to "Static" prior to migration to prevent any reconfiguration after the process completes.

Printer migration

Migrating printers from one server operating system to another is a relatively straightforward process, but must be done with care, especially in a production environment. The actual progress can be accomplished from the Windows Server 2012 R2 Server Manager Print

Management tool, which should be available from the Tools menu. If not, you have to install the Print Services role on the target server. Figure 1-28 shows a portion of the Print Management screen.

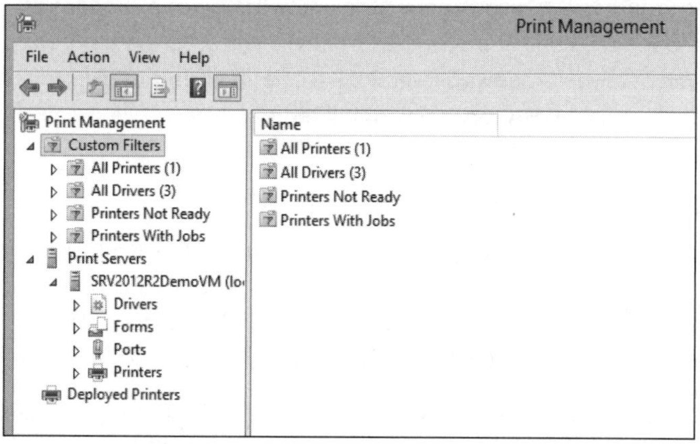

FIGURE 1-28 The Windows Print Management screen

Migrating servers across domains and forests

The biggest challenge of cross-domain migration has to do with credentials and trust. Microsoft provides the Active Directory Migration Tool (ADMT) to simplify the process of migrating objects across domains and forests. The two types supported are interforest and intraforest migration. An *interforest migration* occurs between forests, and an *intraforest migration* occurs between domains within the same forest.

Prior to either migration, you must establish a trust relationship between the two domains. Possibilities here include a one-way or two-way transitive trust.

> **EXAM TIP**
>
> Make sure that you understand the different trusts required for different migration scenarios for the exam. For a scenario in which objects are migrated from a source domain to a target domain, the source domain must trust the target domain. In the scenario in which users are migrated and will access resources in the source domain, a two-way trust is required.

Designing a server consolidation strategy

Microsoft Hyper-V 3.0 has changed the approach to server consolidation, especially for IT shops heavily invested in Microsoft technologies that include System Center. Workloads that traditionally demanded a physical machine, such as an Active Directory domain controller, can now be virtualized and made redundant by using Hyper-V 3.0. Virtualization and Hyper-V represent a key piece of a server consolidation strategy.

To optimize this strategy, it is important to have a general understanding of your network and how the existing pieces fit together. It is also important to know the types of workloads and the level of service required for each one; it drives the target virtualization system from a hardware and redundancy perspective. Windows Server 2012 R2 has built-in clustering features for building out a highly available (HA) system with full redundancy.

Planning for capacity and resource optimization

The Microsoft Assessment and Planning (MAP) Toolkit for Windows Server 2012 R2, shown in Figure 1-29, includes an inventory tool to help assess your current environment and produce a comprehensive report. Version 9.0 of the tool is available from the Microsoft Download Center and includes sample reports, a Getting Started Guide, and a training kit.

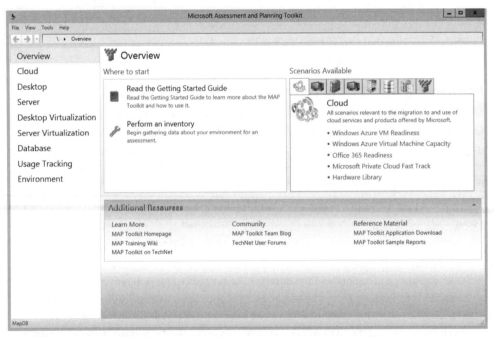

FIGURE 1-29 The Overview page of the Microsoft Assessment and Planning Toolkit

The MAP Toolkit requires the .NET Framework 3.5 run time, which is not installed by default. If you have the Windows Server 2012 R2 ISO file mounted on the X drive, you can use the following command to install it:

```
Dism /online /enable-feature /featurename:NetFx3 /All /Source:X:\sources\sxs
/LimitAccess
```

The source path for the .NET Framework 3.5 run time shown in the previous DISM line, X:\sources\sxs, must point to a valid location for the .NET Framework 3.5 installation files.

Objective summary

- Migrating existing systems to a new operating system is a skill every IT administrator should have because Microsoft delivers new releases of Windows Server on a regular basis.

- The migration of specific roles provides a good way to break down a larger migration process into manageable steps.

- Understanding options such as Microsoft Hyper-V for the consolidation of physical servers can help save operating costs.

- Microsoft provides a wide variety of tools to assist the migration of different roles and workloads to Windows Server 2012 R2.

- It is important to put a good migration plan together before starting the process to identify all the steps necessary and ensure success.

Objective review

Answer the following questions to test your knowledge of the information in this objective. You can find the answers to these questions and explanations of why each answer choice is correct or incorrect in the "Answers" section at the end of this chapter.

1. What roles are good candidates for migration to a new operating system? (Choose all that apply.)

   A. Active Directory domain controllers

   B. Routing and Remote Access Services (RRAS)

   C. VPN server

   D. Isolated test server

2. What tools should be used for a server role migration?

   A. WSMT

   B. Windows SIM

   C. DISM

   D. PowerShell

3. What tools does the MAP Toolkit provide? (Choose all that apply.)

   A. DISM

   B. Capacity planning tool

   C. PowerShell cmdlets

   D. An inventory and reporting tool

Objective 1.4: Plan and deploy Virtual Machine Manager services

With the inclusion of Hyper-V 3.0 in Windows Server 2012, Microsoft provides a production-ready virtualization platform. Improvements in Windows Server 2012 R2 to the storage subsystem have only enhanced the platform and its readiness to support any virtualized workload.

System Center 2012 R2 Virtual Machine Manager (VMM) is the primary management tool for any enterprise-level virtualization deployment. In some cases, it might be cost effective in terms of administration costs for a smaller organization with a significant number of VMs to manage. Either way, a good understanding of VMM is a skill every IT administrator should possess.

This objective covers how to:

- Design Virtual Machine Manager service templates
- Define operating system profiles
- Configure hardware and capability profiles
- Manage services
- Configure image and template libraries
- Manage logical networks

Designing Virtual Machine Manager service templates

VMM is intended to simplify the task of managing large numbers of supporting services. Most modern enterprise applications use a tiered design approach with different services, such as a database, assigned to a specific tier. VMM builds on this approach to enable the creation of service templates to include everything necessary to bring a tier or service online.

You should create a Run As account if you haven't done so. This account is required in a number of different management functions. A Run As account is an alias for a domain administrator account that is used by VMM when performing system management tasks. From the Settings workspace of the VMM management console application, click the Create Run As Account icon to launch the Create Run As Account wizard.

Service templates can include networking, storage, and compute resources configured in a specific way. VMM includes a Service Template Designer for creating these services to be used later when configuring new applications. It comes with a total of four default templates for blank, one-tier, two-tier, and three-tier services. Figure 1-30 shows what the template looks like with the two-tier basic template.

A VM template is a generic description of the specific details required to function in a particular role. At a minimum, the VM template consists of an operating system profile, a hardware profile, and virtual disks. A new VM template can be constructed from an existing baseline template, from a VHD stored in the library, or from an existing VM deployed on the same host.

EXAM TIP

Watch for exam questions that include situations calling for minimizing administrative overhead. For VMM, service templates might be your answer because they allow you to manage multiple entities at the same time as one single entity.

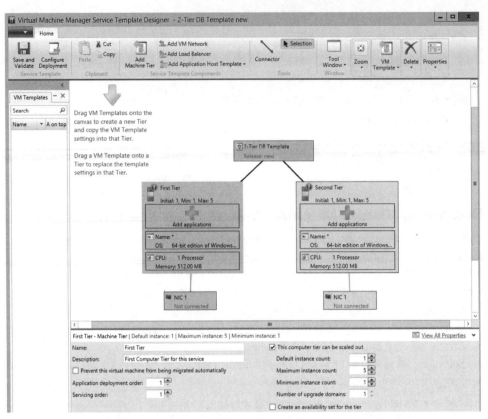

FIGURE 1-30 The Virtual Machine Manager Service Template Designer

Defining operating system profiles

One of the most common tasks related to creating a new VM is operating system installation. VMM enables the creation of a Guest OS Profile containing basic information such as a product key, the default administrator password, and information to join the operating system to a domain.

Figure 1-31 shows the New Guest OS Profile dialog box for entering the domain join information. This dialog box can save an IT administrator both time and energy for every new VM needing to join a domain. You can also configure additional settings by using a previously created answer file to further automate the installation process. A provision to execute commands upon first logon gives you a way to accomplish anything not covered in the basic installation process.

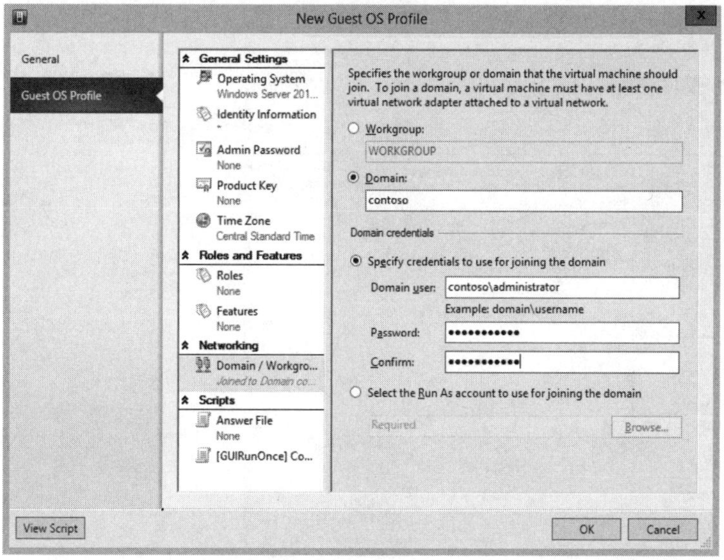

FIGURE 1-31 The New Guest OS Profile Wizard

Configuring hardware and capability profiles

Capability profiles allow an administrator to define the limits of a particular virtualization platform such as ESX, Hyper-V, or XenServer. Configurable items include the number of processors, amount of memory, number of virtual hard drives, and number of network adapters. A capability profile can also be used to set the minimum number of vCPUs or amount of memory to ensure good performance.

Figure 1-32 shows the Create Capability Profile Wizard, which you can launch from the Create icon with the Library workspace selected. A capability profile makes it possible to place limits on memory and number of processors, for example, to improve the compatibility across different hardware platforms.

Figure 1-33 shows the New Hardware Profile Wizard, which enables you to set specific hardware defaults.

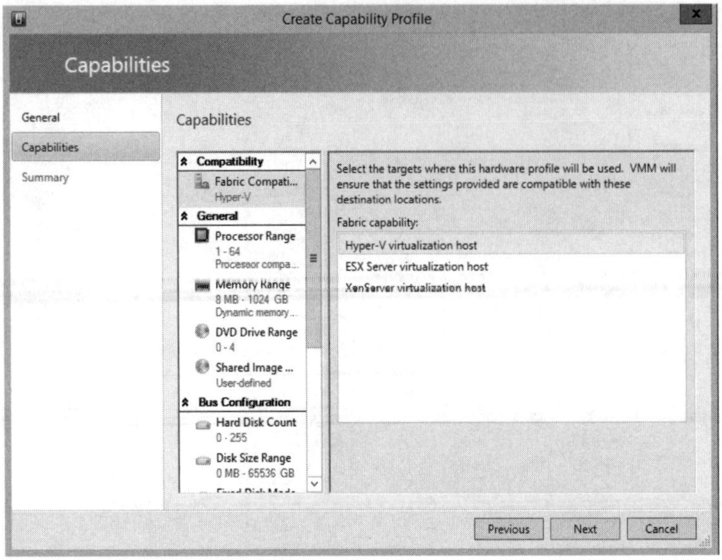

FIGURE 1-32 The Create Capability Profile Capabilities Wizard

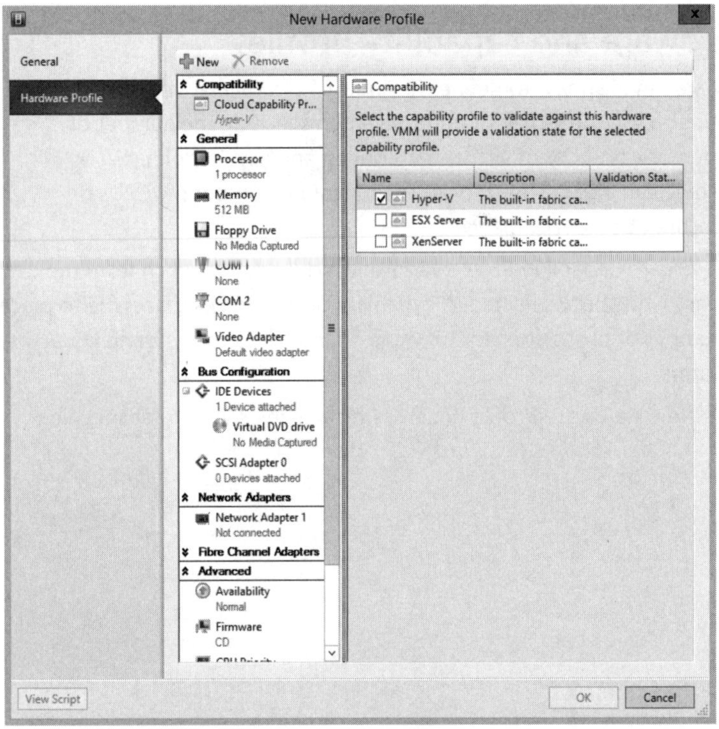

FIGURE 1-33 The New Hardware Profile Wizard

The New Physical Computer Profile Wizard defines specific details needed when deploying new physical hosts with VMM in an environment. Before you launch this wizard, you should have several components properly configured, including at least one logical switch and an operating system image for deployment. Figure 1-34 shows this Hardware Configuration page.

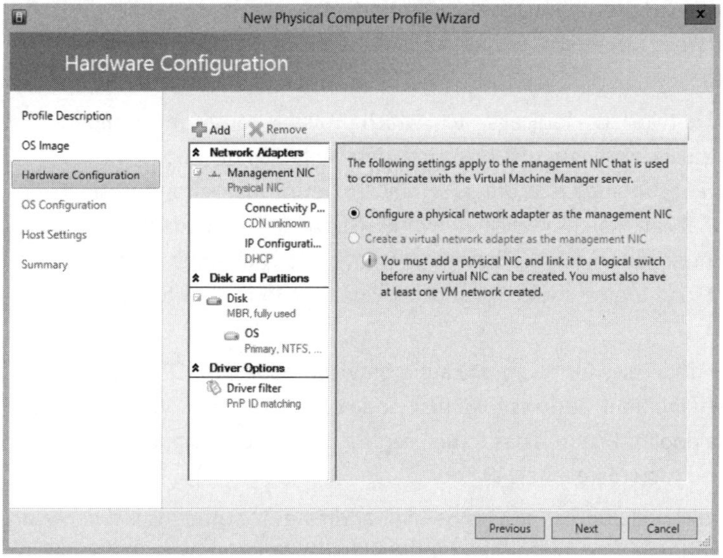

FIGURE 1-34 The New Physical Computer Profile Wizard

Managing services

After a service has been deployed, you can make changes in two ways:

- Update an existing VM to modify its settings
- Deploy a new VM containing all necessary updates

When done with care, in-place changes of an existing VM reduce the risk of service interruption. Deploy a new VM only when the number or scope of changes makes it necessary (for example, a major service pack release with many updates).

Configuring image and template libraries

VMM can store a variety of resources in libraries, including file-based resources such as VHD, ISO, PS1, SQL, ZIP, and other necessary files. Options for configuring the storage location of these files include a typical share on a server and a share on a cluster-shared volume (CSV). The CSV option provides a resilient resource shared throughout the cluster for any host to use.

Templates and profiles are stored in the VMM SQL database unless redirected. For large installations, this database can grow to a significant size. You should keep the SQL database on a system with adequate space to meet the needs of your VMM deployment. (Microsoft provides sizing guidance on the TechNet site.)

Managing logical networks

VMM uses the word "fabric" to group together Infrastructure, Networking, and Storage resources. Grouped under each of these three titles are specific pieces organized according to common functionality. This structure makes managing the different resources a little more intuitive as you search for a specific item needing attention. Managing a logical network involves a number of different pieces and properties, such as virtual local area networks (VLANs) and IP addresses.

One piece of a logical network is a logical switch, which provides consistent configuration information to control virtual switches across hosts in a datacenter. Single-root I/O virtualization (SR-IOV) is a technology that brings significant performance improvements to virtualized networks that can match physical networks. Not all network adapters support SR-IOV, so you have to check your hardware before attempting to enable this capability. Enabling SR-IOV support for a logical switch must occur when the logical switch is created (and it can't be changed).

Every network uses IP addresses for communicating between nodes. DHCP is the most common method of assigning an IP address for a new node on the network. VMM provides the capability to define a pool of IP addresses to be used for a specific network site. With the Create IP Pool Wizard, you can create a new IP Pool.

You can reserve an individual address or a range of IP addresses for other uses if necessary, including any virtual IP addresses you might need for load balancing purposes. IP Pools must be associated with a logical network at the time of creation and can't be changed without deleting the entire logical network and starting over.

> ## *Thought experiment*
> ### Automating with VMM and PowerShell
>
> In this thought experiment, apply what you've learned about this objective. You can find answers to these questions in the "Answers" section at the end of this chapter.
>
> System Center VMM has a large number of moving parts and provides the IT administrator control over a wide range of components. Understanding which tool to use and when to use it is a key skill for any IT administrator in today's virtualized IT environment.
>
> 1. What is the make up of a cloud?
>
> 2. Why should you create service templates?
>
> 3. What steps should you take to deploy a VM in a VMM environment using Windows PowerShell?
>
> Knowing how Windows PowerShell and VMM work together and when to use PowerShell can help automate the management process.

Objective summary

- System Center VMM is a powerful tool with many facets.
- Profiles and templates provide the basis for rapidly deploying and configuring new VMs and their associated services.
- After you learn the basics of building templates and creating new VMs, you can move on to automation.
- You can use PowerShell in conjunction with System Center VMM to customize a wide range of functions.
- System Center VMM can manage every aspect of your virtualization implementation to include other vendors' products.

Objective review

Answer the following questions to test your knowledge of the information in this objective. You can find the answers to these questions and explanations of why each answer choice is correct or incorrect in the "Answers" section at the end of this chapter.

1. Creating a VM template requires what resources? (Choose all that apply.)

    A. A Windows system image

    B. A preconfigured VM

    C. At least one Hyper-V host on which to run the VM

    D. Full installation of Microsoft SQL Server

2. Operating system profiles allow you to specify what parts of an installation?

    A. Administrator name and password

    B. Boot partition size

    C. Custom drivers

    D. System components such as number of virtual CPUs and amount of memory

3. What networking components can be configured when managing logical networks using VMM? (Choose all that apply.)

    A. Switch Ports

    B. VLANs

    C. IP address blocks

    D. MAC addresses

Objective 1.5: Plan and implement file and storage services

Windows Server 2012 R2 brings even more improvements and innovation in the area of storage. The inclusion of storage tiering capabilities brings Windows Server 2012 R2 into parity with many expensive dedicated storage systems. Understanding how to take advantage of these new features will be important for any system administrator.

> **This objective covers how to:**
>
> - Incorporate planning considerations, including iSCSI SANs, Fibre Channel SANs, Virtual Fibre Channel, storage pools, Storage Spaces, and data deduplication
> - Configure the iSCSI Target Server
> - Configure the iSCSI Naming Services (iSNS)
> - Configure the Network File System (NFS)
> - Install Device Specific Modules (DSMs)

Incorporating planning considerations

Well-defined requirements must drive all design, planning, and implementation efforts to ensure that the system is built to meet specified needs. Storage is often quantified in terms of size and speed, but you can also include availability or reliability because they determine how much and the type of redundancy required. Another common requirement source comes from specific workloads. A good understanding of the required types of I/O can help determine the best way to allocate capital funds against traditional and solid-state disks.

Windows Server 2012 R2 includes many storage-related capabilities that should be considered when evaluating any new storage requirements. Many features that were previously available only from high-end storage vendors now come in the box. Offloaded Data Transfer (ODX) is one of these new features with a potential for significant impact on overall performance. The biggest requirement for using ODX is a storage system that provides the appropriate support. Many of the famous and some smaller storage vendors have announced support for ODX, which requires that the system initiating the transfer be running Windows 8, Windows 8.1, or Windows Server 2012 or 2012 R2.

Figure 1-35 shows a typical Hyper-V configuration with a scale-out file server hosting all file shares for use by any host. They are replicated across multiple file servers and use shared storage on the back end. Redundancy is provided through the use of Storage Spaces.

From a Hyper-V perspective, your storage system must support ODX at the logical unit number (LUN) level if you use block storage. Another possibility is to use a Server Message Block (SMB) file share on another system backed by an ODX–capable storage array. A major enhancement delivered with Windows Server 2012 is the inclusion of the SMB 3.0 protocol.

This newest version of the basic network file protocol for Windows adds a number of new capabilities specifically targeted for high availability and reliability. High availability file storage can now be built on top of Windows Server 2012 with a CSV. One common implementation for a CSV is to build a scale-out file server based on multiple physical Windows Server machines and shared serial attached SCSI (SAS) storage.

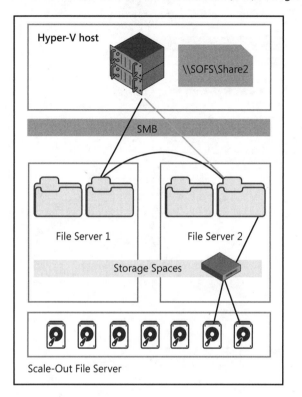

FIGURE 1-35 The scale-out file server configuration

iSCSI and Fibre Channel SANs

The SCSI has been one of the primary disk interface standards for many years. RFC 3720 defines the Internet SCSI, mapping the SCSI architecture and commands onto TCP/IP. To connect to remote disks over a storage area network (SAN), you use the same basic SCSI command structure—but over a network transport. The two most common transports in use today are Ethernet and Fibre Channel. Many traditional SAN architectures used a totally separate network for all storage traffic, typically using Fibre Channel host bus adapters (HBAs), cabling, and switches.

Hyper-V for Windows Server 2012 introduced a new virtual Fibre Channel SAN feature. To use this feature, the host machine must have one or more Fibre Channel HBAs with updated drivers supporting the virtual Fibre Channel. This feature enables workload virtualization with a dependency on Fibre Channel storage.

Figure 1-36 shows the Hyper-V Virtual SAN Manager interface. Clicking the Create button launches a wizard to create a new virtual Fibre Channel SAN directly connected to an HBA and available for use by any VM on the host. The virtual SAN appears to the VM as a dedicated, locally attached device just as if the system were running on physical hardware.

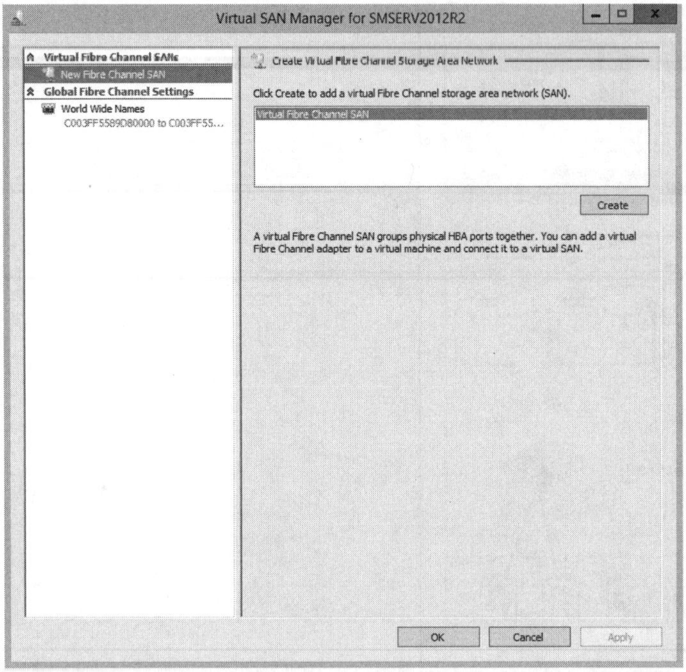

FIGURE 1-36 The Virtual SAN Manager

Storage pools

Microsoft defines a storage pool as "a collection of physical disks that enable you to aggregate disks, expand capacity in a flexible manner, and delegate administration." Windows Server 2012 R2 adds a number of new features to storage pools, including the concept of storage tiers, write-back cache, dual parity, and parity space support for failover clusters. A new rebuild feature uses free space in the storage pool to significantly reduce the amount of time required to repair a storage space after a physical disk failure.

Microsoft uses the term "primordial storage pool" to define all available unallocated physical disks recognized by the operating system. A new named storage pool is then created from this list of available physical disks. Figure 1-37 shows the properties page for a storage pool named TieredPool1. This pool includes both hard disk drives (HDDs) and solid-state disks (SSDs), which allow tiering to be enabled.

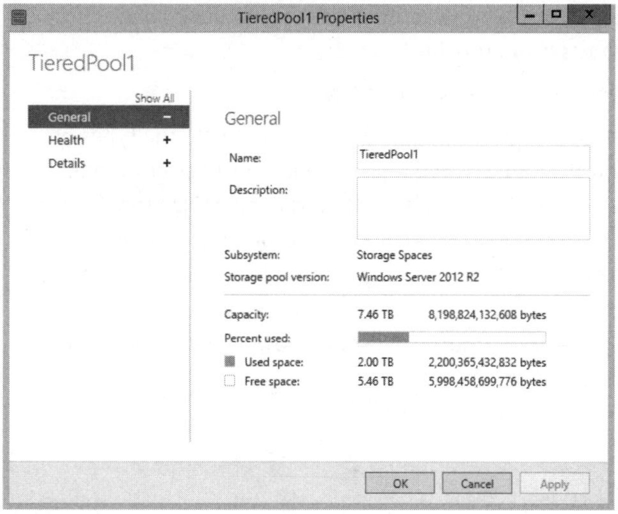

FIGURE 1-37 A storage pool property page

To see the disks in the storage pool named TieredPool1, use the following PowerShell command:

```
Get-StoragePool -FriendlyName TieredPool1 | Get-PhysicalDisk | FT FriendlyName, Size,
MediaType
```

```
FriendlyName      Size              MediaType
------------      -------------     ---------
PhysicalDisk1     3999956729856     HDD
PhysicalDisk2     3999956729856     HDD
PhysicalDisk3     198910672896      SSD
```

New Windows PowerShell cmdlets for managing storage tiers include Get-StorageTier, Get-StorageTierSupportedSize, New-StorageTier, Remove-StorageTier, Resize-StorageTier, and Set-StorageTier.

Storage Spaces

Storage Spaces is a storage subsystem where you can group disks into one or more storage pools. A storage space is a virtual disk created from free space in a storage pool with attributes including resiliency levels, for example. Microsoft introduced Storage Spaces with Windows 8 and Windows Server 2012. Storage spaces resemble hardware redundant arrays of independent disks (RAID) and use some of the same language, such as mirroring, parity, and striping.

Planning a new storage deployment with Windows Server 2012 R2 requires answers to several questions:

- How much storage is needed?
- What level of redundancy is required?

- What levels of performance in terms of input/output per second (IOPS) and throughput should the storage system provide?
- Does the storage system need to provide a clustered system?

After you have answers to these questions, you need to match them with the types of Storage Spaces and understand how they are created (including the new tiered storage capability in Windows Server 2012). A tiered space uses both traditional HDDs and SSDs to provide the best type of storage for each workload. A background process observes the Storage Space to determine which disk blocks have the highest usage and attempts to move them to the faster SSD tier. This process runs at predetermined intervals and uses as much or as little of the available SSD space as needed. Figure 1-38 shows how a tiered storage system works in terms of data moving between tiers.

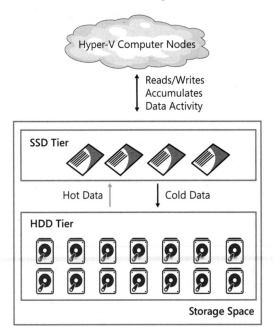

FIGURE 1-38 How a tiered storage system works

Each Storage Space can be configured to have as little or as much redundancy as required. Windows Server 2012 R2 provides for two-way and three-way mirroring for data redundancy (you need a minimum of five physical disks to establish a three-way mirror).

Thin provisioning is the concept of allocating a small fraction of the total capacity of a virtual disk and then growing the allocation as needed. You can initialize a disk with a large capacity but with only a percentage of that capacity physically available. Using this approach helps to minimize a disk-resizing problem if demand outgrows capacity.

Data deduplication

Reducing the amount of duplicated data can have a significant effect on the amount of storage required. Many high-end storage systems have a deduplication feature as a standard part of the operating system. Windows Server 2012 brings this feature into the base operating system as an optionally enabled capability.

Microsoft recommends a number of steps to take when considering and planning for data deduplication:

1. Identify target deployments.

2. Identify specific volumes and the file contents.

3. Run the deduplication evaluation tool to determine savings.

4. Plan the rollout, scalability, and deduplication policies.

Data deduplication must be installed by using either the Add Roles and Features Wizard or Windows PowerShell. Using the wizard, select Server Roles and then select Data Deduplication as shown in Figure 1-39.

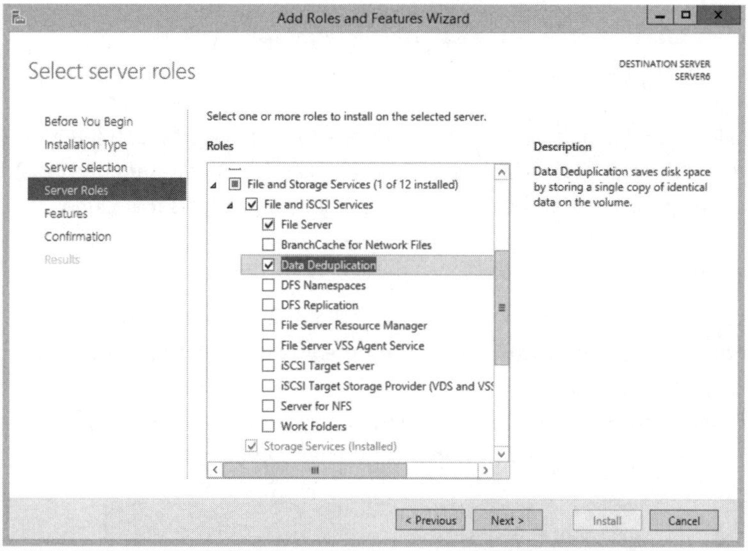

FIGURE 1-39 The Data Deduplication role

After the Data Deduplication role is installed, you have access to the deduplication evaluation tool (DDPEval.exe). The Server Manager File And Storage Services Volumes tab is where you go to enable deduplication on a specific volume. Right-clicking the volume displays a menu of options, including Configure Data Deduplication. Selecting this option displays a dialog box like the one shown in Figure 1-40.

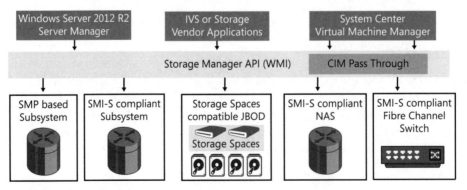

The screenshot shows a dialog window titled "Data (D:\) Deduplication Settings" with the following contents:

Data (D:\)

Data deduplication: [Disabled ▾]
  Disabled
  General purpose file server
  Virtual Desktop Infrastructure (VDI) server

Deduplicate files ol

Type the file extensions that you want to exclude from data deduplication, separating extensions with a comma. For example: doc,txt,png

Default file extensions to exclude: edb,jrs

Custom file extensions to exclude: [   ]

To exclude selected folders (and any files contained in them) from data deduplication, click Add.

[   ] [Add...]
                        [Remove]

[Set Deduplication Schedule...]

                [OK]   [Cancel]   [Apply]

FIGURE 1-40 The Data Deduplication Settings page

This page provides all the configurable options for a deduplicated volume. At present, the two deduplication types are General Purpose File Server and Virtual Desktop Infrastructure (VDI) Server. Other configuration options include file extensions to exclude and folders to exclude.

Storage management

Managing storage resources can be both a difficult and a tedious task. Windows Server 2012 R2 includes a number of SMI-S–compliant storage management features available through Windows PowerShell as well as external management platforms such as System Center VMM. Figure 1-41 shows the different possibilities for managing storage using storage management application programming interfaces (APIs) provided by Windows Server 2012 R2.

Windows Server 2012 R2 Server Manager	IVS or Storage Vendor Applications	System Center Virtual Machine Manager
Storage Manager API (WMI)		CIM Pass Through
SMP based Subsystem	SMI-S compliant Subsystem	Storage Spaces compatible JBOD / Storage Spaces	SMI-S compliant NAS	SMI-S compliant Fibre Channel Switch

FIGURE 1-41 A storage management summary

Configuring the iSCSI Target Server

Windows Server 2012 R2 includes a number of new and improved iSCSI Target Server features and functionality. New in this release is the capability to use VHDX files as the persistence layer behind an iSCSI LUN, bringing with it increased capacity and use of both dynamic and differencing disks.

As with most other Windows Server roles, the iSCSI Target Server role can be installed either through Server Manager or by using the following Windows PowerShell command:

```
Add-WindowsFeature fs-iscsitarget-server
```

iSCSI disks are intended to use one-to-one mappings with a target host device. Traditionally, a large storage vendor provided an expensive SAN that offered block-based storage. In *block-based storage*, a small chunk, or block, of the total storage system is allocated and dedicated to a specific LUN. Physical SCSI disks use LUNs on a host machine to uniquely identify each disk to a controller.

In Windows Server 2012 R2, each iSCSI LUN connects to a VHD as the source. Figure 1-42 shows the New iSCSI Virtual Disk Wizard, which is used to create a new iSCSI Target disk.

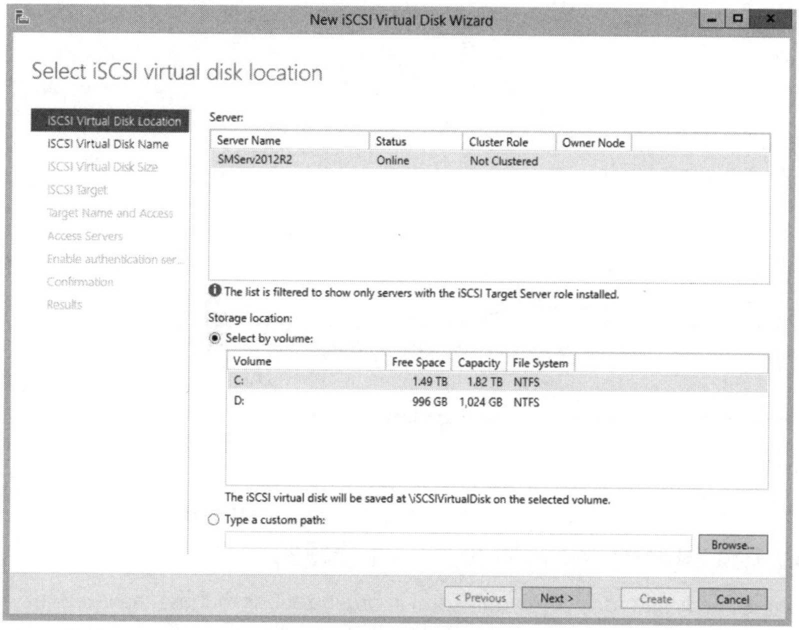

FIGURE 1-42 The New iSCSI Virtual Disk Wizard

You must identify the access server so that initiators can find the target. Options here include IQN, DNS Name, IP Address, or MAC Address. The iSCSI Qualified Name (IQN) is a required part of defining an iSCSI Target and is autogenerated for you by the wizard.

Configuring iSCSI Naming Services (iSNS)

In large networks, the presence of large numbers of iSCSI LUNs can make it difficult for a client to connect to the right target. To help solve this problem, Microsoft provides iSCSI Naming Services (iSNS). It installs as a feature using the Server Manager Add Roles And Features Wizard. Figure 1-43 shows the iSNS Server Properties page with the Discovery Domains tab selected, which is where you can create a new domain with individual iSCSI nodes for easier client access and management. An iSCSI node can be an initiator, target, or management node.

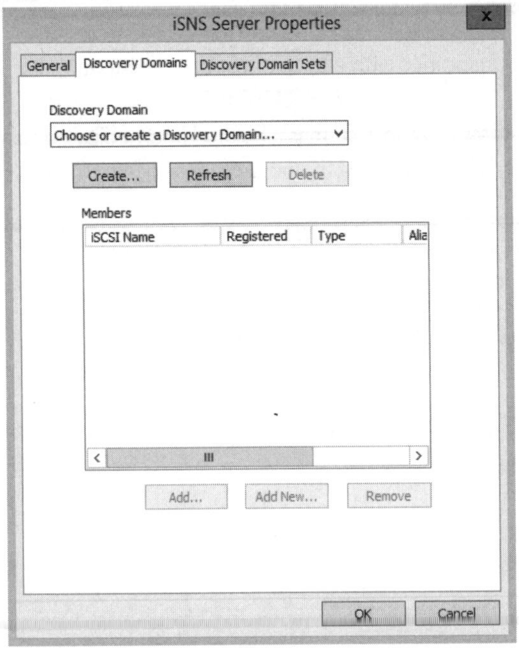

FIGURE 1-43 The iSNS Server Properties page is used to configure iSNS

You can use PowerShell to do the installation as follows:

```
Add-WindowsFeature iSNS
```

Configuring the Network File System (NFS)

Although the Network File System isn't commonly used in organizations that use the Windows operating system exclusively, it is frequently used in UNIX and VMware installations. For ease of management, it makes sense to provide NFS services from your Windows Server 2012 R2 environment if required. NFS is another role-based installation available either through Server Manager or Windows PowerShell. The PowerShell command to install NFS is this:

```
Add-WindowsFeature fs-NFS-Service
```

Figure 1-44 shows the Microsoft Management Console–based management screen for NFS services. One of the key requirements for configuring and managing NFS has to do with mapping users between Active Directory and (potentially) a Linux or UNIX equivalent by using the identity mapping feature of NFS services.

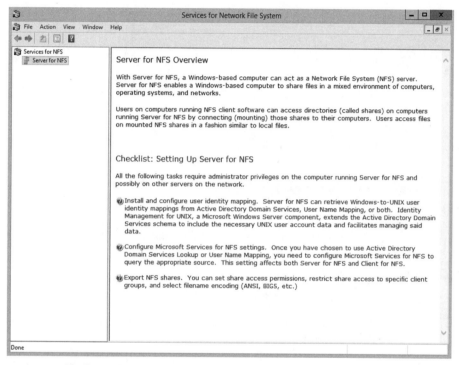

FIGURE 1-44 The Server For NFS Overview page

After the NFS services role is installed, you can create a new NFS share from Server Manager using the New Share Wizard as shown in Figure 1-45.

Authentication options include different levels of Kerberos authentication (see Figure 1-46) or no server authentication for a public NFS share.

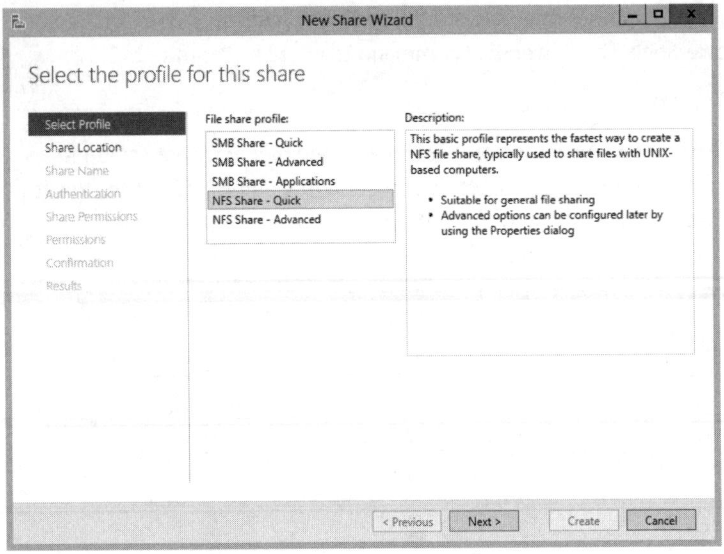

FIGURE 1-45 The New Share Wizard creating an NFS share

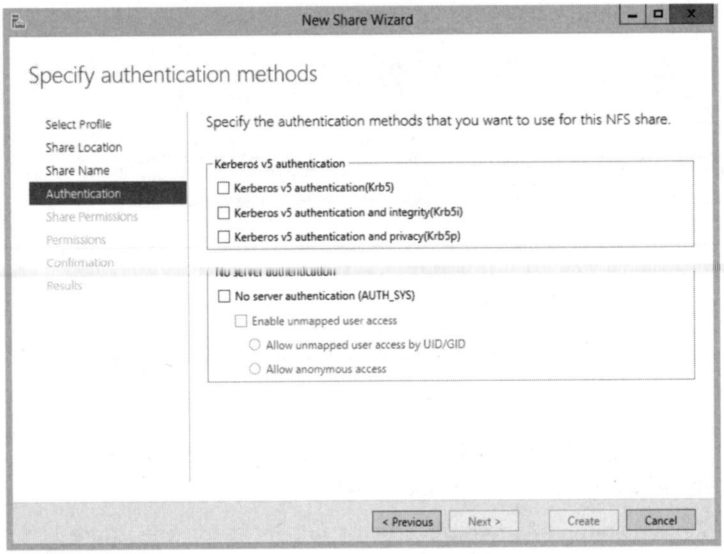

FIGURE 1-46 The New Share Wizard authentication page

Thought experiment

Building a cluster

In this thought experiment, apply what you've learned about this objective. You can find answers to these questions in the "Answers" section at the end of this chapter.

Clusters have become the default method for providing high availability and high reliability of Microsoft services. Consider the following tasks related to establishing a clustered file server:

1. List the hardware required to build out a minimal cluster system.

2. List the steps necessary to create a cluster and provide a clustered file system to the network.

3. List the advantages of using an SMB 3.0 file transport.

Clustering has become much more important to mainstream IT with the advent of Windows Server 2012. Understanding how to build a cluster from a hardware and software perspective is a key skill to have.

Objective summary

- Windows Server 2012 R2 includes a number of new storage features, including storage tiering, flashback read cache, and new management capabilities.

- Storage Spaces replace traditional hardware–based RAID drives.

- Data deduplication can deliver significant space savings and performance improvements.

- Windows Server 2012 R2 is an excellent iSCSI and NFS host.

- A good understanding of the new SMB 3.0 protocol and the requirements to take full advantage of its built-in resiliency should be a priority for any IT administrator.

- Knowing which storage vendors offer ODX support should greatly influence any new purchases of storage equipment.

Objective review

Answer the following questions to test your knowledge of the information in this objective. You can find the answers to these questions and explanations of why each answer choice is correct or incorrect in the "Answers" section at the end of this chapter.

1. Which tools are required to configure an iSCSI Target? (Choose all that apply.)

   A. Server Manager

   B. MMC and the appropriate snap-in

   C. Windows PowerShell

   D. DISM

2. Which security options are available for NFS volumes? (Choose all that apply.)

   A. Kerberos

   B. Active Directory

   C. Clear text

   D. SHA1 hash

3. What is used as the system resource behind an iSCSI LUN?

   A. Direct Attached Disk

   B. Storage Spaces

   C. ReFS volumes

   D. Virtual Disks

Answers

This section contains the solutions to the thought experiments and answers to the objective review questions in this chapter.

Objective 1.1: Thought experiment

1. Building a boot image for a site with different hardware requires a generic boot image with support for common devices. In this case, you could use the boot.wim file for the appropriate version of Windows Server 2012 R2.

2. With a specific hardware target. it's possible to customize the boot image and add any drivers that would normally not be available in the standard install image. To do this, have a copy of the drivers and then use DISM to insert them into the image used for deployment.

3. You can connect to Azure using Windows PowerShell by executing the following two commands:

    ```
    Get-AzurePublishSettingsFile

    Import-AzurePublishSettingsFile
    ```

Objective 1.1: Review

1. **Correct answers:** A, C

    A. **Correct:** Installation images are available on the Windows Server 2012 installation media.

    B. **Incorrect:** Although you can download distribution media from the Microsoft Developer Network (MSDN), they are not generally available from the Microsoft Download Center.

    C. **Correct:** Images can be captured using the WDS tools.

    D. **Incorrect:** It is not possible to capture an image from a running VM.

2. **Correct answer:** B

    A. **Incorrect:** Images for installing an operating system to a new system are either extracted from the distribution media or captured from an existing machine.

    B. **Correct:** Windows SIM is used to build an answer file for use in an automated operating system installation.

    C. **Incorrect:** DISM is used to modify an existing system image to add customized drivers and software.

    D. **Incorrect:** In the context of this chapter, you would use WDS to install a system image on a new computer.

3. **Correct answers:** A, B

   A. **Correct:** Windows PE is part of WDS.

   B. **Correct:** Windows SIM is part of WDS.

   C. **Incorrect:** The Windows Deployment Toolkit is a separate download.

   D. **Incorrect:** The Windows Migration Toolkit is a separate download.

Objective 1.2: Thought experiment

1. Microsoft Azure PowerShell provides the cmdlets necessary to fully automate deploying and managing VMs on the Azure platform. Using PowerShell makes it possible to create a library of scripts that can accomplish repetitive tasks consistently.

2. PowerShell has a built-in help cmdlet, Get-Help, which displays the documentation embedded in each cmdlet. You can also use the command Get-Command along with a filter to show all Azure–related cmdlets.

3. Deploying a VM can be accomplished with just a few PowerShell commands. They require the use of three commands:

   - New-AzureVMConfig -Name "TestVM" -InstanceSize "Small" -Image $image
   - Add-AzureProvisioningConfig -Windows -AdminUserName $un -Password $pwd
   - New-AzureVM -ServiceName "clcTestSvc1" -Location "East US"

Objective 1.2: Review

1. **Correct answers:** A, B, C, D

   A. **Correct:** Having local images available in a geographically diverse network speeds up the process.

   B. **Correct:** It is possible to prestage custom images for remote installation.

   C. **Correct:** Using prestaged images gives a greater measure of control over the deployment process.

   D. **Correct:** Using a local image reduces the bandwidth required over a WAN.

2. **Correct answers:** C, D

   A. **Incorrect:** Server Manager is not the proper tool.

   B. **Incorrect:** Although the network control tool allows you to change settings about adapters, it is not appropriate here.

   C. **Correct:** All GUI management of WDS happens using the MMC snap-in.

   D. **Correct:** PowerShell is a powerful tool and offers a second choice to MMC with the addition of the new cmdlets in this release.

3. **Correct answers:** A, B, C

    A. **Correct:** System Center App Controller is a viable way to deploy a VM to the cloud.

    B. **Correct:** Microsoft Azure PowerShell is another viable method of deploying a VM to the cloud.

    C. **Correct:** Linux support is provided through the Azure command-line tool.

    D. **Incorrect:** Xcopy is not a viable method for deploying a VM to the cloud.

Objective 1.3: Thought experiment

1. Microsoft lists a number of roles that migrate easily, but Hyper-V is probably the most obvious. New benefits with the Windows Server 2012 R2 version of Hyper-V make it a prime candidate, and the migration process is relatively painless. Other roles include remote access, network policy services, and typical file and print roles.

2. The Windows ADK provides the reports needed to determine what roles and services can be migrated either to a newer operating system or up to the cloud.

3. Migrating a file server with named shares would require creating duplicate shares on the target system and then copying files between the systems. Finally, the old server would be disconnected and any default share mappings reset to point to the new system.

Objective 1.3: Review

1. **Correct answers:** B, C

    A. **Incorrect:** A new Active Directory domain controller is typically brought up and configured, and then the old domain controller is decommissioned.

    B. **Correct:** Routing and Remote Access Services (RRAS) have been upgraded with Windows Server 2012 R2 and offer new capabilities not found in previous versions.

    C. **Correct:** A VPN server is now part of RRAS and would also be a good candidate for migration.

    D. **Incorrect:** Although an isolated test server could be easily upgraded, it typically isn't a candidate for migration.

2. **Correct answer:** A

    A. **Correct:** The WSMT offers the best solution for migration.

    B. **Incorrect:** The Windows SIM is used for deploying new systems but not migration.

    C. **Incorrect:** DISM is another tool used primarily in the installation process.

    D. **Incorrect:** PowerShell is a powerful tool, but not the right choice here.

3. **Correct answers:** B, D

    A. **Incorrect:** DISM is not part of the MAP Toolkit.

    B. **Correct:** The MAP Toolkit includes a capacity planning tool.

    C. **Incorrect:** PowerShell cmdlets are not part of the MAP Toolkit.

    D. **Correct:** The MAP Toolkit includes an inventory and reporting tool.

Objective 1.4: Thought experiment

1. At the lowest level, a cloud is made up of VMs connected together and to the outside world by virtual networks and some type of storage. Microsoft uses the term "Fabric" to describe the "plumbing" required to make a cloud functional.

2. Service templates make deploying new services much simpler. Specifically, they are designed to create identical applications or services based on the same template. The key is consistency and simplification of the overall process.

3. Deploying a VM in a VMM environment can take advantage of the PowerShell cmdlets installed with VMM. You can see these cmdlets by clicking the View Script button provided by the VMM console. For example, the NewVmFromVmConfig cmdlet creates a new VM using a previously defined configuration template.

Objective 1.4: Review

1. **Correct answer:** B

    A. **Incorrect:** A Windows system image is not required for creating a new VM.

    B. **Correct:** Using a previously configured VM is a valid option.

    C. **Incorrect:** Although you need a Hyper-V host on which to run a VM, it is not required for creating a new VM.

    D. **Incorrect:** Although SQL Server is used behind the scenes in VMM, it is not required for creating a new VM.

2. **Correct answer:** A

    A. **Correct:** Default administrator name and password are part of a Guest OS profile.

    B. **Incorrect:** Boot partition size is not part of a Guest OS profile.

    C. **Incorrect:** Custom drivers can be added using DISM, but not in a Guest OS profile.

    D. **Incorrect:** System components are configured in hardware profiles.

3. **Correct answers:** A, B, C, D

    A. **Correct:** Switch ports can be configured when managing logical networks.

    B. **Correct:** VLANs can be configured when managing logical networks.

    C. **Correct:** IP address blocks are a key piece of logical networks and can be configured.

    D. **Correct:** It is possible to create custom MAC address pools from VMM.

Objective 1.5: Thought experiment

1. Creating a cluster requires a minimum of two independent nodes plus storage available to both nodes.

2. Creating a clustered file share requires a minimum of two nodes with shared "just a bunch of disks" (JBOD)–based storage. The cluster wizard takes you through the steps required to actually create the cluster and add storage.

3. SMB 3.0 provides the underlying protocol for highly available storage and includes new features and services to provide timely failover. They require all client and server machines to be running Windows Server 2012 or 2012 R2, or Windows 8 or 8.1.

Objective 1.5: Review

1. **Correct answers:** A, B, C

    A. **Correct:** Server Manager provides multiple management points for creating and managing iSCSI Targets.

    B. **Correct:** MMC is a valid tool for making changes to the iSCSI Target Server.

    C. **Correct:** Windows PowerShell includes iSCSI cmdlets for creating and managing the service.

    D. **Incorrect:** DISM is not used for iSCSI Target management.

2. **Correct answers:** A, B

    A. **Correct:** Kerberos is the primary method.

    B. **Correct:** Connections can be made between Active Directory credentials and equivalents.

    C. **Incorrect:** Clear text is not an option.

    D. **Incorrect:** SHA1 is not used for this case.

3. **Correct answer:** D

    A. **Incorrect:** Direct Attached Disks can be used to store the virtual disks but are not directly assignable as an iSCSI Target LUN.

    B. **Incorrect:** Although the virtual disk can reside on a Storage Spaces volume, it is not the direct source of an iSCSI Target LUN.

    C. **Incorrect:** ReFS volumes are not recommended for iSCSI virtual disks.

    D. **Correct:** A virtual disk is the resource behind an iSCSI LUN.

CHAPTER 2

Design and implement network infrastructure services

Certain services have been a part of computer networks for decades and are largely unchanged. The intent of having computers networked is to facilitate communication between them, which is impossible without a standard set of services making this communication possible. This chapter discusses two of these services: The Dynamic Host Configuration Protocol (DHCP) provides IP address and basic configuration information to clients on a network; the Domain Name System (DNS) provides a way for computers to refer to each other using names that are more human-friendly. You'll also take a look at some alternatives to these services and some scenarios in which they might not be entirely necessary. Finally, you'll look at the new IP address management solution provided in Windows Server 2012, a tool that has the potential to ease the headaches felt by system administrators for years.

Objectives in this chapter:

- Objective 2.1: Design and maintain a Dynamic Host Configuration Protocol (DHCP) solution
- Objective 2.2: Design a name resolution solution strategy
- Objective 2.3: Design and manage an IP address management solution

Objective 2.1: Design and maintain a Dynamic Host Configuration Protocol (DHCP) solution

The Dynamic Host Configuration Protocol (DHCP) has two primary roles in a network: to provide IP addressing information and basic network configuration settings. A DHCP server typically provides (at a minimum) an IP address and subnet mask for the client device, the IP address of the router or gateway, and one or more IP addresses for Domain Name System (DNS) servers that will be used to perform name resolution.

The process of designing a DHCP solution involves many factors. The overall network design is a driving force in DHCP server placement, as well as the configuration applied to each server. DHCP broadcast requests do not traverse network routers by default, so DHCP relay agents are often used in large networks to assist in routing these DHCP requests to a DHCP server that can respond. DHCP scopes are also typically driven by the overall network configuration. Not only do scopes provide the pools of IP addresses but they also can be used to provide configuration information for clients on a specific network segment using DHCP options such as the subnet mask to be used or the IP address of the router for that network segment.

In addition to the network, the services used within a network should also be considered when designing a DHCP solution. Most networks use DNS for name resolution, and DHCP options provide a simple method of providing DNS server addresses to clients. Some network services such as Windows Deployment Services (WDS) actually require a DHCP server be available to provide IP addresses and configuration information to network clients.

Windows Server 2012 offers several tools with which to make your DHCP infrastructure design more flexible. DHCP options are used to provide configuration such as IP addresses for routers and DNS servers. A key part of your DHCP design is understanding where and how these options should be applied. For example, the router IP address is typically determined by subnet and can often be easily applied to a DHCP scope. On the other hand, DNS servers are often the same across an enterprise, making them good candidates to be configured at the server level. A new feature in Windows Server 2012, *DHCP policies*, are even more of an improvement. Using conditions based on the client's MAC address, vendor class, or even fully qualified domain name (FQDN), DHCP options can be applied to clients meeting the conditions of the policy.

Because DHCP is so critical to almost every aspect of your corporate network, it is essential to ensure high availability for DHCP services throughout your network. Several high-availability options are provided to DHCP server administrators in Windows Server 2012, and each has scenarios in which it can be the best solution. Choosing the appropriate high-availability method for different network scenarios and use cases is a critical aspect of designing a complete DHCP solution.

> **This objective covers how to:**
>
> - Design a highly available DHCP service and planning for interoperability
> - Implement DHCP filtering
> - Implement and configure a DHCP management pack
> - Maintain a DHCP database

Designing a highly available DHCP service

Due to the nature of DHCP, it is important to have the service available to the network at all times. In addition to ensuring that client computers can reach servers on the network to function properly, many network services actually rely heavily on the configuration information provided by DHCP servers on the network. Windows Server 2012 R2 provides several methods of ensuring that your DHCP services are highly available.

Because DHCP clients use broadcast traffic to find a DHCP server and request an IP address, you can't simply place two DHCP servers on the same network segment because they can provide conflicting information, causing significant problems for DHCP clients. An additional concern is that DHCP broadcast requests travel only as far as the local network router by default, requiring the use of a DHCP relay agent in order to pass DHCP requests on to the appropriate DHCP server. Any high-availability solution needs to take these networking intricacies into account.

Split scope

The oldest high-availability trick in the DHCP book is to use split scopes. DHCP scopes are used to provide a specific range of IP addresses for a portion of your network as well as the configuration information needed for that network segment. A *split scope* is typically configured with identical scopes on both servers, but the scope is split by using opposing exclusion ranges to prevent the two servers from offering the same IP address to a client. By splitting the scope in two and configuring two separate DHCP servers to handle a portion of the scope, you can better ensure that a DHCP server is always available to your network.

A typical split-scope deployment is configured with a primary server that provides 80 percent of the address space and a secondary server responsible for the remaining 20 percent. An optional delay can also be configured on the secondary server to ensure that the primary server handles the majority of the address leases. Although split-scope configuration used to be a manual process, Windows Server 2012 provides a wizard-based means to configure a split-scope deployment (see Figure 2-1).

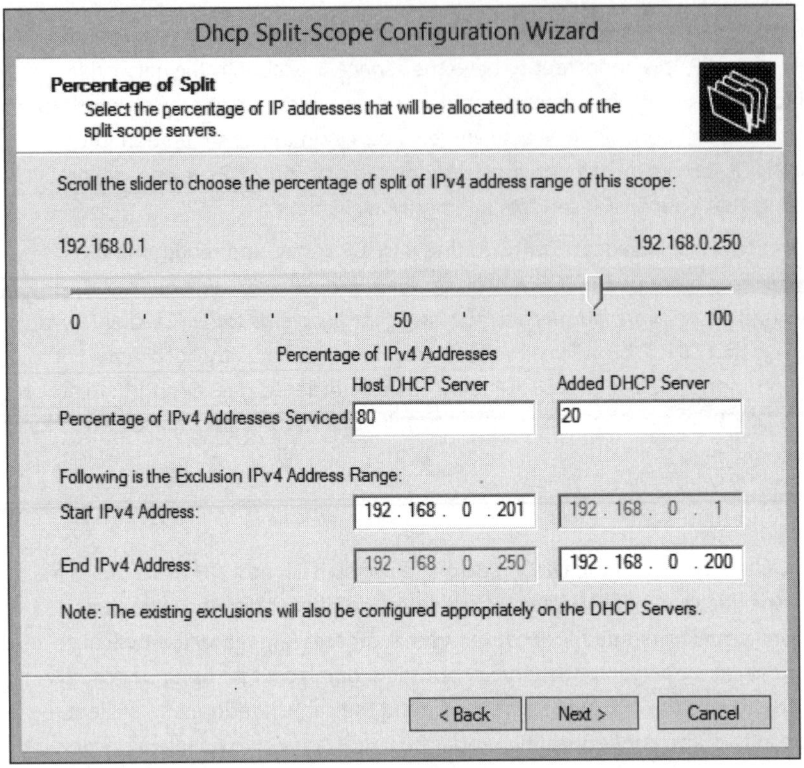

FIGURE 2-1 DHCP split scopes are the de facto standard for high availability

As with many aspects of life, there are pros and cons to using a split-scope implementation. A benefit of using this approach is the fact that legacy DHCP servers can participate in a split-scope implementation, although they might require manual configuration. The key disadvantage of split-scope implementation is that each DHCP server is capable of serving only a portion of your DHCP scope. If a DHCP server becomes unavailable, only a percentage of the scope is available for use until the server is reconfigured or the other DHCP server is restored to service. A key differentiator between a split-scope configuration and other high-availability options is that the two servers do not share or synchronize IP address leases, configuration information, or the DHCP database.

DHCP failover clustering

Another method of achieving the high availability typically found with DHCP services is *failover clustering*. Failover clusters require a minimum of two servers, known as *cluster nodes*, and can support up to 64 nodes. Failover clusters use shared storage to access and maintain the same DHCP database. A basic failover cluster configuration is shown in Figure 2-2.

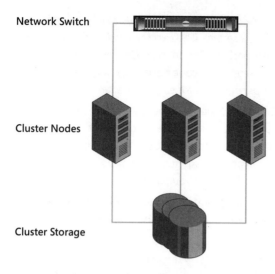

Network Switch

Cluster Nodes

Cluster Storage

FIGURE 2-2 Failover clusters require shared storage in order to maintain a consistent DHCP database

A failover cluster composed of multiple cluster nodes appears to network clients as a single host even if one node becomes unavailable, making it a good candidate for high availability. Although a failover cluster has the potential to provide a high level of reliability, it has significant hardware requirements for DHCP servers. Cluster nodes must be able to simultaneously access shared storage using Serial Attached SCSI, Fibre Channel, or iSCSI. A potential weakness of failover clusters is having the shared storage being a single point of failure. Hardware compatibility can be verified using the Validate Configuration Wizard.

Failover clustering is installed as a feature in Windows Server 2012 R2. After the feature is installed, the DHCP role must be added to the cluster using the Failover Cluster Manager. This process involves configuring the hostname and IP address for the cluster, as well as selecting the storage device. Additional nodes can be added to the failover cluster using the Add Node Wizard in the Failover Cluster Manager. A high-level overview of the steps to implement a DHCP failover cluster is as follows:

1. Configure appropriate networking and shared storage between servers.

2. Install the Failover Clustering feature on each server by using the Add Roles and Features Wizard.

3. Create the cluster using the Create Cluster Wizard.

4. Deploy and configure the DHCP role within the failover cluster.

DHCP failover

Windows Server 2012 introduced a new option for DHCP high availability in *DHCP failover,* which creates a partnership between two DHCP servers, enabling them to share the responsibility for a scope. It is important to understand the distinction between DHCP failover and failover clustering. Although using DHCP in a failover cluster requires a cluster first be deployed, DHCP failover is a function of the DHCP service. The two servers synchronize their databases and recognize the availability of their partner. Although DHCP failover partnerships are created between two servers, they are on a scope-by-scope basis, meaning that one DHCP server can have different DHCP failover partnerships for each scope it hosts.

When planning for reliability in your DHCP service, keep in mind the networking limitations of the DHCP. Because DHCP broadcasts do not traverse routers by default, it is important to plan for these broadcasts to reach a secondary server if the primary is unavailable. If your secondary server is located in another subnet, it might be necessary to configure DHCP relay even if your primary server is local to your clients.

DHCP failover supports two modes: load balancing mode and hot standby mode. The choice between the two modes is made during completion of the Configure Failover Wizard, as shown in Figure 2-3.

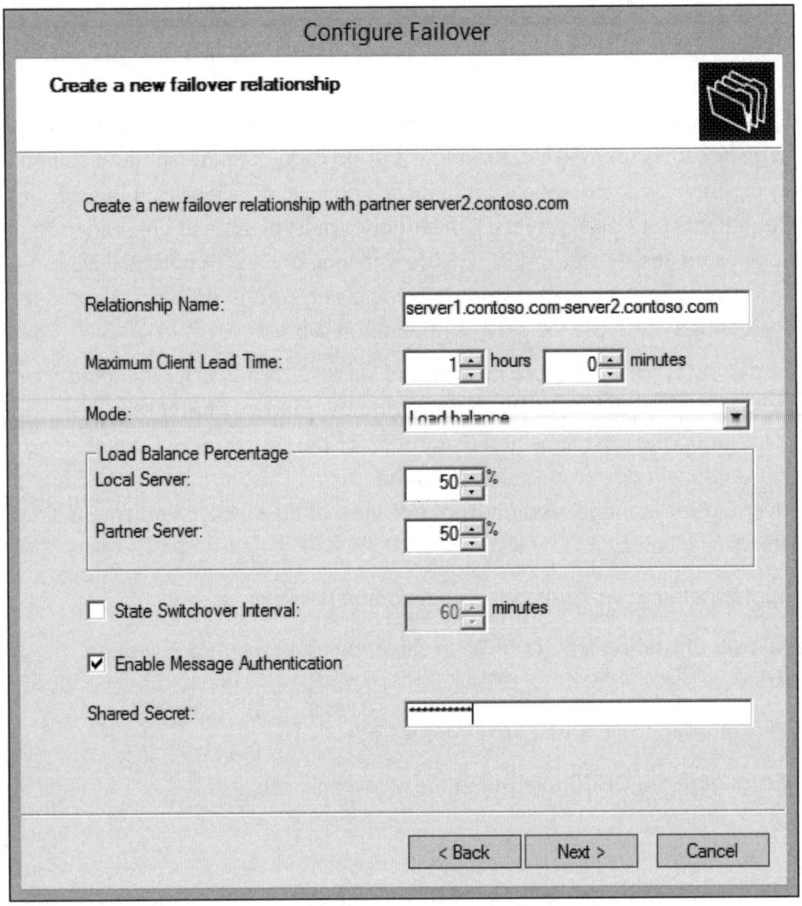

FIGURE 2-3 Configuring DHCP failover in load balancing mode

LOAD BALANCING MODE

Load balancing mode enables you to divide the workload between the two servers, either splitting the load evenly or prioritizing one server over another. Unlike a split-scope configuration, however, each server can provide the full range of IP addresses if the partner server is unavailable. Figure 2-4 illustrates two DHCP servers operating in load balancing mode, distributing the workload evenly between the two servers. The diagram illustrates the two DHCP servers alternating the responsibility of responding to DHCP requests. If desired, the load can be balanced unevenly, using a weighted load to have one server provide an increased percentage of the workload.

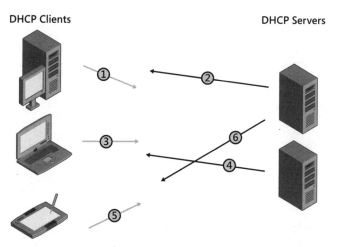

FIGURE 2-4 Two DHCP servers in a failover relationship operating in load balancing mode

HOT STANDBY MODE

Hot standby mode enables a secondary server to take over if the primary DHCP server is unresponsive for a predetermined amount of time. Because the necessary database changes are synchronized and not centrally stored, DHCP failover in hot standby mode is a good fit for a standby server located off-site. It can be beneficial for organizations in which having multiple servers at each location is difficult due to budget constraints or management workload.

In hot standby mode, the primary server is configured to accept all incoming DHCP requests, whereas the partner server is configured with a slight delay and reserves a percentage of the IP address pool for itself. If a DHCP lease is provided by the standby server, as shown in Figure 2-5, the lease duration is set based on the Maximum Client Lead Time (MCLT), which can be configured during the creation of the failover partnership.

Another function of the MCLT is to define how long the standby server should wait to take on the primary role after losing communication with the primary server. When the standby server loses communication with its partner, it enters a communication interrupted state. If communication has not been reestablished by the end of the MCLT duration, it remains in this state until manually changed to the partner down state by an Administrator. Alternatively, the failover partnership can automatically switch to the partner down state based on the value of the State Switchover Interval. A hot standby server cannot offer the DHCP scope's full IP address pool to clients until it enters the partner down state.

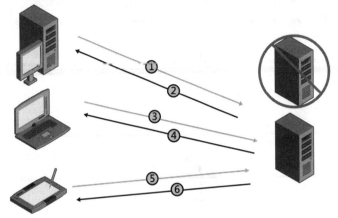

DHCP Clients

DHCP Servers

FIGURE 2-5 DHCP failover in hot standby mode

 EXAM TIP

Your knowledge of new features is typically assessed often throughout the exams, so you should be intimately familiar with DHCP failover. Specifically, you should know how to configure it, how it functions when one server becomes unavailable, and what types of scenarios are best for different configurations.

DHCP interoperability

At the top of this section, we mentioned how critical DHCP is to your entire infrastructure. This is especially true when viewed through the lens of DHCP interoperability, or how DHCP interacts with other services in your network. The simple process of connecting a computer to the network and authenticating to Active Directory depends largely on DHCP providing the IP address and DNS information for the client to contact a domain controller. A key aspect of planning and designing a DHCP implementation is to understand what configuration options must be in place and where they should be configured.

In a modern network, particularly one using Active Directory, DHCP and DNS go hand in hand. Often, DHCP clients receive their DNS server configuration through DHCP options, listing one or more DNS servers. Your DHCP server can also be used to perform dynamic updates of DNS records, keeping name resolution to clients consistent and up to date. DHCP–based DNS dynamic updates are just one method of keeping client resource records (RRs) updated and are typically used with legacy clients. Computers using Windows Vista,

Windows Server 2008, or a later operating system perform dynamic updates using the DNS client and DHCP client services. DNS dynamic updates are configured in the properties for the IP type node, as shown in Figure 2-6.

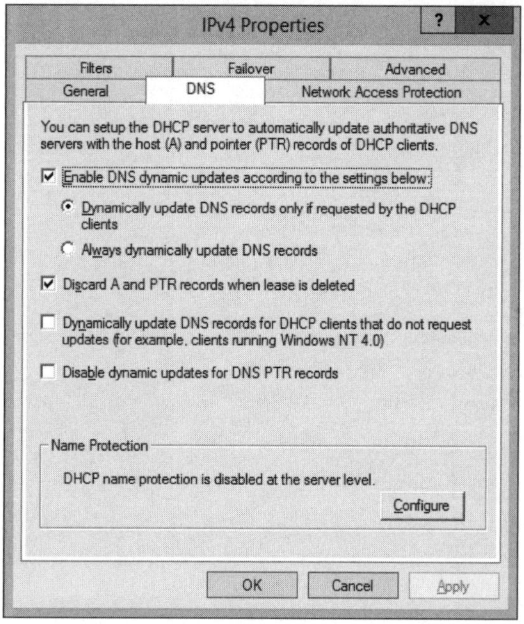

FIGURE 2-6 Configuring DNS dynamic updates from the DHCP server

Two new features in Windows Server 2012 R2 relate specifically to DHCP interoperability with DNS. Starting with Windows Server 2012 R2, you can configure DHCP to create or update only DNS A records for clients instead of both A records and pointer (PTR) records. The other new capability in Windows Server 2012 R2 is the ability to create a DHCP policy condition based on the FQDN of the DHCP client. It can be used to register DHCP clients using a specific DNS suffix or even configure DNS registration for guest devices such as workgroup computers or bring-your-own-device (BYOD) scenarios.

Another service that can be implemented in conjunction with DHCP is *Network Access Protection (NAP)*, which is a service used to constrain or manage a client's network connectivity based on specific criteria such as the client's health, method of connectivity, or type of hardware. A critical aspect of NAP is the need to evaluate the client computer prior to full network connectivity being established, making DHCP one service that can be used as an enforcement method. Although DHCP is a valid NAP enforcement method, it is by far the weakest because it can be bypassed by simply configuring a static address. Although NAP is officially deprecated in Windows Server 2012 R2, it is still part of this exam. (We'll delve into NAP more in Chapter 3.) Enforcement of NAP can be configured for individual scopes or enabled on all scopes, as shown in Figure 2-7.

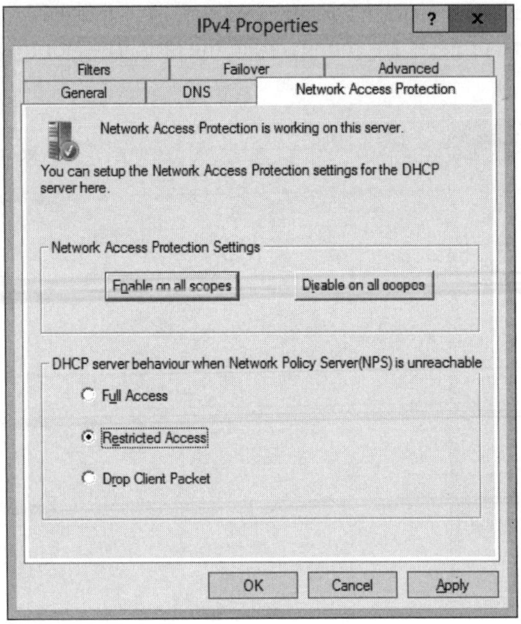

FIGURE 2-7 Enabling NAP enforcement using DHCP

DHCPv6

By this time, you are probably aware of the limitations of IPv4 due to network size and specifically the explosion of the Internet. You also probably know that IPv6 is the solution for the IP address crunch, at least for the foreseeable future. The IPv6 standard supports client autoconfiguration, so IPv6 clients are capable of generating and configuring themselves to use their own unique IPv6 addresses. DHCP for IPv6 (DHCPv6) can operate in both stateful and stateless modes, in line with the IPv6 standard.

Stateless DHCPv6 allows clients to use IPv6 autoconfiguration to obtain the IPv6 address, but provides additional configuration information such as DNS servers. Stateless mode requires minimal configuration, making it an especially good fit for organizations not yet fully invested in IPv6.

A stateful DHCPv6 implementation provides both the IPv6 address and additional configuration to clients. As with DHCP for IPv4, DHCPv6 requires configuration of scopes in order to offer IP addresses to DHCP clients; however, the scope configuration process differs somewhat from its counterpart. Table 2-1 lists the options found in the New Scope Wizard for a DHCPv6 scope.

TABLE 2-1 Configuration options for DHCPv6 scopes

Option	Description
Name	Used to identify and reference the scope.
Description	A longer description used to explain the purpose and use of the scope.
Prefix	A /64 IPv6 prefix for the address space served by the DHCPv6 scope.
Preference	Allows for the use of multiple DHCPv6 servers on the same network. DHCP clients use the server with the highest preference value.
Exclusions	Denotes a range of IPv6 addresses that should not be offered to clients.
Preferred Lifetime	The amount of time an autoconfigured IPv6 address remains in the tentative or preferred states.
Valid Lifetime	The amount of time an autoconfigured IPv6 address remains in a valid state.

In addition to offering a vast number of IP addresses, IPv6 has several other differences from IPv4. The DHCPv6 request process differs significantly from IPv4 communication between client and server. Table 2-2 lists the communication steps involved in DHCPv6 and their IPv4 equivalents.

TABLE 2-2 DHCPv6 message types

Type	Message	Description	IPv4 equivalent
1	Solicit	Broadcast sent by the client to locate servers.	DHCPDiscover
2	Advertise	Server response to Solicit message, communicating availability of DHCP.	DHCPOffer
3	Request	Direct communication with DHCP server, asking for configuration information that includes an IPv6 address.	DHCPRequest
4	Confirm	Client communicates with any available DHCP server to determine the validity of the address it was assigned.	DHCPRequest
5	Renew	Client communicates directly with the DHCP server that provided the previous lease, requesting an extension of the IP address lease and updates for other configuration information.	DHCPRequest
6	Rebind	When no response is received from a Renew message, the client requests an extension for the IP address and updated configuration information.	DHCPRequest

Type	Message	Description	IPv4 equivalent
7	Reply	Server message to the client in response to a Solicit, Request, Renew, or Rebind message. Also used to supply configuration information in response to an Information-Request message, confirmation or denial in response to a Confirm message, and acknowledgment of a Release or Decline message.	DHCPAck
8	Release	Allows the client to notify the DHCP server that it is no longer using the assigned addresses.	DHCPRelease
9	Decline	Used by the client to notify the server that one or more of the assigned addresses are already in use.	DHCPDecline
10	Reconfigure	Sent by the server to notify the client that that new or updated configuration information is available, indicating that the client should run a Renew and Reply or Information-Request and Reply to get the updated configuration.	N/A
11	Information-Request	Used by the client to request updated configuration information without an IPv6 address.	DHCPInform
12	Relay-Forward	Allows a DHCP relay agent to forward communication to another relay agent or a DHCP server.	N/A
13	Relay-Reply	Response from a DHCP server to a Relay-Forward message. Must be relayed by other relay agents to the originating relay agent and then to the client.	N/A

Implementing DHCP filtering

DHCP filtering enables you to exert more fine-grained control over which clients receive IP addresses from your DHCP server. Although DHCP filtering might be unwieldy for an entire enterprise network, it can be very useful for smaller, more secure segments of your network.

DHCP filters can be created by using either an Allow or Deny rule, and are configured using a full MAC address to target a specific client or a partial MAC address with wildcards to target network adapters from a specific vendor. Filters can be created at the server or scope level, and they must be enabled before use. Some examples of valid MAC addresses include these:

- C4-85-08-26-54-A8
- C4-85-08-26-54-*
- C4-85-08-26-*-*

One example using DHCP filtering is in a datacenter environment. Although many servers have static IP address assignments by design, this is not always the case. You can also have workstations within your datacenter network for management purposes, but you probably want to limit the computers that can connect on this network. DHCP filtering can be part of the solution to limiting the computers that can gain access to your datacenter network.

Creating a DHCP filter can be included as part of the provisioning process for new servers or workstations.

A new feature in Windows Server 2012, *DHCP Policies*, takes the concept of filtering a step further. Where filters can be used to only allow or deny a DHCP lease, policies allow you to configure specific DHCP options based on a client's MAC address, user class, vendor class, or several other criteria. Windows Server 2012 R2 even allows you to create a policy condition based on a client's FQDN.

When DHCP policies are incorporated into your DHCP design plan, you open up capabilities such as registering DNS records for non-domain DHCP clients. In this scenario, you would create a condition in which the client's FQDN did not match that of your domain and then configure DHCP option 015 (DNS Domain Name) with the DNS suffix used to register non-domain devices.

EXAM TIP

DHCP policies are not mentioned specifically in the exam objectives, but the feature is entirely new in Windows Server 2012, and the ability to use a client's FQDN was added in Windows Server 2012 R2. Be prepared to answer questions on this topic.

Implementing and configuring a DHCP Management Pack

Even with the configuration and management tools provided by default in a Windows Server 2012 R2 install, Microsoft offers an additional level of control when used with Microsoft System Center 2012. This holds true with DHCP because Microsoft offers the DHCP Management Pack as part of Microsoft System Center 2012 Operations Manager. The DHCP Management Pack enables you to centrally monitor and manage several key aspects of DHCP servers throughout your network, including the following:

- DHCP server health
- DHCP failover status
- DHCP database health
- DHCP security health
- DHCP performance
- DHCP configuration changes

The DHCP Management Pack does require Microsoft System Center 2012 and specifically targets DHCP servers running Windows Server 2012 or later. Additional management packs are available for use with DHCP servers running older versions of Windows Server.

Maintaining a DHCP database

Windows Server 2012 R2 DHCP servers store configuration and lease information in a database. The location of this database can be configured in the DHCP server properties, as shown in Figure 2-8. The DHCP server's database can be manually backed up or restored through the Actions context menu. An automated backup runs every 60 minutes by default. The location of this backup can also be configured in the DHCP server properties, and the interval can be modified by editing the BackupInterval value in the registry key found in HKEY_LOCAL_MACHINE\SYSTEM\CurrentControlSet\Services\DHCPServer\Parameters.

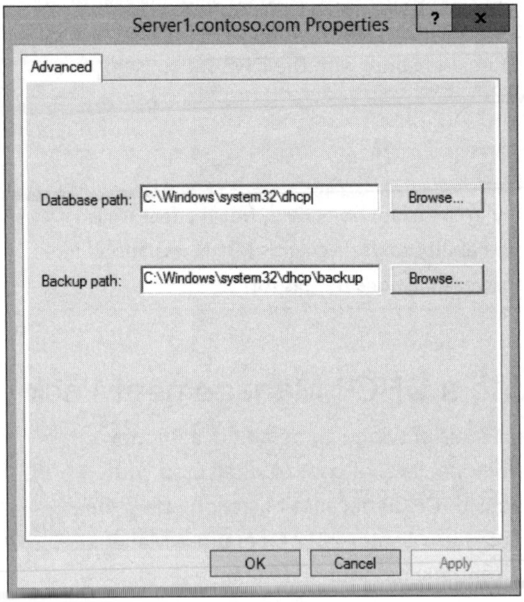

FIGURE 2-8 Configuring DHCP database and backup locations

It might be necessary to periodically resolve mismatches in the DHCP server database. You can do this by choosing Reconcile All Scopes at the IPv4 or IPv6 level, or Reconcile At The Scope Level in the DHCP Management console.

Thought experiment
Planning a highly available DHCP implementation

In this thought experiment, apply what you've learned about this objective. You can find answers to these questions in the "Answers" section at the end of this chapter.

You are being consulted on updating a large corporation's DHCP implementation. This organization has a corporate headquarters with a centralized datacenter and multiple branch offices. Each branch office has a single server operating as a DHCP server, DNS server, and domain controller. The corporation's IT department is located entirely at its headquarters and it needs to be able to efficiently monitor and manage DHCP services throughout the company.

An additional corporate requirement is to ready its network for IPv6. The IT department wants to minimize the configuration workload for its IPv6 implementation for the time being.

Finally, your client wants to allow guest devices on the network, but needs to be able to distinguish these guest devices from those that are corporate-owned in DNS.

Answer the following questions based on this scenario:

1. What DHCP high-availability technique is the best fit for this company? What level of service would be provided by servers at each branch? At headquarters?

2. How would you meet the requirement to efficiently monitor and manage DHCP throughout the company? What other requirements must be in place to implement this solution?

3. What type of IPv6 addressing would honor the IT department's request to minimize configuration workload?

4. Is there a capability within DHCP to control how DHCP clients are registered in DNS? If so, what is it?

Objective summary

- Split scopes are the traditional method of providing high availability, but they limit the IP address pool when one DHCP server is unavailable.

- Using DHCP in a failover cluster enables you to distribute your DHCP load across two or more servers, but requires shared storage and adds complexity to your deployment.

- DHCP failover is a new feature in Windows Server 2012 that allows you to partner two DHCP servers that then synchronize their DHCP databases to provide high availability.

- DHCP failover in load sharing mode actively shares the DHCP workload between two servers, although hot standby mode allows one DHCP server to serve DHCP clients with a second server used only when the first is unavailable.

- DHCP interoperates with several other critical network services, including DNS, enabling the automatic creation or update of DNS records when a DHCP lease is renewed. In Windows Server 2012 R2, this capability is more flexible, allowing you to limit these updates to only A records rather than to A and PTR records.

- New DHCP policy capabilities in Windows Server 2012 R2 enable you to create policies based on a client's FQDN, allowing you to dynamically modify the registered DNS suffix or handle DNS registration for workgroup computers or guest devices.

- DHCP filtering provides a means to restrict what computers are allowed to query the DHCP server by pattern matching the client's MAC address.

- The DHCP Management Pack for Microsoft System Center 2012 allows various aspects of DHCP to be managed and monitored at an enterprise-wide level.

Objective review

Answer the following questions to test your knowledge of the information in this objective. You can find the answers to these questions and explanations of why each answer choice is correct or incorrect in the "Answers" section at the end of this chapter.

1. DHCP failover supports two modes. What is the name of the mode that configures both partner servers to share the responsibility for responding to DHCP clients with the entire pool of addresses?

    A. Split scope

    B. Hot standby

    C. Load balancing

    D. Failover cluster

2. What is the maximum number of nodes that can be used in a DHCP failover cluster?

    A. 2

    B. 6

    C. 10

    D. 64

3. What is the recommended high-availability method for an organization with multiple branch offices and a central datacenter?

   A. Split scope

   B. DHCP failover in hot standby mode

   C. DHCP failover cluster

   D. DHCP failover in load balancing mode

4. What duration is used when a DHCP client obtains a lease from a hot standby server?

   A. The lease duration for the scope

   B. The lease duration for the DHCP server

   C. Until the primary DHCP server returns to service

   D. The value of the Maximum Client Lead Time

5. Which of these services supports interoperability with DHCP but is not a recommended solution?

   A. DNS

   B. Active Directory

   C. VPN

   D. NAP

6. How would you use DHCPv6 to provide only network configuration information to a client, not an IP address itself?

   A. DHCP filtering

   B. Stateless DHCP

   C. DHCP options

   D. Stateful DHCP

7. How frequently is the DHCP database backed up by default?

   A. 30 minutes

   B. 60 minutes

   C. 12 hours

   D. 24 hours

Objective 2.2: Design a name resolution solution strategy

DNS has the potential to be the single most critical aspect of your network. Resolving names to IP addresses is critical for network services and human usability, particularly in an industry moving to IPv6. Even beyond name resolution, DNS is used to direct computers to critical services such as email or Active Directory.

One significant area of focus for DNS recently is security. Due to the nature of the service, it can be catastrophic if a malicious user can register a DNS record that could then be used to direct traffic to a server under the user's control. Windows Server 2012 R2 takes some important steps in securing your DNS servers and ensuring that names are registered and resolved correctly and securely. Knowing what attack vectors are likely to be used to target your DNS infrastructure and which features in DNS can be used to mitigate potential areas of risk are probably the most critical aspects of designing a DNS deployment. The conceivable damage from an attacker being able to manipulate DNS is boundless because almost any network traffic can be diverted if the name resolution process becomes compromised.

Although not the only security feature provided for DNS, Domain Name System Security (DNSSEC) is a huge part of validating name resolution. Although DNSSEC was available in Windows Server 2008 R2, it was not until Windows Server 2012 that DNS zones could be signed while online. Another factor to be considered in the design phase of your DNS infrastructure is the performance overhead DNSSEC requires. A DNSSEC signed zone has four times the number of RRs of an unsigned zone. For file-backed DNS zones, this means four times the disk space is used by DNS; Active Directory–integrated zones have to plan for a significant increase in memory consumption. Similarly, DNS queries will result in an increase of network traffic, as RRs are queried and validated.

When the DNS structure is designed for an organization, the makeup of that structure is obviously an aspect that should be carefully planned. The structure of DNS is created using zones and zone delegations. Understanding the name resolution process and how other services such as Active Directory integrate with DNS will be driving forces in your DNS infrastructure design.

This objective covers how to:

- Configure secure name resolution using DNSSEC
- Support DNS interoperability
- Manage DNS replication using application partitions
- Provide name resolution for IPv6
- Support single-label DNS name resolution
- Design a DNS zone hierarchy

Configuring secure name resolution

Because name resolution is such a critical aspect of your network infrastructure, it is critical to ensure that all aspects are secure and can be trusted. Windows Server 2012 R2 includes tools to secure your DNS servers, protecting them from false DNS registrations. You also have the ability to use DNSSEC to add a validation process to DNS queries, preventing a malicious user from spoofing a response to a DNS client.

DNS infrastructure security

A large part of making your DNS infrastructure secure is designing your infrastructure and topology with security in mind. Features such as Active Directory–integrated DNS zones improve replication performance and security as well as allow for secure dynamic updates. Using file-backed DNS zones requires you to choose between completely disabling dynamic updates or leaving your DNS infrastructure open to significant attack. Likewise, limiting zone transfers to only known hosts should be one of the first things configured in your DNS zones.

Another aspect of your DNS infrastructure that needs planning is the support of DNS queries from both internal and external sources. Most organizations do not need every host on their network to be available to the Internet, so you should not allow their names to be resolved by Internet hosts. There are multiple ways of segregating your DNS infrastructure in this way. First, you can have a separate DNS structure for internal and external queries. Often a DNS server providing responses to the Internet has its RRs configured manually, thus preventing false resource records from being created in your zone. Another method of segregating your DNS is to have separate namespaces for your internal and Internet-facing hosts, such as contoso.local and contoso.com, respectively.

Outgoing DNS queries are another area to design for security. If every DNS server in your network is allowed to directly perform Internet DNS queries, this could unnecessarily expose these servers to attack. A better practice is to designate one or more DNS servers to perform external queries and configure the remainder of your DNS servers to refer external queries to these servers, either through forwarding or root hints.

Domain Name System Security (DNSSEC)

DNSSEC is a set of Internet Engineering Task Force (IETF) standards that adds a validation process to DNS queries using digital signatures. Digital signatures are used in DNSSEC to sign individual records as well as relationships up and down the hierarchy, providing a method to ensure a chain of trust throughout a recursive DNS query.

DNSSEC requires DNS servers and networking hardware that support EDNS0. It also requires the use of large DNS packets, which are enabled by EDNS0. In cases where networking hardware does not support EDNS0, DNS queries and validation might not occur properly.

A typical DNS query works recursively through several steps in a process. A typical recursive DNS query is shown here:

1. The DNS client begins the name resolution process by checking the local DNS cache, including names listed in the local Hosts file, which is preloaded into the cache when the DNS client service starts. The client cache also includes information from previous successful DNS name resolution queries. Cached RRs are retained for the duration of the Time To Live (TTL) value.

2. If the DNS query is not resolved in step 1, the client queries its preferred DNS server.

3. The client's preferred DNS server attempts to match the queried domain name against the zones it hosts.

4. If the DNS query cannot be resolved using the DNS server's own zones, the DNS server cache is searched for a match. These cached RRs are stored after successful name resolution queries and last for the duration of the RR's TTL.

5. After the preferred DNS server determines that it cannot resolve the DNS query internally, it begins a recursive query through the DNS namespace. Beginning with the Internet root DNS servers, as defined in the root hints, the DNS server queries through the DNS namespace from top to bottom until it contacts a DNS server that can provide a response to the query.

6. After a response is provided to the recursive DNS server, it caches the response locally and provides a response to the DNS client.

7. After the DNS client receives its response, it also caches the response for future use.

If recursion is disabled on the DNS server or a DNS client does not request recursion, an iterative process can be used to resolve the DNS name. An iterative DNS query is quite similar to a recursive query, except the client performs each of the queries instead of using the preferred DNS server. When using an iterative query, the client receives a response containing the DNS server that matches the requested domain name most closely. Using this newly identified DNS server, the client continues to query through the DNS hierarchy until it resolves the domain name.

Several response types can be returned by DNS servers in response to queries, each with a different meaning to the querying client or server. An overview of the various DNS query responses is provided in Table 2-3.

TABLE 2-3 DNS query responses

Type	Description
Authoritative	Indicates a response from a server with direct authority over the requested DNS name.
Positive	Returns one or more RRs matching the name and record type requested by the query.

Type	Description
Referral	Contains data differing from the requested record type. An example is a CNAME record that matches the query when an A record is requested. Referral responses can also be used in iterative queries.
Negative	Can indicate that the queried name is nonexistent or no records matching the name and type were found.

ATTACK METHODS

When a malicious user chooses DNS as a target, the goal is typically to compromise a DNS query to provide a false reference to a server under the attacker's control. If successful in returning a false query to a recursive DNS server, the attacker controls not only what server this traffic gets directed to but also the TTL value of the cached record, resulting in continued traffic for a prolonged period of time.

One potential method for an attacker to compromise a DNS query is to intercept the DNS query from either the client or the DNS server. If able to get between the corporate DNS server performing recursive queries and the authoritative DNS server for the record being requested, the attacker could provide a response containing whatever values he or she wants. This type of attack, shown in Figure 2-9, is known as a *man-in-the-middle (MITM) attack*.

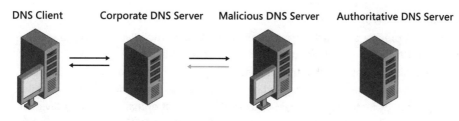

DNS Client   **Corporate DNS Server**   **Malicious DNS Server**   **Authoritative DNS Server**

FIGURE 2-9 An MITM attack requires a malicious user to intercept DNS query traffic

A second form of DNS attack does not require the attacker to step into the process, but does require some luck or (more precisely) some time. In this scenario, the attacker does not attempt to intercept the DNS query; instead, the malicious user simply attempts to predict a query response and trick the recursive DNS server into accepting this response.

Figure 2-10 shows this type of attack, referred to as *spoofing*. The difficulty of a spoofing attack is that the malicious user has to not only correctly guess or predict the name and record type being requested but also the XID, a 16-bit random value that must match the DNS request, as well as the ephemeral port (a random port selected from the DNS socket pool) being used for the specific query. With enough time and resources, both the XID and the port used can potentially be compromised by a skilled attacker.

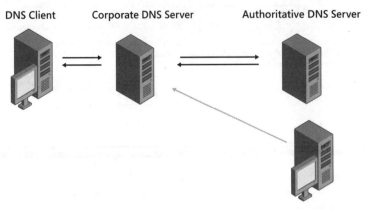

DNS Client   **Corporate DNS Server**   **Authoritative DNS Server**

Malicious DNS Server

FIGURE 2-10 Using spoofing, a malicious user attempts to predict the information required for a DNS response while providing information used to direct network traffic to a server of the attacker's choosing

In both scenarios, the attackers are attempting to perform cache poisoning. By inserting information of their design into the corporate DNS cache, they can direct Internet traffic to their own servers to exploit whatever information passes.

SECURE NAME RESOLUTION

DNSSEC does not prevent an attacker from intercepting DNS traffic or attempting to spoof the response to DNS queries. Instead, DNSSEC-enabled queries allow the recursive DNS server and DNS client to validate that the responses they receive are valid and come from a trusted DNS server. This validation is enabled by using digital signatures to sign and validate zone delegations in order to create a chain of trust from the root domain down to individual corporate domains, as well as signatures for individual RRs within a DNSSEC signed zone. By validating these digital signatures at each step in the query process, a DNS server can ensure that the responses being received are correct and have not been provided by a malicious user.

DNSSEC capability is communicated and negotiated within the DNS query through the use of flags, or single bits of data within the query. DNS clients and servers indicate whether they are DNSSEC-aware and capable of returning signed responses through the use of these flags throughout the DNS query process. Table 2-4 lists the flags used to indicate different aspects of DNSSEC capability.

TABLE 2-4 DNS flags used with DNSSEC

Flag	Usage	Description
DO (DNSSEC OK)	Query	Indicates that a DNS client or recursive DNS server is DNSSEC-capable, and DNSSEC signed responses should be sent if possible.

Flag	Usage	Description
AD (Authenticated Data)	Response	Declares that a response has already been validated. The AD bit is typically set by the recursive server in the response sent to the DNS client. DNS clients such as Windows 8 cannot perform DNSSEC validation, but can require that the response be authenticated.
CD (Checking Disabled)	Query	Indicates to the DNS server that the resulting response should be returned even if the response has not been validated. The default functionality with the bit cleared (CD=0) requires that the response be validated before being returned. Typically, a recursive DNS server performs the DNSSEC validation, so it doesn't require the response to be previously validated because it would have been handled internally. DNS clients normally leave the bit clear, accepting only responses that have already been through validation.
AA (Authoritative Answer)	Response	Although not DNSSEC-specific, the AA flag indicates that the response came directly from a DNS server that is authoritative for the zone containing the name being queried. If a client has set the AD flag requiring DNSSEC validation, the AA bit can be returned instead. It occurs when the corporate DNS server being queried by the client hosts the DNS zone containing the name being queried. DNSSEC validation in this scenario would be redundant and unnecessary.

A typical DNS query validated using DNSSEC would progress in the following way (see Figure 2-11):

1. A DNS client queries its preferred DNS server, indicating that it is DNSSEC-aware.

2. The corporate DNS server begins performing a recursive query, starting with the DNS root domain. It, too, indicates that it is DNSSEC-aware using the DO bit.

3. A DNS root server then replies to the query from the corporate DNS server, providing the DNS RRs for the requested child domain, the Resource Record Signature (RRSIG) record used to sign those records, and the DS record used to sign the relationship between the parent and child domains. The recursive DNS server queries one of the DNS servers in charge of the child domain, comparing the key in the DS record with that of the DNSKEY record in the child domain.

4. If the delegation is validated, the recursive DNS server continues the query process by querying the DNS server for the child domain. If the response includes another delegation, the validation process continues recursively through the DNS structure as shown in steps 3 and 4.

5. After a DNS server containing the requested RR is reached, the record is returned along with the corresponding RRSIG record. If the requested record name and type do not exist, the NSEC or NSEC3 and RRSIG record are returned, indicating a negative response.

6. Whether the response is positive or negative, the response is validated to ensure that the response is legitimate. If the DNS client is DNSSEC-aware, the response from the corporate DNS server includes the AD bit set to 1, indicating a validated response.

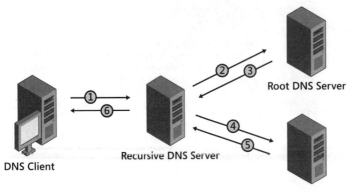

FIGURE 2-11 A typical DNS query uses recursion to resolve the DNS name

CHAIN OF TRUST

Each DNSSEC signed zone has a trust anchor, which is designated by a DNSKEY record. These DNSKEY records contain the public key for either the zone signing key (ZSK) or key signing key (KSK) used to sign the zone. Parent domains refer to a delegation using a DS record, indicating that the child zone is DNSSEC aware. These DS records are not automatically created either during the delegation creation process or at zone signing, but must be manually created to provide validation for the delegation. This DNSKEY-to-DS pairing creates the chain of trust that can be validated throughout the name resolution process, ensuring that a malicious user is not posing as a legitimate DNS server.

In a corporate DNS infrastructure, trust anchors must be distributed to each DNS server that provides DNS responses for a particular zone. When using Active Directory–integrated DNS zones, this process can be automated from the Trust Anchor tab of the DNSSEC properties for the zone. Windows Server 2012 also adds the Trust Points node in DNS Manager, allowing you to quickly determine where trust points are configured within your DNS structure.

ZONE SIGNING

A DNS zone becomes capable of providing DNSSEC signed responses through the zone signing process. Although Windows Server 2008 R2 supports DNSSEC, it supports zone signing only while the zone is online. Windows Server 2012 and following support online signing of DNS zones. During the zone signing process, keys are created and then used to create signatures for each RR in the zone.

Each RR typically found in a DNS zone, such as A and CNAME records, has two additional RRs associated with it after the zone is signed. The RRSIG record type contains the digital signature used to validate the RR (see Figure 2-12). Either a Next Secure (NSEC) or Next Secure 3 (NSEC3) record is created to validate a negative response from a DNS server when a requested record does not exist. NSEC3 records have the additional benefit of preventing *zone walking*, by which an attacker could enumerate all the RRs in your zone. Additionally, this NSEC or NSEC3 record has an RRSIG record of its own. The net result is at least four times the number of RRs per DNSSEC signed zone, which could have an impact on performance because additional memory and storage capacity might be needed.

server1	Host (A)	192.168.1.134
server1	Host (A)	192.168.0.1
server1	IPv6 Host (AAAA)	2002:6cb9:8988:e472:d907:...
server1	RR Signature (RRSIG)	[A][Inception(UTC): 1/4/2...
server1	RR Signature (RRSIG)	[AAAA][Inception(UTC): 1...

FIGURE 2-12 RRSIG RRs provide digital signatures for each A or AAAA RR

Table 2-5 describes the DNS RRs used by DNSSEC.

TABLE 2-5 DNS RRs introduced by DNSSEC

Resource record	Description
DS	Used to secure a delegation, contained in the parent zone.
DNSKEY	Pairs with the DS record in the parent zone to secure a delegation. Stores a public key for the zone.
NSEC (Next Secure)	Used to secure negative responses for nonexistent RRs.
NSEC3 (Next Secure 3)	Secures negative responses, but prevents zone walking by malicious users.
RRSIG (Resource Record Signature)	Contains signatures for individual RRs, including NSEC and NSEC 3 records.

In Windows Server 2012, DNS zones can be signed by using the Zone Signing Wizard found under DNSSEC in the context menu for the zone (shown in Figure 2-13) or by using the Invoke-DnsServerZoneSign PowerShell cmdlet.

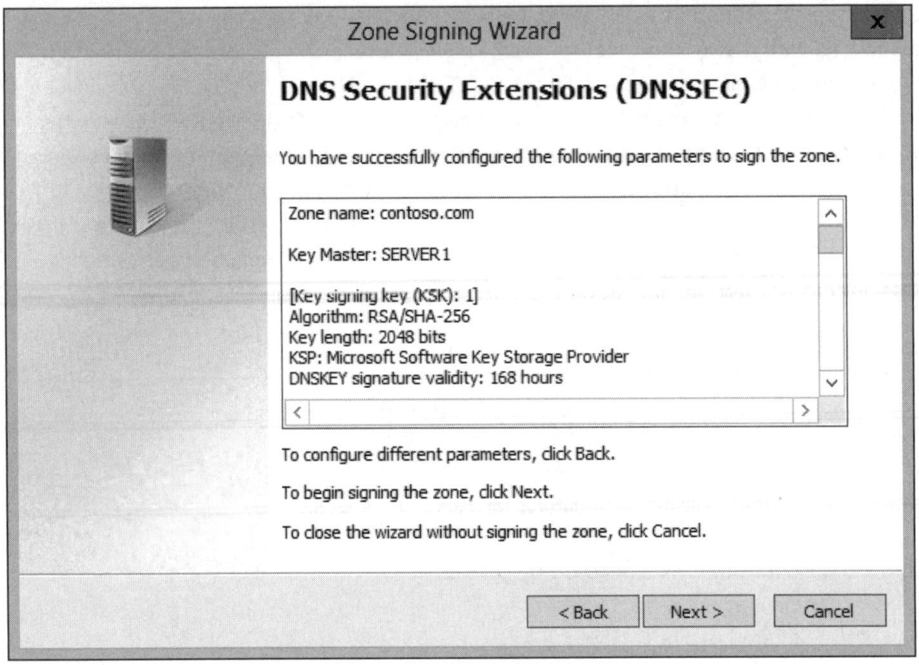

FIGURE 2-13 Completing the DNSSEC Zone Signing Wizard

KEY MANAGEMENT

The key to DNSSEC, quite literally, are the keys used to sign RRs. For each DNSSEC signed zone, the Key Master is responsible for managing and maintaining the keys used for that zone. The Key Master role can be transferred by using either the Key Master tab in the DNSSEC properties window or the Reset-DnsServerZoneKeyMasterRole cmdlet. Transfer of the Key Master role is possible only with Active Directory–integrated zones.

Two keys are typically used for DNSSEC signed zones. The KSK is used to digitally sign the ZSK; the ZSK is used to sign the remaining RRs in the zone. From a DNSSEC standpoint, there is no real difference between the two keys; in fact, the same key can be for both purposes. The benefit afforded by using both key types has to do with balancing the need for frequent key rollover for security purposes and the need to minimize the administrative overhead involved with the key rollover process. The two key types can be managed in the DNSSEC properties for the zone using the KSK and ZSK tabs.

Key rollover is the process of changing the keys used to create digital signatures. Because this key is what protects the integrity of your DNS infrastructure, it is important to change it periodically, much like requiring users to change their passwords. The problem is that the existing keys have been used to sign RRs, which often have been replicated to other servers, published to a parent zone, or cached on a recursive DNS server. To prevent scenarios in which name resolution queries cannot validate correctly due to mismatched keys, there are two key rollover methods that allow you to change your DNSSEC keys without interfering with the name resolution process.

Double Signature rollover involves generating and using two keys rather than one. For the ZSK, it results in the size of the zone being doubled because each RR must be signed using each ZSK. For KSK rollover, only the corresponding DNSKEY record must be duplicated, and communication to the parent zone needs to happen only once to provide an updated DS record.

Key Pre-publication also creates two keys, but the process differs after that. When used for the ZSK, only the DNSKEY record is duplicated. After the key rollover is performed, the zone is signed using the second key; the original is retained until all cached signatures would have expired. In the case of the KSK, Key Pre-publication duplicates the DNSKEY and publishes the associated DS record to the parent zone. After the DS record has been fully propagated through the DNS servers for the parent zone, the original DS record is removed, and the new KSK is put into service. Table 2-6 enumerates the pros and cons of pairing each key rollover method with the two key types.

TABLE 2-6 Pros and cons of key rollover methods

Key type	Rollover method	Comments
ZSK	Double Signature	Pro: Key rollover can be accomplished in three steps. Con: The size of the DNS zone doubles.
ZSK	Key Pre-publication	Pro: Size of the zone is not doubled. Pro: Key can be manually changed quickly in the case of a compromised ZSK. Con: Requires four steps rather than three.
KSK	Double Signature	Pro: Needs only one communication with the parent zone.
KSK	Key Pre-publication	Con: Requires two interactions with the parent zone: one to add the new key and another to remove the old. Con: Could result in "security lameness," in which the parent has a DS record that is not matched by a DNSKEY in the child. In this scenario, the child zone might be marked as bogus by a validator.

Due to the requirements of the rollover processes for the two key types, it is recommended to use Key Pre-publication for the ZSK and Double Signature for the KSK. Automatic rollover for both key types can be enabled in the ZSK and KSK tabs in the DNSSEC properties for the zone. The automated key rollover process uses the recommended rollover method for each key type.

NAME RESOLUTION POLICY TABLE

The Name Resolution Policy Table (NRPT) is used to configure the way DNS clients in Windows Vista, Windows Server 2008, and later perform their name resolution. Managed within Group Policy, the NRPT allows you to configure the DNS client based on domain names or wildcard matches. Using NRPT, you can configure the way computers in your organization use DNSSEC, when validation should be required, and even when IPsec should be used to encrypt communication between the DNS client and the DNS server.

Policies in the NRPT can be applied using several methods, which are listed in Table 2-7.

TABLE 2-7 Criteria for applying policies in the NRPT

Type	Description
Suffix	Can be used to target a specific domain, including child or top-level domains.
Prefix	Affects only queries for a specific host name. For example, an entry of *server1* would affect queries for server1.contoso.com or server1.west.contoso.com.
FQDN	Applies only to a specific host and is configured as the FQDN for a specific computer.
Subnet (IPv4)	Allows you to configure NRPT entries for reverse lookups within an IPv4 subnet.
Subnet (IPv6)	Allows you to configure NRPT entries for reverse lookups within an IPv6 subnet.
Any	Configures the default policy, which will apply to all DNS queries not matched by another policy.

As an example, your organization might want to perform DNSSEC-enabled queries for external DNS queries, but needs to force validation for internal name resolution. In this scenario, two entries are created in the NRPT, one for the contoso.com suffix, and the other for *Any*. Both policies are configured to use DNSSEC, but only the contoso.com policy requires name and address data validation.

The NRPT is shown in Figure 2-14 and can be found in the Group Policy Management Editor under Computer Configuration\Policies\Windows Settings\Name Resolution Policy. Additionally, the client NRPT can be viewed using the Get-DnsClientNrptPolicy cmdlet.

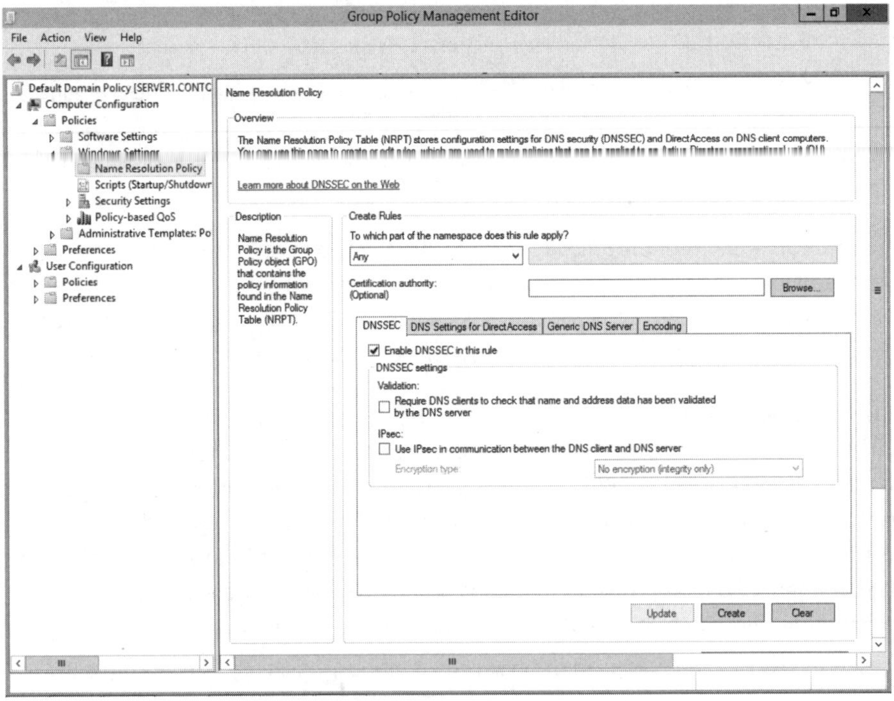

FIGURE 2-14 Configuring the NRPT

MORE INFO **DNSSEC**

For more information on DNSSEC, visit *http://technet.microsoft.com/en-us/library/
jj200221.aspx*. For more information on new DNSSEC features in Windows Server 2012, visit
http://technet.microsoft.com/en-us/library/dn305897.aspx#DNSSEC. For more information
on changes to DNSSEC in Windows Server 2012 R2, visit *http://technet.microsoft.com/
en-us/library/dn305898.aspx#DNSSEC*.

EXAM TIP

DNSSEC has received some significant new capabilities in both Windows Server 2012 and
Windows Server 2012 R2. Make sure you know what new features are available in each
edition and have a good understanding of DNSSEC.

DNS socket pool

DNS servers use a range of ports known as the DNS socket pool to reply to DNS queries.
Using a pool of addresses provides a level of protection against DNS spoofing attacks by
requiring a malicious user to correctly guess the randomly selected response port in addition
to a random transaction ID. Increasing the size of your DNS socket pool reduces the odds of
an attacker correctly guessing the port number being used for a DNS response.

Windows Server 2012 has a default DNS socket pool size of 2,500 that can be adjusted to
between 0 and 10,000. Exclusions can also be made when a port range is already being used
by another service.

To configure the socket pool size, use the following command:

```
dnscmd /Config /SocketPoolSize <value>
```

An exclusion range can be added to prevent interference with other applications or
services using this command:

```
dnscmd /Config /SocketPoolExcludedPortRanges <excluded port ranges>
```

Although increasing the size of the DNS socket pool reduces the odds of an attacker
compromising a DNS query, by itself this is not enough of a security measure to protect your
DNS infrastructure from attack. It is recommended that you manage the size of the DNS
socket pool in addition to implementing other measures such as DNSSEC.

Cache locking

DNS clients and servers make heavy use of caching to expedite DNS queries. Rather than
performing a full recursive DNS query when resolving a name, both the client and server will
typically cache the response for later use. The amount of time a query response is cached is
determined by a TTL value assigned to the RR.

Although a DNS response is cached, it can be updated if new information about the RR is obtained. A potential vulnerability known as *cache poisoning* involves the possibility of an attacker updating a cached record with false information and a long TTL value. When cache poisoning occurs, it allows an attacker to direct users to a server under his or her control.

To prevent cache poisoning, the DNS server role has supported *cache locking* since Windows Server 2008 R2, whereby updates to cached records are restricted for a percentage of the record's TTL. For example, if the cache locking value is set to 50, cached records will not be allowed to update for the first half of the TTL. The default cache value is set to 100, meaning updates are not allowed to cached records until the TTL has fully expired. The cache value can be configured using the following command:

```
Set-DnsServerCache -LockingPercent <percent>
```

In addition to configuring cache locking, the Set-DnsServerCache cmdlet can also set the maximum size of the DNS cache, the maximum TTL values for positive and negative responses, and other security-related settings for the DNS server cache.

Supporting DNS interoperability

In a network that depends largely on Active Directory, it is usually beneficial to use DNS servers running Windows Server because of the tight integration between Active Directory and DNS. When a client connects to the network and attempts to authenticate to a domain controller, DNS is the service used to locate a nearby domain controller. When a domain controller is added to the domain, it not only creates A and PTR records in the DNS zone but service location (SRV) records are also created for clients to find a server to perform authentication. Figure 2-15 shows some of the SRV records used to direct clients to Active Directory domain controllers through both Kerberos and LDAP, as well as the _mcds.contoso.com zone. Many other services and applications, such as Microsoft Exchange and Lync, use SRV records in DNS to refer clients to the appropriate server.

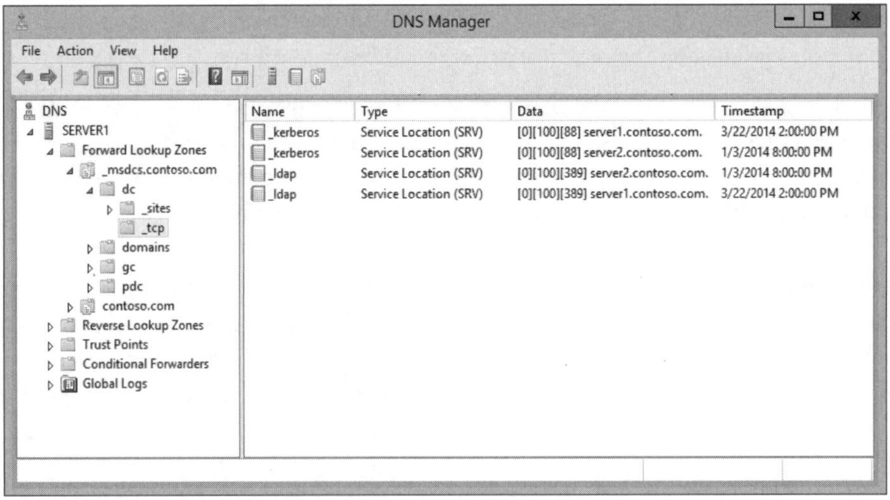

FIGURE 2-15 SRV records used for Active Directory

DNS servers running Windows Server do support interoperability with the Berkeley Internet Name Domain (BIND) software that is an alternative DNS server for UNIX platforms. Interoperability with BIND must be enabled in the DNS server properties by selecting the Enable BIND Secondaries check box on the Advanced tab.

EXAM TIP

Name resolution touches so many other aspects of your infrastructure that DNS is one of the most important topics when studying for this exam. DNS interoperability with other services is crucial for understanding and diagnosing problems with everything from Remote Access to Active Directory.

Managing DNS replication with application partitions

Not properly planning for DNS replication can have a performance impact on your network. If your DNS servers are not strategically placed within your network with properly configured replication, all sorts of performance issues could result.

Application partitions, also known as *directory partitions*, are part of the Active Directory database that control replication between domain controllers in your domain and forest. Active Directory-integrated DNS zones can have the following replication scopes:

- To all DNS servers running on domain controllers within the domain
- To all DNS servers running on domain controllers within the forest
- To all domain controllers within the domain
- To domain controllers within the directory partition

To fine-tune the replication of your DNS zone, you can create custom application directory partitions and selectively choose which domain controllers should receive a copy of your DNS zone.

To illustrate the utility of using application partitions to define replication scope, Figure 2-16 shows a simple Active Directory forest. Each domain in the forest contains three domain controllers, two of which are also DNS servers. For this scenario, consider the need to replicate the contoso.com zone to one DNS server in each domain. Choosing to replicate to all DNS servers operating as domain controllers in the domain results in two instances of the DNS zone, both in the contoso.com domain. Expanding to DNS servers on domain controllers in the entire forest results in your zone being hosted on six separate servers throughout the forest. Replicating to all domain controllers within the domain doesn't meet the requirement, either. Only by creating an application directory partition and adding one DNS server/domain controller from each domain can the requirement be met.

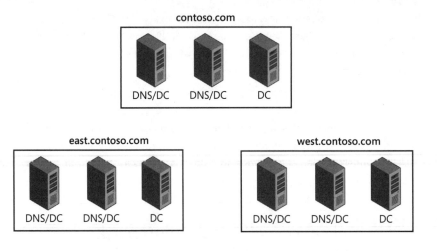

contoso.com

DNS/DC   DNS/DC   DC

east.contoso.com

DNS/DC   DNS/DC   DC

west.contoso.com

DNS/DC   DNS/DC   DC

FIGURE 2-16 A simple Active Directory forest structure showing the utility of application partitions

There are three steps to configure DNS zone replication to domain controllers within an application partition. The first is to create the application partition by using the following command:

```
AddDnsServerDirectoryPartition < Partition FQDN >
```

The second step is to include one or more domain controllers in the application partition by using this command, specifying the –ComputerName parameter if a remote server is to be added instead of the computer running the command:

```
Register-DnsServerDirectoryPartition <Partition FQDN> -ComputerName <ServerName>
```

The final step of configuring your DNS zone to replicate using an application partition is to configure replication in the DNS zone properties window. On the General tab, click the Change button next to Replication, select the option for replication within a directory partition and then choose the partition you want to use for the zone (see Figure 2-17).

FIGURE 2-17 Choosing a directory partition as the DNS replication scope

Providing name resolution for IPv6

DNS for IPv6 clients is not significantly different from that for IPv4. The biggest difference is in the creation of RRs: Instead of using A records for name resolution, IPv6 hosts require AAAA (quad-A) records.

Reverse lookups also function in the same way as IPv4 reverse lookups. When used to create a reverse lookup, the New Zone Wizard allows you to choose between IPv4 and IPv6, as shown in Figure 2-18. The wizard continues by asking for an IPv6 address prefix that is configured using the prefix combined with the length, as in FE80::/64. Finally, you configure dynamic updates for the reverse lookup zone.

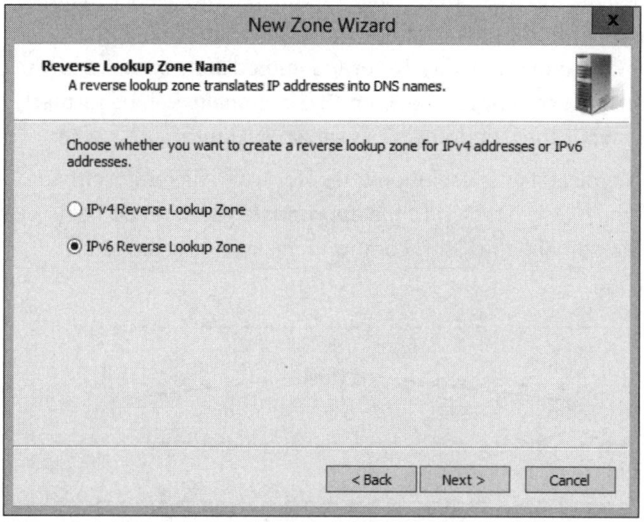

FIGURE 2-18 Creating a reverse lookup zone for IPv6

Supporting single-label DNS name resolution

Single-label DNS name resolution refers to queries for names without a DNS hierarchy. Whereas host1.contoso.com is an FQDN, host1 is a single-label DNS name. In most cases, the requirement for a query of this sort stems from a legacy application that was designed to use Windows Internet Name Service (WINS) for name resolution. In some cases, this sort of query can be handled through the use of DNS suffixes, but there can be a significant performance impact if the number of DNS suffixes on a client becomes too large.

A better solution for single-label DNS name resolution is through the use of a *GlobalNames Zone (GNZ)*. A GNZ allows you to support single-label DNS name resolution throughout a forest without having to query every domain using DNS suffixes. In fact, Windows Server 2012 uses the GNZ before using DNS suffixes by default, thereby improving name resolution performance. The GNZ can be enabled and configured using the Set-DnsServerGlobalNameZone PowerShell cmdlet.

Designing a DNS zone hierarchy

The structure created by DNS is useful for many reasons. First is the performance offered by simplifying the traversal of such a hierarchy. Within a few levels of DNS, you can limit the number of possible results from millions to just a handful. Another benefit of DNS is the separation provided between domains and subdomains, enabling management to be delegated to an organization or even split between corporate branches.

DNS zone hierarchy

A DNS zone hierarchy refers to the tree-like structure defining the parent-child relationships within DNS. The DNS structure begins with the root domain, designated by a dot (.). In most FQDNs, the dot is assumed. Up one level from the root domain are the top-level domains such as .com, .net, .edu, and .gov (to name just a few). Following immediately after are private or corporate domains such as microsoft.com or technet.com. These domains can be further divided into support.microsoft.com or other subdomains, as shown in Figure 2-19.

When a DNS client performs a typical name resolution query for *www.microsoft.com*, the DNS server begins at the root domain (.), is directed to the appropriate top-level domain (.com), progresses to the corporate domain (microsoft.com), and finally is directed to an individual host (www.microsoft.com).

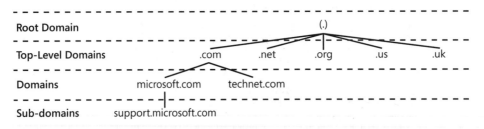

FIGURE 2-19 A basic illustration of the structure provided by the DNS namespace

DNS zone delegation

DNS zone delegations define the parent-child relationships within a DNS hierarchy. In Windows Server 2012, a zone delegation is created by using the New Delegation Wizard (shown in Figure 2-20), which is found by right-clicking a zone in DNS Manager and choosing New Delegation.

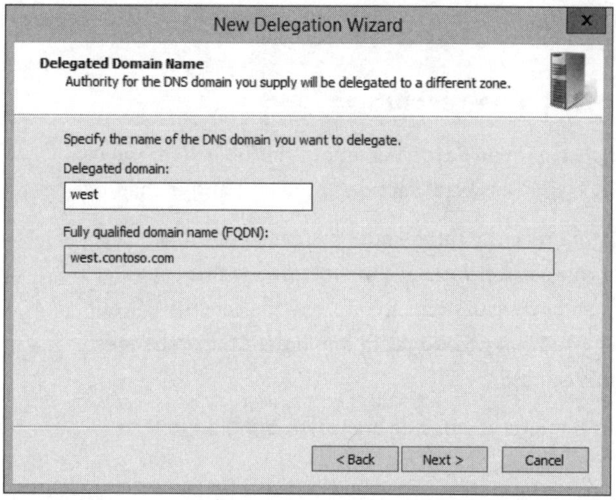

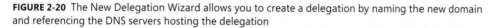

FIGURE 2-20 The New Delegation Wizard allows you to create a delegation by naming the new domain and referencing the DNS servers hosting the delegation

Through the process of completing the New Delegation Wizard, several things happen. First, the new DNS zone is created. Second, RRs are created in the parent zone referencing the new delegation. A name server (NS) record contains the name of the new child domain as well as the name server, whereas an A (or AAAA) record is created to resolve the name server to its IP address. This allows the parent domain to refer DNS clients to the child to resolve names within that domain.

Disjoint namespaces

A *disjoint namespace* is one whose Active Directory and DNS namespaces do not match. The most common configurations for disjoint namespaces are a multidomain Active Directory forest paired with a single DNS zone or a single Active Directory domain with multiple DNS zones.

Disjoint namespaces do require some manual configuration and maintenance. The DNS records used to refer clients to domain controllers are created automatically based on the client's Active Directory domain. If this domain differs from the desired location, these RRs must be created and managed manually.

Some applications are developed under the assumption that the Active Directory and DNS namespaces will match. When implementing a disjoint namespace, ensure application compatibility through proper testing.

In this thought experiment, apply what you've learned about this objective. You can find answers to these questions in the "Answers" section at the end of this chapter.

Your company's DNS infrastructure recently came under increased scrutiny due to a security breach suffered by a competitor. You have been tasked with evaluating the existing DNS configuration and offer solutions to improve the security of your DNS implementation. However, you have no budget to implement these changes because of the current economic climate.

Upon evaluation, you find several things you decide are worth bringing to the attention of your superiors:

- Your DNS zones are file backed.
- Each of your DNS servers is configured to use DNS root servers for recursive name resolution.
- DNS records are dynamically updated.
- Your corporation uses the fabrikam.com zone to provide name resolution from both internal and external DNS clients.
- DNSSEC is not currently implemented.
- All your DNS servers are domain controllers, and each is running Windows Server 2012 R2.

Answer the following questions based on this scenario:

1. What security features are you missing out on because your DNS zones are file backed? Do any of the other criteria listed increase your concern over this finding? Which piece of information makes resolving this vulnerability a simple fix?

2. Do you have any concern about your DNS servers being configured to use DNS root servers directly? Is there any security or performance benefit to using this configuration?

3. How big a weakness is using the same domain for internal and external name resolution? What steps could you take to mitigate these risks?

4. What benefit would the implementation of DNSSEC provide? What sort of performance impact can you expect from implementing DNSSEC?

Objective summary

- There are several inherent performance and security benefits to using Active Directory–integrated DNS zones, including secure zone transfers and secure dynamic updates to DNS RRs.

- DNSSEC uses digital signatures to provide a validation process for DNS name resolution queries, including zone delegation, individual RRs, and negative responses for nonexistent RRs.

- DNSSEC uses several new RRs to provide validation: DS and DNSKEY records validate the relationship between a parent domain and a child, RRSIG records validate individual RRs such as A or alias (CNAME) records, and negative responses are validated using NSEC and NSEC3 records. NSEC3 records also prevent zone walking.

- Windows Server 2012 introduced the capability to sign a DNS zone while online, and Windows Server 2012 R2 provides the capability to use a DNS server hosting a file backed DNS zone to perform the Key Master role.

- The DNS socket pool, the range of ports used to provide DNS responses, can reduce the likelihood of an attacker correctly guessing the random port used for a DNS response.

- Cache locking configures how soon into a cached RR's TTL the record can be updated. By default, cache locking is set to a value of 100, meaning that updates will not be accepted until after the TTL has fully expired.

- Replication of Active Directory–integrated DNS zones can be fine-tuned using application partitions.

- When DNS suffixes are not a feasible option for single-label DNS name resolution, the GlobalNames Zone (GNZ) can be used.

- The DNS structure is built using zone delegation, which identifies a child domain's relationship to its parent. This relationship is defined by an NS record and an A record in the parent zone.

- Disjoint namespaces are those whose DNS namespace does not match its Active Directory namespace; RRs required for Active Directory to function must be created manually in this configuration.

Objective review

Answer the following questions to test your knowledge of the information in this objective. You can find the answers to these questions and explanations of why each answer choice is correct or incorrect in the "Answers" section at the end of this chapter.

1. What security feature is offered by DNSSEC?

   A. Encrypted zone transfers

   B. Validated name resolution

   C. Secure dynamic updates

   D. Prevention of cache poisoning

2. Which of the following DNSSEC RRs validate the relationship between a parent and child domain? (Choose all that apply.)

   A. DS

   B. SOA

   C. NS

   D. DNSKEY

3. What capability is provided to manage the way DNS clients use DNSSEC for validated name resolution?

   A. EDNS0

   B. DO flag

   C. NRPT

   D. CD flag

4. What process results in the size of the DNS zone increasing by four times?

   A. Key rollover

   B. Recursion

   C. Zone delegation

   D. Zone signing

5. How would you manage the range of ports used for replies to DNS queries?

   A. Enable cache locking

   B. Use Active Directory–integrated zones

   C. Implement application pools

   D. Configure the DNS socket pool

6. What type of value is used to configure DNS cache locking?

A. Percentage of the RR's TTL value

B. Number of days

C. Number of hours

D. Percentage of a day

7. What benefit is offered by using application pools to manage DNS zone replication?

A. Increased control over replication

B. Secure zone transfers

C. Capability to replicate to DNS servers that are not domain controllers

D. Interoperability with BIND servers

8. Which type of RR is not used for IPv6 hosts?

A. CNAME

B. A

C. NS

D. AAAA

9. What methods can be used to provide single-label DNS name resolution? (Choose all that apply.)

A. Zone delegation

B. DNS suffixes

C. GlobalNames zone

D. Disjoint namespaces

10. What RRs are used to create a zone delegation? (Choose all that apply.)

A. NS

B. CNAME

C. A

D. DS

11. What aspect of your DNS infrastructure must be handled manually in disjoint namespaces?

A. Secure dynamic updates

B. SRV records for Active Directory domain controllers

C. DNSSEC zone signing

D. Zone transfers

Objective 2.3: Design and manage an IP address management solution

One of the new features in Windows Server 2012 that was a long time coming is IP Address Management (IPAM). The IPAM feature lets you monitor and manage DHCP servers, DNS servers, and IP address spaces throughout your enterprise in a single interface. Through the IPAM provisioning process, scheduled tasks are deployed on DHCP and DNS servers. These scheduled tasks are used to retrieve information from these servers, aggregating this data on the IPAM server.

The information within IPAM can be monitored to forecast IP address usage and diagnose problem areas at a glance. Thresholds can be configured to flag IP address pools or scopes approaching capacity. IPAM provides several ways to group and organize different collections of data, including the ability to configure custom fields.

After your IP usage data is captured and organized, IPAM features multiple capabilities for analyzing the data it contains. Comprehensive auditing, including the ability to track the IP address used by computers and users, allows you to track IP address usage over time for security and compliance needs. Windows PowerShell cmdlets provide import and export capability for IP utilization data, giving administrators great flexibility over where their data comes from and what they can do with it.

> **This objective covers how to:**
> - Manage IP addresses with IPAM
> - Provision IPAM
> - Plan for IPAM server placement
> - Manage IPAM database storage
> - Configure role-based access control with IPAM
> - Configure IPAM auditing
> - Manage and monitor multiple DHCP and DNS servers with IPAM
> - Migrate IP addresses
> - Configure data collection for IPAM
> - Integrate IPAM with Virtual Machine Manager (VMM)

Managing IP addresses with IPAM

DHCP and its associated IP address pools have always been an area that requires monitoring to ensure that the pool of available IP addresses does not run out. If an address pool runs out of addresses, users might not be able to access the network. The introduction of the IPAM feature in Windows Server 2012 provides administrators with an out-of-the-box tool for monitoring and managing IP address usage throughout the enterprise.

IPAM on Windows Server 2012 enables you to track usage of both public and private IP address pools. Windows Server 2012 R2 integrates with the Microsoft System Center 2012 R2 Virtual Machine Manager (VMM) to manage IP addresses used in a virtual environment.

IPAM not only allows you to monitor IP address usage but several aspects of managing your DHCP infrastructure can also be performed using IPAM. In Windows Server 2012, management capabilities include configuring scopes and allocating static IP addresses. With Windows Server 2012 R2, you can manage DHCP failover, DHCP policies, and DHCP filters, to name a few.

There are some limitations as to where IPAM can be installed and how many servers it can manage. IPAM cannot be installed on a domain controller. DHCP servers can have the IPAM feature installed, but automatic DHCP server discovery is disabled. IPAM has been tested to support the following numbers:

- 150 DHCP servers
- 500 DNS servers
- 40,000 DHCP scopes
- 350 DNS zones

IPAM supports monitoring of a single Active Directory forest, and only domain joined computers can be monitored. IPAM can manage only DHCP or DNS servers that run on Windows Server 2008 and later, but data from third-party or legacy servers can be imported into the IPAM database using Windows PowerShell cmdlets such as Import-IpamRange or Import-IpamSubnet. Auditing and usage data contained in IPAM is not purged automatically, but can be purged manually as needed.

Provisioning IPAM

In addition to installing the IPAM feature, there are several steps involved in provisioning IPAM, or configuring communication between servers running the DHCP and DNS server roles and the IPAM server. This is the most critical and most complex step of deploying IPAM. There are two ways to handle IPAM provisioning: using Group Policy or manually.

Group Policy-based provisioning

Because of the number of steps involved in provisioning IPAM and the number of servers typically requiring configuration, most organizations should use Group Policy to implement IPAM because it automates much of the process.

IPAM features the Provision IPAM Wizard to walk you through the majority of the IPAM provisioning process, allowing you to choose a database type and location, and begins the process of creating IPAM-related Group Policy Objects (GPOs) using a prefix of your choosing. Figure 2-21 shows the Provision IPAM Wizard at the Select Provisioning Method step.

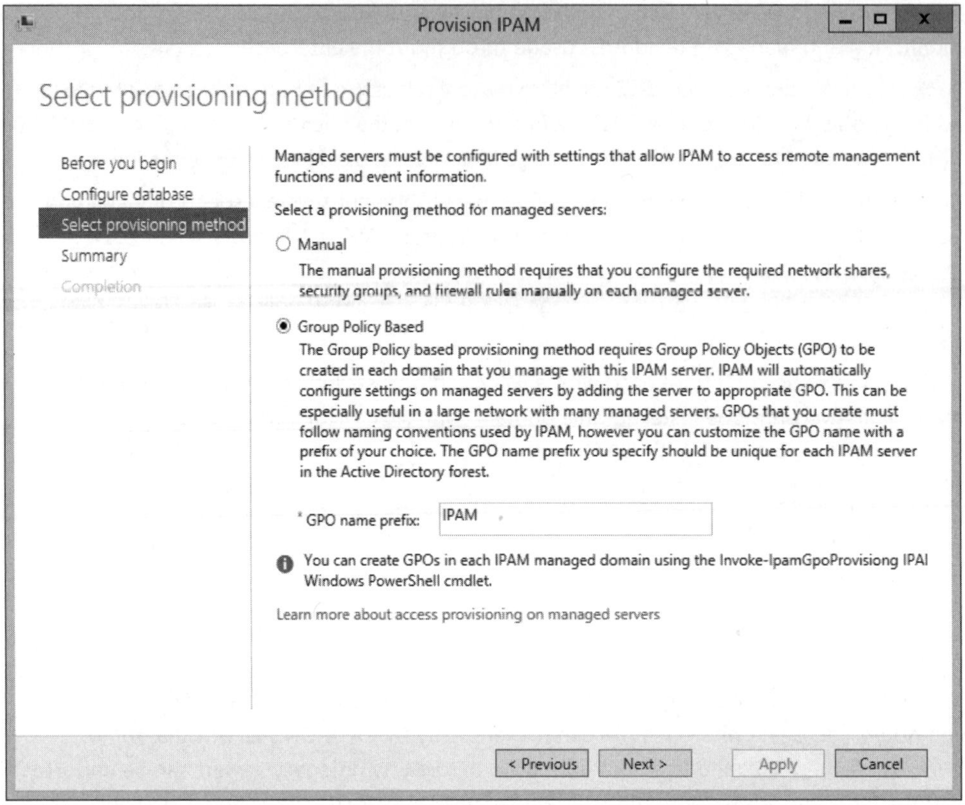

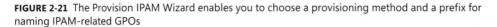

FIGURE 2-21 The Provision IPAM Wizard enables you to choose a provisioning method and a prefix for naming IPAM-related GPOs

These GPOs are not actually created and linked to a domain until the Windows PowerShell cmdlet Invoke-IpamGpoProvisioning is run. This cmdlet creates three GPOs and links them to the domain specified using the -Domain parameter. The following command is an example of creating these GPOs in the **contoso.com** domain, using a prefix of **IPAM** and an IPAM server name of **IPAM1**:

```
Invoke-IpamGpoProvisioning –Domain contoso.com –GpoPrefixName IPAM –IpamServerFqdn
IPAM1.contoso.com –Force
```

Next, you must configure the IPAM server to begin server discovery by clicking the Start Server Discovery link in the IPAM section of Server Manager. The Configure Server Discovery sheet requires you to choose a domain and the types of servers to discover. The server discovery process can take some time, depending on the size of your network and the number of servers to be discovered.

As servers are discovered, their management status must be set to Managed so IPAM can begin fully monitoring and managing them. Only users with domain administrator privileges can mark servers as managed. Individual servers can also be added manually by clicking Add Server in the Tasks menu.

EXAM TIP

The IPAM provisioning process sets it apart from other tools you're familiar with in Windows Server. Ensure that you know each of the steps in Group Policy–based provisioning and have a general understanding of what each step does in the provisioning process.

Manual provisioning

Although Group Policy–based provisioning is the best option for most scenarios, understanding the manual provisioning process ensures that you know the requirements for provisioning IPAM and configuring each server type.

Provisioning IPAM manually requires you to make the necessary configuration changes to each server that you want to manage with IPAM. Each server can be configured through the manual application of the IPAM GPOs, or individual settings can be applied to each server. These changes include modifying firewall rules, adding security groups and modifying memberships, configuring file shares, and restarting services. Each managed server type (DNS, DHCP, and domain controller) has a separate set of requirements and a different process for manual provisioning. After you manually provision the required servers, the server discovery process can begin, and you can configure servers as managed in IPAM.

Creating a security group in Active Directory to contain IPAM servers is recommended prior to manually provisioning IPAM. Group Policy–based provisioning uses the IPAMUG group in Active Directory to give IPAM servers membership in local security groups.

DHCP SERVERS

Several requirements must be met before IPAM can retrieve data from DHCP servers. Incoming traffic from IPAM to the DHCP server must be allowed through the Windows Firewall using the following built-in rules:

- DHCP Server (RPC-In)
- DHCP Server (RPCSS-In)
- File and Printer Sharing (NB-Session-In)
- File and Printer Sharing (SMB-In)
- Remote Event Log Management (RPC)
- Remote Event Log Management (RPC-EPMAP)
- Remote Service Management (RPC)
- Remote Service Management (RPC-EPMAP)

Because IPAM communicates directly with DHCP servers, the IPAM server must be given access to DHCP resources through membership in the DHCP Users local security group. In addition, membership in the Event Log Readers group is used to audit DHCP-related events. After the IPAM server is given membership in the appropriate groups, the DHCP Server service must be restarted.

For monitoring IP address utilization, IPAM requires access to the DHCP audit file location, which is contained in the C:\Windows\System32\DHCP folder by default. This folder should be shared as dhcpaudit, with Read permissions given to the IPAM server or the Active Directory group containing the IPAM servers. Best practices dictate that the default permissions for the Everyone group should be removed from this share.

DNS SERVERS

For monitoring and managing DNS servers, inbound IPAM traffic must be allowed through the Windows Firewall. As with DHCP servers, the following rules are predefined and need only be enabled:

- RPC (TCP, Incoming)
- DNS (UDP, Incoming)
- DNS (TCP, Incoming)
- RPC Endpoint Mapper (TCP, Incoming)
- Remote Service Management (RPC-EPMAP)
- Remote Service Management (NP-In)
- Remote Service Management (RPC)
- Remote Event Log Management (RPC-EPMAP)
- Remote Event Log Management (RPC)

If the DNS server is also a domain controller, membership in the Event Log Readers group in Active Directory must be provided to the IPAM server to monitor DNS events. If the DNS server is not a domain controller, the local Event Log Readers group should be used.

Monitoring of the DNS server's event log must also be enabled for the IPAM server, which is accomplished by modifying the CustomSD value in the HKLM\SYSTEM\CurrentControlSet\Services\EventLog\DNS Server registry key. To enable event logging, you must first find the security identifier (SID) value that belongs to the IPAM server's Active Directory computer object. A computer object's SID can be retrieved using the Get-ADComputer PowerShell cmdlet. The CustomSD value must be modified, with the following string being appended to the end of the existing value: (A;;0x1;;; <IPAM SID>).

To enable management of DNS servers, IPAM must be given DNS administration permissions. On DNS servers also operating as a domain controller, the IPAM server or a group in which it has membership must be added to the Security tab of the DNS server properties window. For management of other DNS servers the IPAM server should be added to the local Administrators group.

DOMAIN CONTROLLERS

To enable monitoring of Active Directory domain controllers or NPS servers, the following two Windows Firewall rules must be enabled:

- Remote Event Log Management (RPC-EPMAP)
- Remote Event Log Management (RPC)

Membership in the Event Log Readers security group in Active Directory provides IPAM the capability to monitor domain controllers. NPS servers can give access to event logs through membership in the local Event Log Readers group.

Planning for IPAM server placement

A big aspect of planning an IPAM deployment is determining the placement of each IPAM server, which could come down to incremental management levels (discussed in the next section) or reasons that are purely geographic. Regardless of the reasoning, there are two primary strategies for IPAM server placement: distributed and centralized.

A *distributed* IPAM deployment typically places one IPAM server in each site in the enterprise, as illustrated in Figure 2-22. This configuration allows for delegation of management tasks and control over address spaces. Each IPAM server is configured to discover and manage servers within its area of control.

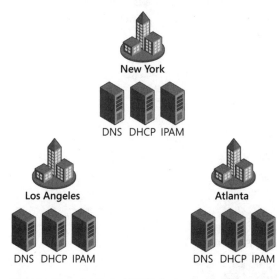

FIGURE 2-22 A distributed IPAM deployment with an IPAM server deployed in each location

Centralized IPAM deployments feature a single IPAM server, typically at corporate headquarters. This scenario works better for organizations that have a centralized IT presence or little to no server footprint at branch locations. Figure 2-23 shows a centralized IPAM deployment.

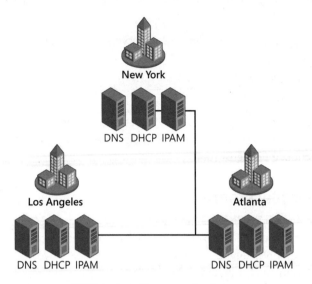

FIGURE 2-23 IPAM deployed in a centralized placement

Large organizations can opt for a hybrid of these two situations, as shown in Figure 2-24. IPAM provides no means of synchronizing databases, but servers can be configured as managed in multiple IPAM servers. Another option is to leverage the IPAM Import and Export cmdlets to move data between servers, providing visibility at multiple levels of the organization.

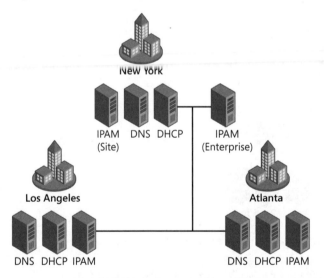

FIGURE 2-24 A hybrid IPAM deployment, with an IPAM server in each location and a second IPAM server deployed at corporate headquarters to monitor and manage IP address utilization throughout the enterprise

Managing IPAM database storage

Windows Server 2012 R2 also introduces the capability to store the IPAM database in an external Microsoft SQL database instead of the default Windows Internal Database (WID). This storage option not only increases performance and reliability but also provides additional methods of accessing, analyzing, and reporting on the data collected. The choice between database storage types is presented during the provisioning process, or the Move-IpamDatabase cmdlet can be used as shown here:

```
Move-IpamDatabase -DatabaseServer "ContosoDB" -DatabaseName "IpamDB" -DatabaseAuthType
Windows
```

Using role-based access control with IPAM

Deploying IPAM servers in each corporate location is one way to delegate control to local administrator groups, but it is not the only method to bring access control to your organization. *Role-based access* is the preferable method of defining access control over IPAM servers because it provides much more control over the actions that an administrator can perform and the objects that can be controlled.

Although Windows Server 2012 included default groups that gave you some control over an administrator's access to IPAM, Windows Server 2012 R2 takes this to an entirely new level by making role-based access completely configurable and providing a much finer level of control. Role-based access control for IPAM in Windows Server 2012 R2 manages access control by breaking permissions down into three separate aspects: roles, access scopes, and access policies.

Roles

An IPAM role is a selection of operations that an administrator can perform. By selecting the management tasks appropriate to a user group or administrative role, you can provide users with access to perform their tasks without giving them the ability to affect other areas within IPAM. Several built-in roles are included with IPAM in Windows Server 2012 R2, as shown in Table 2-8.

TABLE 2-8 Default IPAM roles in Windows Server 2012 R2

Name	Description
DNS record administrator	Manages DNS RRs.
IP address record administrator	Manages IP addresses, but not IP address spaces, ranges, blocks, or subnets.
IPAM administrator	Manages all settings and objects in IPAM.
IPAM ASM administrator	Completely manages IP addresses.
IPAM DHCP administrator	Completely manages DHCP servers.

Name	Description
IPAM DHCP reservations administrator	Manages DHCP reservations.
IPAM DHCP scope administrator	Manages DHCP scopes.
IPAM MSM administrator	Completely manages DHCP and DNS servers.

Custom roles can also be created and should be defined by your organizational structure or business rules. Custom role creation is shown in Figure 2-25.

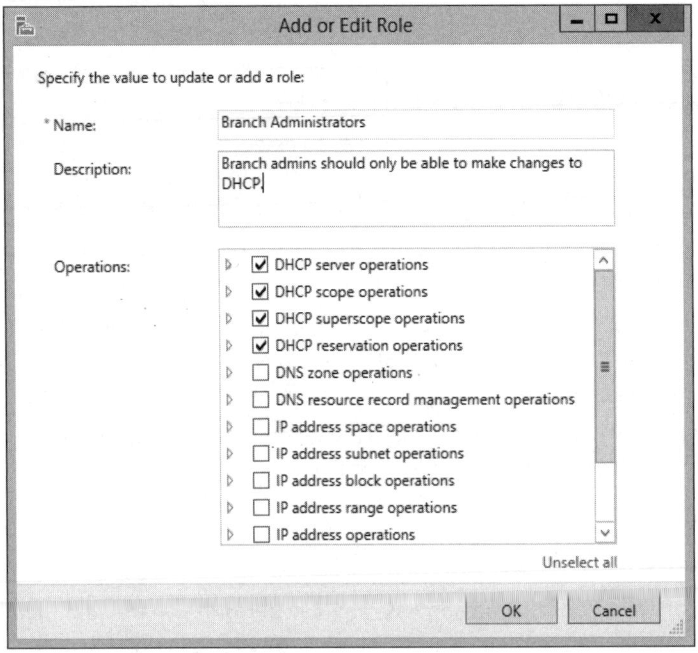

FIGURE 2-25 Creating a new IPAM role, providing DHCP administration to branch administrators

Access scopes

Access scopes can be used to define the objects an administrative user can monitor or manage. By default, only the Global access scope is provided in Windows Server 2012 R2, providing access to all objects in IPAM. Additional access scopes can be added, as shown in Figure 2-26, and the default access scope can be changed from the Global access scope. Because access scopes are defined in a hierarchy, users with access to the Global access scope can always monitor and manage all objects within IPAM.

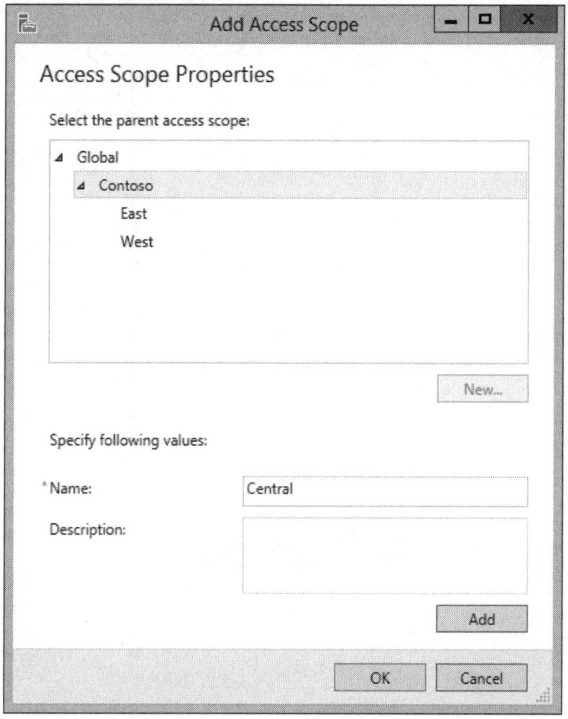

FIGURE 2-26 Managing IPAM access scopes

Rather than defining a set of criteria or rules for access scopes, individual objects such as IP address blocks, DHCP scopes, and DNS zones must be placed within an access scope. At this time, none of the PowerShell cmdlets in the IpamServer module supports automated configuration of the access scope.

Access policies

Access policies combine the role and access scope with a user or group, allowing you to assign access to perform specific actions on certain objects to a group of users. Configured using the Add Access Policy window, which is shown in Figure 2-27 and is accessed through the Tasks menu, a user or security group is associated with one or more role and access scope pairings. This allows a single group to be given the ability to perform one role within one access scope and another role in a different access scope.

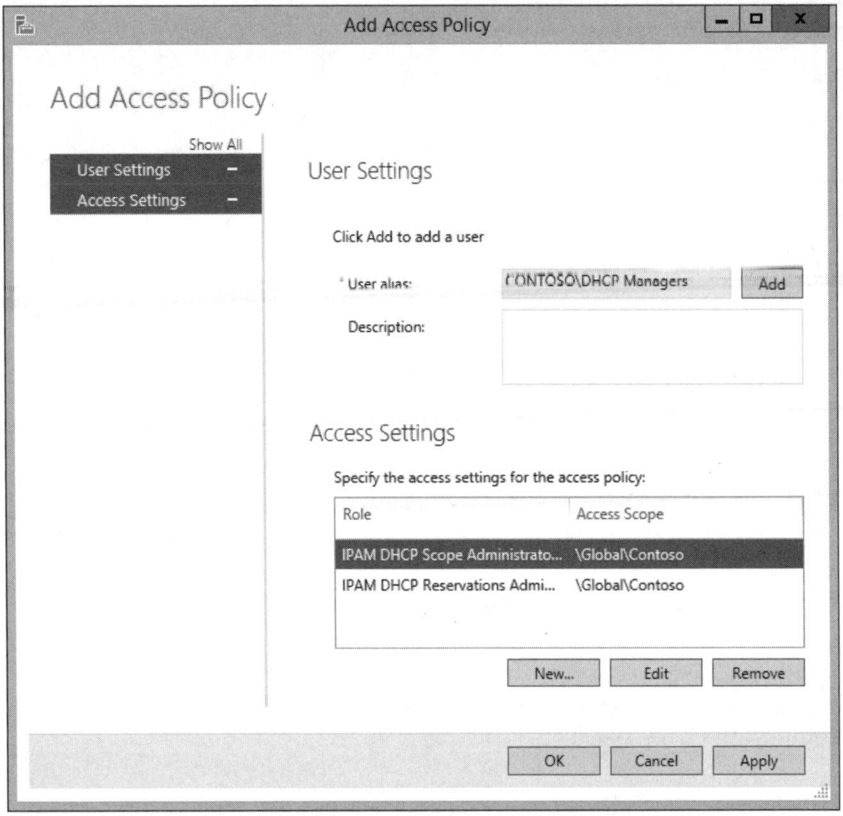

FIGURE 2-27 Creating a new access policy: combining an Active Directory security group with IPAM roles and access scopes

EXAM TIP

Role-based access control in IPAM is a change in Windows Server 2012 R2. Make sure that you understand the differences between roles, access scopes, and access policies, as well as how to configure each.

Configuring IPAM auditing

IPAM simplifies the task of auditing IP-related events. IP address assignment can be tracked using event data retrieved from DHCP servers, DNS servers, and domain controllers. Due to the types of events catalogued on these servers, IPAM enables you to view address assignments based on IP address, host name, or even user name by selecting the appropriate view in the bottom-left corner of the IPAM console (see Figure 2-28).

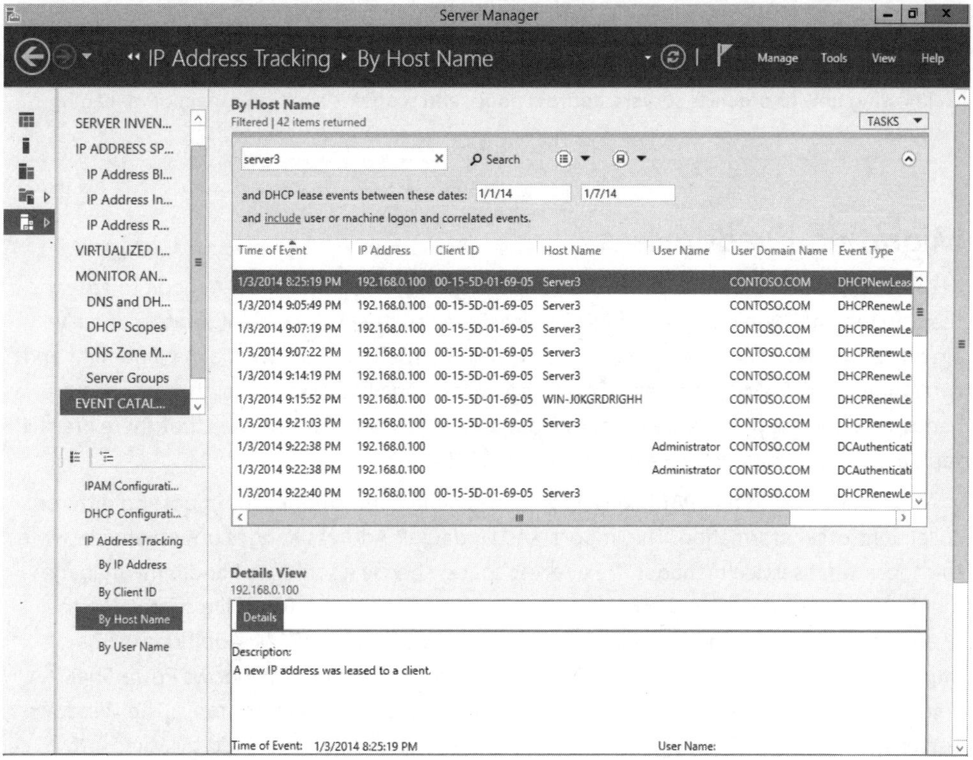

FIGURE 2-28 Auditing IP address assignments by host name (even records that predate the host name changes are shown)

DHCP and IPAM configuration events can also be audited, easing the troubleshooting process and allowing you to monitor configuration changes made by administrators with delegated permissions.

Audit records remain in the IPAM database indefinitely and must be manually purged using the Purge Event Catalog Data option from the Tasks menu. Purging these audit records have no impact on the event logs of the managed servers.

Managing and monitoring multiple DHCP and DNS servers with IPAM

IPAM provides several methods to view data grouped or aggregated from multiple servers, and in some cases to even edit or configure multiple objects simultaneously.

IPAM enables you to create server groups to monitor and manage multiple servers that share configuration similarities. This functionality is quite different from the similarly named server group feature in Server Manager. Rather than manually adding servers to a group, IPAM allows you to choose one or more criteria on which to create the group, such as site, building, or floor. New servers added to the network that meet the criteria of the group are automatically added.

Migrating IP addresses

Because IPAM is a new feature in Windows Server 2012, efforts have been made to ease the workload of spinning up the IPAM service. Much of the process is automated, as we've already discussed, but some scenarios don't lend themselves to automatic management and configuration in IPAM. Third-party DHCP servers or static IP addresses might require more hands-on effort than address ranges managed by Microsoft DHCP servers, but there are still tools available to migrate these addresses into IPAM.

The Tasks menu in the IPAM console provides quite a few options for importing different collections of IP information. The Import And Update IP Address Ranges option enables you to choose what service manages the address space, choose a server to handle the management of these addresses, and provide a comma-separated values (CSV) file containing the IP address information for the range you want to manage using IPAM. Additionally, the Import-IpamAddress, Import-IpamRange, and Import-IpamSubnet Windows PowerShell cmdlets can facilitate the migration from other IP address management tools. The Windows Server 2012 IPAM/DHCP integration module, a PowerShell script provided by Microsoft, allows you to quickly read DHCP leases into IPAM using the Invoke-IpamDhcpLease cmdlet. The Windows Server 2012 IPAM/DHCP integration module can be downloaded from *http://gallery.technet.microsoft.com/scriptcenter/Windows-Server-2012-f44cefce*. A comprehensive list of PowerShell cmdlets useful for managing IPAM data imports and exports is listed in Table 2-9.

TABLE 2-9 PowerShell cmdlets used for importing or exporting IPAM data

Cmdlet	Description
Export-IpamAddress	Exports all IP addresses from the specified address family from IPAM to a CSV file.
Import-IpamAddress	Imports IP addresses from a CSV file into the IPAM database. Can be used to migrate from a third-party IPAM solution.
Export-IpamRange	Extracts all IP address ranges from a specific address family.
Import-IpamRange	Imports IP address ranges from the given CSV file into the IPAM database.
Export-IpamSubnet	Exports subnets configured in IPAM to a CSV file, allowing for modification, analysis, or import into another IPAM server.
Import-IpamSubnet	Allows automated configuration of subnets within IPAM through the use of a properly formatted CSV file.
Invoke-IpamDhcpLease	Imports DHCP leases and reservations directly from a DHCP server into an IPAM database.

Configuring data collection for IPAM

As part of the IPAM provisioning process, several scheduled tasks are created in order to facilitate data collection. Table 2-10 shows the default frequencies of these tasks. If you have provisioned IPAM using Group Policy, these frequencies can be adjusted within the GPOs.

TABLE 2-10 IPAM data collection tasks

Task	Frequency
AddressExpiry	1 day
AddressUtilization	2 hours
Audit	1 day
ServerAvailability	15 minutes
ServerConfiguration	6 hours
ServerDiscovery	1 day
ServiceMonitoring	30 minutes

These tasks (with the exception of ServerDiscovery) can be run manually from the IPAM console by selecting one or more servers in the Server Inventory section and choosing Retrieve All Server Data from the context menu. Figure 2-29 shows these tasks as they are listed in Task Scheduler under the Microsoft\Windows\IPAM node.

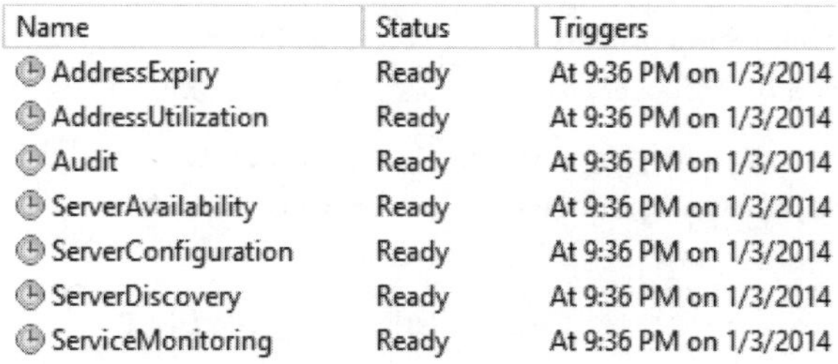

Name	Status	Triggers
AddressExpiry	Ready	At 9:36 PM on 1/3/2014
AddressUtilization	Ready	At 9:36 PM on 1/3/2014
Audit	Ready	At 9:36 PM on 1/3/2014
ServerAvailability	Ready	At 9:36 PM on 1/3/2014
ServerConfiguration	Ready	At 9:36 PM on 1/3/2014
ServerDiscovery	Ready	At 9:36 PM on 1/3/2014
ServiceMonitoring	Ready	At 9:36 PM on 1/3/2014

FIGURE 2-29 IPAM data collection tasks

Integrating IPAM with Virtual Machine Manager (VMM)

For organizations making extensive use of virtual machines (VMs) using Hyper-V, the addition in Windows Server 2012 R2 of integration between IPAM and Virtual Machine Manager (VMM) is a huge benefit. Not only can IPAM monitor and manage network services and IP address usage in your physical network but also logical networks created within VMM. IPAM can be integrated with one or more VMM servers using the IPAM integration plugin for VMM, which manages communication between the VMM and IPAM servers. IPAM servers are added in VMM through the Add Network Service Wizard, found under Networking in the Fabric pane.

Not only can virtual address space usage be tracked but IPAM and VMM also synchronize address space data, usage, and even alerts. Additionally, address spaces can be created within IPAM, and the changes are visible in the VMM console. Conversely, virtual networks and IP address pools created in VMM are automatically displayed in IPAM.

Thought experiment
Planning an enterprise-wide IPAM deployment

In this thought experiment, apply what you've learned about this objective. You can find answers to these questions in the "Answers" section at the end of this chapter.

You have been hired at a corporation with a nationwide presence. Your new company has a corporate headquarters, four regional headquarters, and branches distributed throughout each region. Datacenters reside in both the corporate and regional headquarters. Each branch has a single server operating as a domain controller, DNS server, and DHCP server.

One of the first tasks in your new job is to plan for the implementation of IPAM throughout the enterprise. Your primary goal is to provide increased control and visibility of the servers and IP address space within each region.

How would you plan your IPAM implementation based on this scenario?

1. Given the requirements and the organizational structure, what type of deployment would you use and where would you place IPAM servers?

2. How would you manage the provisioning process for each regional IP department to have visibility and control over DHCP servers within its region?

3. What tool would you use to allow regional administrators to have access to DHCP servers, scopes, and IP addresses without giving them control over DNS or IPAM?

4. How could regional administrators use IPAM to view similarly configured DHCP servers together?

5. The CIO wants to receive monthly reports illustrating IP address utilization from each region. What tool does IPAM provide that would facilitate these reports?

6. Why might there be some trouble auditing IP address usage for users travelling between regions if a distributed IPAM deployment is used?

Objective summary

- IPAM is a feature that monitors and manages IP address utilization, DHCP servers, DNS servers, and domain controllers.

- Windows Server 2012 R2 adds integration with the Microsoft System Center 2012 R2 VMM to the IPAM toolset.

- An additional feature of IPAM in Windows Server 2012 R2 is the capability to use an external database running Microsoft SQL Server.

- IPAM must be provisioned to begin server discovery and data collection. This process can be handled through Group Policy or manual provisioning.

- The IPAM provisioning process involves creating firewall rules, managing file shares, configuring groups and permissions, and implementing scheduled tasks.

- IPAM servers can be deployed using a centralized or distributed strategy, or a hybrid of the two.

- Role-based access control is introduced in Windows Server 2012 R2, allowing you to create a permissions structure based on roles, access scopes, and access policies.

- IPAM allows for auditing of IP address usage as well as DHCP and IPAM configuration.

- IPAM handles data collection through scheduled tasks running on the IPAM server and provisioned DHCP servers, DNS servers, and domain controllers.

Objective review

Answer the following questions to test your knowledge of the information in this objective. You can find the answers to these questions and explanations of why each answer choice is correct or incorrect in the "Answers" section at the end of this chapter.

1. What is the first step of implementing IPAM on your network?

   A. Starting server discovery

   B. Performing a gpupdate /force on each DHCP server

   C. Configuring each server as managed

   D. Provisioning IPAM

2. What tool on your network facilitates the IPAM provisioning process?

   A. Group Policy

   B. DHCP configuration options

   C. Windows PowerShell

   D. Microsoft System Center 2012

3. When using the manual provisioning method, which of the following tasks are typically required for provisioning servers? (Choose all that apply.)

   A. Enabling rules in Windows Firewall

   B. Creating file shares

   C. Restarting the server

    D. Assigning group membership

4. On which type of server role can IPAM *not* be installed?

    A. DHCP

    B. DNS

    C. Active Directory domain controller

    D. NPS

5. Which IPAM deployment method is best for organizations with IT support at each location, but no centralized IT department at a corporate headquarters?

    A. Centralized

    B. Distributed

    C. Hybrid

    D. Manual

6. Which of the following *cannot* be managed by IPAM?

    A. Windows Server 2012 domain controller

    B. Windows Server 2008 DNS server

    C. Windows Server 2003 DHCP server

    D. Windows Server 2012 R2 DHCP failover

7. Which PowerShell cmdlet allows you to populate IPAM with IP addresses from a properly formatted CSV file?

    A. Import-IpamAddress

    B. Import-IpamRange

    C. Import-IpamSubnet

    D. Invoke-IpamDhcpLease

8. Which aspect of role-based access control defines the operations an administrator can perform?

    A. Roles

    B. Access scopes

    C. Access policies

    D. Security groups

9. Which IPAM role allows an administrator to monitor and manage DHCP failover relationships within IPAM, while limiting the ability to perform other management tasks?

   A. IPAM administrator

   B. IPAM DHCP administrator

   C. IPAM DHCP scope administrator

   D. IP address record administrator

10. What types of information can an administrator use to audit IP address usage? (Choose all that apply.)

    A. IP address

    B. Host name

    C. User name

    D. Connection type

11. What scheduled task is *not* run when the Retrieve All Server Data option is initiated for a server?

    A. AddressUtilization

    B. Audit

    C. ServerDiscovery

    D. ServiceMonitoring

Answers

This section contains the solutions to the thought experiments and answers to the lesson review questions in this chapter.

Objective 2.1: Thought experiment

1. DHCP failover in hot standby mode is the ideal solution. In this situation, the local DHCP servers would be configured as the primary server in hot standby mode, and the server residing in the datacenter would be configured as the hot standby.

2. A DHCP Management Pack is best suited to monitor and manage DHCP servers on a large scale. The customer has to implement Microsoft System Center 2012 to use this functionality.

3. DHCPv6 in a stateless configuration would allow the IT department to provide network configuration to DHCP clients without providing an IPv6 address.

4. In Windows Server 2012 R2, DHCP filters can be used to manage DNS registration at this level.

Objective 2.1: Review

1. **Correct answer:** C

    A. **Incorrect:** A split-scope DHCP configuration results in two DHCP servers sharing a workload, but it is not part of DHCP failover, and each server is responsible for only a portion of the address pool.

    B. **Incorrect:** Hot standby mode is used when one server is to be inactive until the primary server is unavailable.

    C. **Correct:** Load balancing mode allows both partner DHCP servers to provide the full pool of addresses. If one server becomes unavailable, the second server continues to serve the full address pool.

    D. **Incorrect:** A DHCP failover cluster provides the full pool of addresses and can be split between two or more active servers, but is not part of DHCP failover.

2. **Correct answer:** D

    A. **Incorrect:** Two nodes are the minimum number of nodes for DHCP failover clusters and are the maximum for DHCP failover.

    B. **Incorrect:** DHCP failover clusters support more than six nodes.

    C. **Incorrect:** Failover clusters can be larger than 10 nodes.

    D. **Correct:** The maximum number of nodes supported for DHCP failover clustering is 64.

3. **Correct answer:** B

   A. **Incorrect:** Although a split-scope configuration would work in this situation, it is not ideal because split scope doesn't continue to provide the full pool of addresses.

   B. **Correct:** DHCP failover in hot standby mode is the optimal solution because the on-site server responds to all DHCP requests. If the primary server goes down, the off-site hot standby can provide the full pool of addresses.

   C. **Incorrect:** A DHCP failover cluster is not the best fit because a failover cluster requires shared storage, which means that the two servers are typically co-located.

   D. **Incorrect:** DHCP failure in load balancing mode would work, but there is potential for performance problems due to the remote server responding to requests when the local server is still operational.

4. **Correct answer:** D

   A. **Incorrect:** The scope's lease duration is not used until the standby server enters the partner down state.

   B. **Incorrect:** Lease durations are configured at the DHCP scope level.

   C. **Incorrect:** Even if the primary DHCP server returns to service, the client's lease duration is determined by using the Maximum Client Lead Time configured in the failover partnership.

   D. **Correct:** The Maximum Client Lead Time determines both the lease time for DHCP leases provided by the standby server and the amount of time between the primary server becoming unresponsive and the hot standby server going into partner down mode.

5. **Correct answer:** D

   A. **Incorrect:** DHCP can and should be used to provide DNS information to clients. In some cases the DHCP server should be used to perform dynamic updates to the DNS server.

   B. **Incorrect:** DHCP is not directly interoperable with Active Directory.

   C. **Incorrect:** Virtual private network (VPN) services or DirectAccess can make use of DHCP; the decision to do so depends largely on the VPN infrastructure and scope.

   D. **Correct:** DHCP interoperability with NAP is not recommended because it is the weakest of the NAP enforcement methods. Also, NAP is deprecated in Windows Server 2012 R2.

6. **Correct answer:** B

   A. **Incorrect:** DHCP filtering enables you to choose which clients to provide addresses to, but doesn't allow you to provide configuration information without IP addresses.

   B. **Correct:** Stateless DHCPv6 is used to provide configuration information without IP addresses. The IPv6 addresses are acquired through autoconfiguration.

   C. **Incorrect:** DHCP options provide configuration settings through DHCP, but they must be used in conjunction with stateless DHCPv6 to meet the requirement.

   D. **Incorrect:** Stateful DHCPv6 provides both the configuration information and an IPv6 address.

7. **Correct answer:** B

   A. **Incorrect:** 30 minutes is incorrect.

   B. **Correct:** The DHCP automatic database backup runs every 60 minutes by default. Both the frequency and the backup location can be modified.

   C. **Incorrect:** 12 hours is incorrect.

   D. **Incorrect:** 24 hours is incorrect.

Objective 2.2: Thought experiment

1. File-backed DNS zones miss out on several security benefits enjoyed by Active Directory–integrated zones, most notably secure dynamic updates and zone transfers. The fact that dynamic updates are being allowed in a file-backed zone is a huge concern, but the issue should be easy to resolve because each DNS server is also a domain controller.

2. Ideally, you will have a limited number of DNS servers configured to perform external name resolution. This situation reduces the visibility of your DNS servers to the outside world and also increases the value of caching on these servers, which improves performance.

3. Using the same domain for internal and external name resolution opens the possibility for outside sources to determine host names of internal computer names and IP addresses. Implementing a separate DNS infrastructure specifically for resolving external name resolution requests enables you to selectively choose which computers can be resolved by external DNS clients.

4. DNSSEC simply provides a validation process for DNS name resolution. There are inherent performance impacts due to the zones quadrupling in size, resulting in increased memory and storage needs.

Objective 2.2: Review

1. **Correct answer:** B

   A. **Incorrect:** DNSSEC does not offer encryption, nor does it secure zone transfers.

   B. **Correct:** DNSSEC validates name resolution through a chain of trust and digitally signed RRs.

   C. **Incorrect:** DNSSEC has no impact on dynamic updates. To secure dynamic updates, you must use an Active Directory–integrated zone.

   D. **Incorrect:** DNSSEC does not protect cached records; you should consider cache locking instead.

2. **Correct answers:** A, D

   A. **Correct:** To validate a child, DS records reside in a parent domain.

   B. **Incorrect:** SOA records are used in all DNS zones and are not specific to DNSSEC.

   C. **Incorrect:** NS records are used by parent zones to indicate a delegated zone and are not specific to DNSSEC.

   D. **Correct:** DNSKEY records correspond to the DS record hosted in the parent zone.

3. **Correct answer:** C

   A. **Incorrect:** EDNS0 is the standard that increases the length of the DNS packet. This is required for DNSSEC traffic, but does not manage how clients use DNSSEC for validation.

   B. **Incorrect:** The DO flag indicates to the DNS server that the client is DNSSEC-capable, but the DO flag is governed by the NRPT.

   C. **Correct:** The NRPT is used to configure the way DNSSEC is used for validation, what domains it should be used to validate, and whether a valid response is required.

   D. **Incorrect:** The CD flag allows DNS clients, or more typically the recursive DNS server, to allow for responses that have not yet been validated by DNSSEC.

4. **Correct answer:** D

   A. **Incorrect:** Key rollover does not result in a drastic expansion in the size of the DNS zone.

   B. **Incorrect:** Recursion has no impact on the size of a DNS zone.

   C. **Incorrect:** Zone delegation does not significantly increase the size of a DNS zone.

   D. **Correct:** Zone signing creates three additional DNSSEC RRs to provide validated responses and negative responses to DNS queries.

5. **Correct answer:** D

   A. **Incorrect:** Cache locking is used to prevent cached RRs from being updated.

   B. **Incorrect:** Active Directory–integrated zones allow for secure dynamic updates and replication, but do not alter how the DNS server responds to name resolution queries.

   C. **Incorrect:** Application pools are used to manage DNS server replication, but do not change how DNS queries are handled.

   D. **Correct:** The DNS socket pool manages which ports can be used for responding to DNS queries.

6. **Correct answer:** A

   A. **Correct:** Cache locking configures how soon TTL updates to the RR should be allowed. This value is set to 100 by default, which means that no updates are allowed until the full TTL has expired.

   B. **Incorrect:** Cache locking is not configured by a number of days.

   C. **Incorrect:** You cannot configure cache locking as a number of hours.

   D. **Incorrect:** Cache locking is not configured as a percentage of a day.

7. **Correct answer:** A

   A. **Correct:** Application pools offer increased control over DNS replication by allowing you to select the domain controllers to be part of the replication scope.

   B. **Incorrect:** The use of application pools indicates that the zone is Active Directory–integrated, so replication is used rather than zone transfers. Regardless, this is not a function of application pools.

   C. **Incorrect:** Application pools require Active Directory–integrated DNS zones, which can be hosted only on DNS servers that are also domain controllers.

   D. **Incorrect:** BIND compatibility is not dependent on application pools.

8. **Correct answer:** B

   A. **Incorrect:** CNAME records use only name values rather than IP addresses, so they function the same way for IPv4 or IPv6 hosts.

   B. **Correct:** A records accept only IPv4 addresses, so they are replaced by AAAA records with IPv6 hosts.

   C. **Incorrect:** NS records refer to the name server's host name, which is contained within a corresponding A or AAAA record.

   D. **Incorrect:** AAAA records replace A records for IPv6 hosts.

9. **Correct answers:** B, C

    A. **Incorrect:** Zone delegations are used to create the hierarchical structure of DNS, whereas single-label DNS names are devoid of any structure.

    B. **Correct:** DNS suffixes can sometimes be used to resolve single-label DNS names.

    C. **Correct:** The GlobalNames zone is used strictly for resolving single-label DNS names.

    D. **Incorrect:** Disjoint namespaces occur when an Active Directory domain differs from the DNS domain.

10. **Correct answers:** A, C

    A. **Correct:** NS records contain the host name of the name server used to provide name resolution for the child zone.

    B. **Incorrect:** CNAME records are aliases for A records and are not typically used for zone delegations.

    C. **Correct:** An A record is required to resolve the name contained in the NS record to an IP address.

    D. **Incorrect:** DS records are used only in DNSSEC signed zones. Although they do refer to a child domain, they are not part of the zone delegation.

11. **Correct answer:** B

    A. **Incorrect:** Secure dynamic updates can be handled in a disjoint namespace, although they require some additional configuration.

    B. **Correct:** The SRV records used to refer clients to Active Directory domain controllers must be created manually in a disjoint namespace.

    C. **Incorrect:** DNSSEC signed zones can still be used in disjoint namespaces.

    D. **Incorrect:** Zone transfers are not complicated by the use of disjoint namespaces.

Objective 2.3: Thought experiment

1. Given the requirements, a distributed IPAM deployment is most likely.

2. Perform the IPAM provisioning process in each region, referencing the regional IPAM server. If each region is its own domain, this process can be done at the domain level. If the Active Directory domain structure does not match regional divisions, there might need to be a more advanced Group Policy configuration or manual provisioning.

3. Role-based access is the best method to provide this type of control over security.

4. Server groups enable you to combine servers with configuration similarities.

5. The IPAM Windows PowerShell cmdlets such as Export-IpamAddress, Export-IpamRange, and Export-IpamSubnet can be used to create CSV files for analysis and reporting.

6. A distributed IPAM deployment means that auditing across regions has to be handled across multiple IPAM servers.

Objective 2.3: Review

1. **Correct answer:** D

   A. **Incorrect:** The server discovery process does not take place until IPAM provisioning has occurred.

   B. **Incorrect:** Updating Group Policy helps accelerate the provisioning process, but provisioning must occur first.

   C. **Incorrect:** In IPAM, configuring servers as managed occurs after provisioning and server discovery.

   D. **Correct:** Provisioning IPAM begins the configuration process of the servers that IPAM manages.

2. **Correct answer:** A

   A. **Correct:** IPAM features automated provisioning through the use of Group Policy.

   B. **Incorrect:** DHCP configuration options cannot be used to provision IPAM.

   C. **Incorrect:** There are aspects of the provisioning process that are accomplished using Windows PowerShell, and it can be a good tool for a manual provisioning process, but Group Policy provides a better solution in most cases.

   D. **Incorrect:** Microsoft System Center 2012 is not part of the IPAM provisioning process.

3. **Correct answers:** A, B, D

   A. **Correct:** Each of the server types requires configuration of firewall rules to facilitate communication with the IPAM server.

   B. **Correct:** File shares are sometimes required during IPAM provisioning, as in the case of DHCP auditing.

   C. **Incorrect:** IPAM provisioning does not typically require servers to be restarted.

   D. **Correct:** Group membership is often required to give IPAM the permissions required to monitor and manage different server types.

4. **Correct answer:** C

   A. **Incorrect:** IPAM can be installed on a DHCP server, but automatic DHCP discovery will be disabled.

   B. **Incorrect:** DNS servers can also function as IPAM servers.

   C. **Correct:** Domain controllers cannot run the IPAM feature.

   D. **Incorrect:** IPAM can be installed on a NPS server.

5. **Correct answer:** B

   A. **Incorrect:** Centralized deployments of IPAM are best suited for organizations in which IT support is primarily centralized, and network services such as DHCP and DNS are managed from corporate headquarters.

   B. **Correct:** A distributed IPAM deployment allows IT support at each location to monitor and manage its own DHCP servers, DNS servers, and domain controllers.

   C. **Incorrect:** A hybrid deployment isn't necessary in this situation because no centralized IT department exists.

   D. **Incorrect:** Manual provisioning could certainly be used in this scenario, but it doesn't specifically address the need for distributed deployment.

6. **Correct answer:** C

   A. **Incorrect:** Windows Server 2012 domain controllers are monitored to provide information for auditing purposes.

   B. **Incorrect:** DNS servers can be monitored and managed from IPAM, including those using Windows Server 2008.

   C. **Correct:** Windows Server 2003 is not supported to be managed or monitored with IPAM.

   D. **Incorrect:** DHCP failover relationships in Windows Server 2012 R2 can be monitored and managed using IPAM.

7. **Correct answer:** A

   A. **Correct:** The Import-IpamAddress cmdlet is used to import IP address information into IPAM from a file.

   B. **Incorrect:** Import-IpamRange allows you to acquire data pertaining to the full IP address range, not individual addresses.

   C. **Incorrect:** The Import-IpamSubnet PowerShell cmdlet populates IPAM with data from your organization's subnets. Information about specific IP addresses is not included.

   D. **Incorrect:** Invoke-IpamDhcpLease is part of the Windows Server 2012 IPAM/DHCP integration module, and is used to import IP address information directly from a DHCP server, not a CSV file.

8. **Correct answer:** A

   A. **Correct:** Roles determine what actions can be performed by an administrator.

   B. **Incorrect:** Access scopes control the areas an administrator can manage.

   C. **Incorrect:** Access policies combine a role, access scope, and security group or user to apply permissions to administrators.

   D. **Incorrect:** Security groups can contain users, but cannot limit a user's access without being tied to a role and an access scope using an access policy.

9. **Correct answer:** B

   A. **Incorrect:** The IPAM administrator role would give administrators the ability to manage DHCP failover relationships, but would provide several other abilities as well.

   B. **Correct:** Administrators given the IPAM DHCP administrator role can manage all aspects of DHCP within IPAM, including failover relationships.

   C. **Incorrect:** IPAM DHCP scope administrators do not have the necessary permissions to manage failover relationships.

   D. **Incorrect:** The IP address record administrator role does not provide the ability to administer DHCP servers or failover relationships.

10. **Correct answers:** A, B, C

    A. **Correct:** IPAM audits can be conducted to determine what computers and users have obtained a particular IP address.

    B. **Correct:** Using a host name, IPAM can be audited to determine which IP addresses have been obtained by a specific computer.

    C. **Correct:** Collecting data from DHCP, DNS, and domain controllers allows IPAM to provide audits by user name.

    D. **Incorrect:** IPAM does not provide a means to audit by network connection type.

11. **Correct answer:** C

    A. **Incorrect:** The AddressUtilization task is one of six tasks initiated when data collection is triggered manually.

    B. **Incorrect:** The Audit task runs when the Retrieve All Server Data option is used in Server Inventory.

    C. **Correct:** ServerDiscovery is not executed during a manual data collection.

    D. **Incorrect:** ServiceMonitoring gets triggered during the manual data-collection process.

CHAPTER 3

Design and implement network access services

With how integral to our business lives our computers, files, and applications have become, much of our daily work requires access to network resources. The obvious trade-off of this scenario is the potential of not being able to accomplish certain aspects of our daily routine without having access to the network resources we count on.

This chapter delves into the tools available in Windows Server 2012 R2 that allow you to provide network access to users who do not have physical access to your network. Several solutions are supported that will provide different types of access depending on the type of resource and security required. The remote access features available in Windows Server 2012 R2 range from the traditional (VPN), to the modern (DirectAccess), to the cutting-edge (Web Application Proxy). Each of these features can be used in your enterprise to support a different kind of user, or you can pick and choose to meet the needs of your users.

A large part of the remote access discussion centers on security. Virtual private network (VPN) connections and remote access are particular areas of concern for security professionals because the purpose of the solution is to allow corporate resource access to users throughout the world. Ensuring that only authorized users access your network is key, and several techniques to help your network to remain safe will be discussed. We also discuss how to protect your network clients, both internal and through VPN, by using Network Access Protection (NAP) and Network Policy Server (NPS).

Scalability is also a topic of interest for remote access, particularly when discussing site-to-site VPN used to link corporate locations into a single logical network. Ensuring that your remote access solution is resilient and highly available is a crucial aspect of maintaining a corporate network that spans multiple locations.

Objectives in this chapter:
- Objective 3.1: Design a VPN solution
- Objective 3.2: Design a DirectAccess solution
- Objective 3.3: Design a Web Application Proxy solution
- Objective 3.4: Implement a scalable remote access solution
- Objective 3.5: Design and implement a network protection solution

Objective 3.1: Design a VPN solution

A VPN connection has been the solution for accessing resources on the corporate network while outside the bounds of the physical network. Several protocols are available for VPN communication, each with different levels of security and configuration requirements. Even though VPN has been around for years, do not mistake its longevity for obsolescence. Most corporations still use VPN solutions to support legacy or third-party clients, and will continue to do so for the foreseeable future.

One area that is relatively new to the discussion is the use of a VPN to connect to resources in Microsoft Azure. Using a site-to-site VPN, you can ensure secure communication between corporate resources in the cloud and on-premises resources. Service providers large and small can provide similar functionality to their customers—secure connectivity to their own applications—using the new multitenant site-to-site VPN feature in Windows Server 2012 R2.

> **This objective covers how to:**
> - Deploy certificates
> - Configure firewalls
> - Use client/site-to-site connections
> - Understand bandwidth requirements
> - Understand protocol implications
> - Connect to Microsoft Azure IaaS
> - Use the Connection Manager Administration Kit (CMAK) for VPN deployment configurations

Deploying certificates

Several aspects of VPN configuration either have the option to use certificates to improve security or an outright requirement for certificates to be used. Three standard VPN tunneling protocols are supported by Windows Server 2012 R2: PPTP, L2TP, and SSTP. Each of these protocols supports certificate-based authentication and encryption of some sort, as shown in Table 3-1.

TABLE 3-1 VPN protocol support for certificate-based authentication and encryption

VPN protocol	Authentication method
PPTP	EAP-TLS
L2TP	IPsec
SSTP	SSL

With certificate-based authentication, a key aspect is ensuring that the client trusts the server performing the authentication. There are multiple ways to achieve this trust relationship between client and server. For domain clients, an internal Certificate Authority (CA) allows you to configure computers to trust the corporate CA as well as enable autoenrollment for client certificates. If a public CA is used, a client-server trust typically exists already, but authentication using client certificates becomes difficult. A hybrid certificate deployment, in which your enterprise CA uses a root certificate from a trusted third party, allows you to combine the strengths of both options: automatic enrollment of domain members and inherent trust from external clients. Figure 3-1 shows an example of a hybrid certificate deployment.

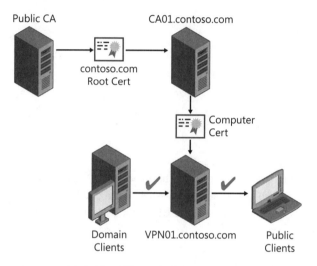

FIGURE 3-1 A hybrid certificate deployment

Client certificate enrollment can be accomplished in a number of ways. Typically, Group Policy is used for clients to automatically obtain certificates from the CA without any user intervention or knowledge. For clients that are not domain members, web-based enrollment can be used to obtain the necessary certificates to authenticate.

EXAM TIP

Certificates are used heavily throughout remote access. Some use cases call for certificates issued by an internal enterprise CA; others are best served using a certificate from a public CA. Knowing when and where to use certificates from different CAs is critical.

Configuring firewalls

Firewall rule configuration is important for enabling VPN traffic to reach remote access servers on your network. In addition to allowing incoming traffic on these ports, there is the potential for remote access servers to also function as VPN clients for site-to-site connections.

In this case, outbound traffic on these ports might need to be enabled as well. Rules enabling client traffic to traverse internal firewalls should also be created when the remote access server is hosted in a perimeter network (also known as a demilitarized network or DMZ). Table 3-2 contains a list of the ports used for VPN connectivity.

TABLE 3-2 Network ports used by VPN protocols

Port	Protocol	Use
TCP 1723	PPTP	PPTP tunnel
GRE (value 47)	PPTP	PPTP pass-through
UDP 500	L2TP	IKEv1/IKEv2 (IPsec)
UDP 4500	L2TP	IKEv1/IKEv2 (IPsec)
TCP 1701	L2TP	L2TP tunnel
ESP (value 50)	L2TP	IPsec
TCP 443	SSTP	SSTP tunnel

Besides the VPN protocols, various other protocols used for address translation and transition technologies might also need to be allowed to traverse the firewall. When using the 6to4 protocol, port 41 must be allowed through the edge firewall. If the public IPv6 address space is used for remote access, both TCP port 50 and UDP port 500 must be allowed through to the remote access server.

Using client/site-to-site connections

Over the years, VPN connections have evolved from a technology primarily used to connect clients to their workplace into one often used to secure corporate traffic between locations. Through the use of site-to-site VPN, illustrated in Figure 3-2, Internet-based connectivity can be used instead of dedicated network infrastructure to allow network traffic between sites and branches.

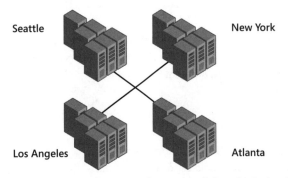

FIGURE 3-2 Site-to-site VPN allows you to link multiple sites into a single logical network

Windows Server 2012 R2 extends the capabilities for VPN connectivity by allowing for multitenant site-to-site or remote access connectivity. This functionality is designed for hosting environments or service providers with a need to provide secure connectivity directly from remote clients to individual Hyper-V virtual networks or virtual local area networks (VLANs).

EXAM TIP

Multitenant site-to-site VPN is a crucial piece of the Microsoft hybrid cloud strategy and is a new feature in Windows Server 2012 R2. Windows 8.1 also introduces auto-triggered VPN, which can be used to allow modern apps to automatically make a VPN connection. These and other new remote access features can be seen on the exam. More information on new remote access features in Windows Server 2012 R2 and Windows 8.1 can be found here: *http://technet.microsoft.com/en-us/library/dn383589.aspx*.

Understanding bandwidth requirements

Some requirements for remote access are simply intuitive. The bandwidth requirements are proportional to the number of clients you expect to use the remote access solution and how heavy you expect the usage to be. Particular attention should be paid to the differentiation between upload and download speeds provided by your Internet connection. Because many Internet providers provide high download speeds with a fraction of the available upload bandwidth, it can become problematic for users trying to access resources from outside the corporate network.

When designing your VPN solution, consider the Internet connections available within each site and within the organization as a whole. If one site has a significantly more robust Internet connection (see the New York location in Figure 3-3), it might make sense to centralize remote access servers to that site. If remote access traffic is expected to be heavy, it might make sense to have a dedicated Internet connection for remote access purposes to provide optimal performance. Users of site-to-site VPN might consider the use of rate limiting to prevent the Internet connection from being saturated by VPN traffic.

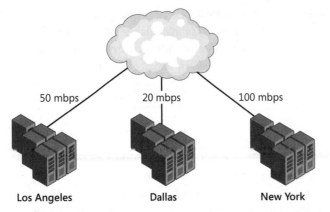

50 mbps   20 mbps   100 mbps

Los Angeles   Dallas   New York

FIGURE 3-3 The bandwidth available to individual sites might dictate where your VPN infrastructure should be deployed

Understanding protocol implications

Several factors contribute to the decision about which VPN protocols to support in an organization. Security is always important, and in remote access scenarios both the authentication process and the VPN tunnel must be considered. Compatibility with clients is another important point to evaluate because newer VPN protocols might not be supported by all VPN clients. Additionally, some protocols handle firewall and NAT traversal better than others, making them better suited for clients connecting through networks found in homes, hotels, or even coffee shops. Performance can also be affected by the choice of protocol and should be a key aspect of any remote access design process.

Security is an important aspect of your VPN infrastructure, largely because it bypasses any physical security measures you might have in place. As already stated, both the authentication process and the VPN tunnel must be secured. Each protocol handles these factors differently; although each offers strong security, understanding the differences and requirements is important. Point to Point Tunneling Protocol (PPTP) supports Extensible Authentication Protocol-Transport Layer Security (EAP-TLS) authentication using certificates. Encryption of the PPTP tunnel is accomplished with Microsoft Point-to-Point Encryption (MPPE), which uses keys generated by the EAP-TLS authentication process. PPTP does not provide data confidentiality, so data can be modified in transit without being discovered. Layer 2 Tunneling Protocol (L2TP)/Internet Protocol security (IPsec) relies on IPsec for authentication, data integrity, and encryption using Data Encryption Standard (DES) or Triple DES (3DES) with keys generated through the Internet Key Exchange (IKE) negotiation process. IPsec requires a public key infrastructure (PKI) to issue computer certificates for client-server authentication, adding some complexity to an L2TP/IPsec deployment. Secure Socket Tunneling Protocol (SSTP) relies on the Secure Sockets Layer (SSL) for encryption, data integrity, and encapsulation while using EAP-TLS for authentication. Of the three traditional VPN protocols mentioned here, only SSTP supports two-factor authentication such as smart cards.

For clients to connect to your VPN implementation, they must support the protocol you choose. SSTP supports only clients using Windows Vista Service Pack 1 (SP1) or later, making it the most restrictive of the three options. L2TP/IPsec and PPTP both support clients using Windows XP and later.

Additional compatibility factors are the networking aspects of the three choices. The SSTP use of SSL makes it the best option for traversing Network Address Translation (NAT) or firewall devices. L2TP/IPsec supports NAT traversal, but might encounter problems on networks with more restrictive firewalls. PPTP requires a NAT device with a NAT editor capable of properly translating and routing the VPN tunnel.

Performance differences between the three VPN protocols discussed here have much to do with the type of encryption and encapsulation being used. Because PPTP uses the least amount of encryption and encapsulation, there is less overhead on both client and server to handle these processor-intensive operations. L2TP/IPsec encapsulates each packet four to six times, resulting in increased overhead on each end of the tunnel and making the processor performance of the remote access server critical.

Connecting to Microsoft Azure IaaS

Microsoft Azure enables you to connect your cloud-based virtual machines (VMs) and applications to your local network through the use of an Azure virtual network and site-to-site VPN connectivity. This functionality is very similar to the multitenant site-to-site VPN connectivity introduced in Windows Server 2012 R2. Not only can you name the connection and specify the VPN information but you can also configure local IP address pools and IP subnets. Point-to-site connectivity is also supported for scenarios in which only a few devices require connectivity to the virtual network, rather than an entire site.

A critical requirement for connecting your organization to an Azure virtual network is a public IPv4 address (public IPv6 addresses are not currently supported). A virtual network is configured using the Azure management portal, shown in Figure 3-4, or manually through the use of network configuration files.

Configuration of a virtual network using network configuration files typically involves exporting an existing virtual network configuration, making modifications to the XML file, and importing the network configuration file. Using manual configuration is an efficient way to rapidly deploy multiple virtual networks with similar configurations.

> **MORE INFO   NETWORK CONFIGURATION FILES**
>
> Using network configuration files involves manually editing the XML files exported from the Azure management portal. More information on this process can be found here: *http://msdn.microsoft.com/en-us/library/azure/jj156097.aspx*.

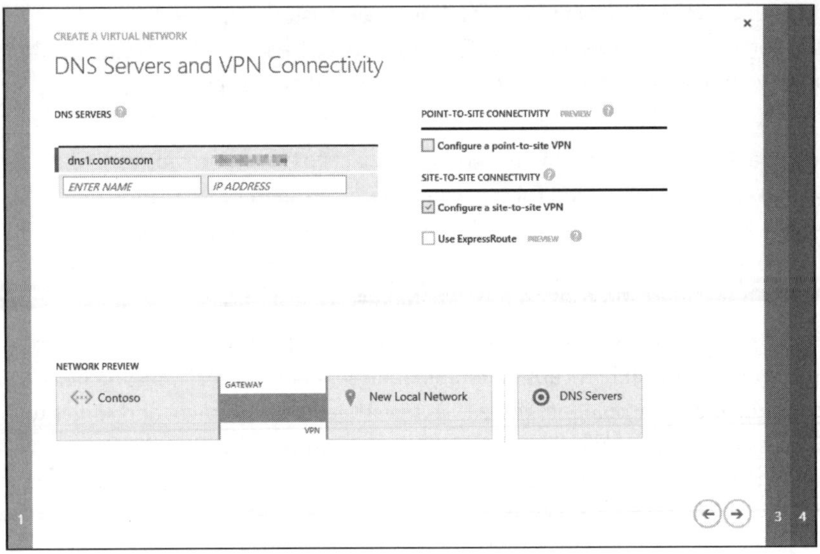

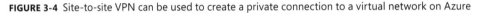

CREATE A VIRTUAL NETWORK

DNS Servers and VPN Connectivity   ×

DNS SERVERS   **POINT-TO-SITE CONNECTIVITY**   PREVIEW

| dns1.contoso.com | | ☐ Configure a point-to-site VPN
| ENTER NAME | IP ADDRESS |

                                                   SITE-TO-SITE CONNECTIVITY

                                                   ☑ Configure a site-to-site VPN

                                                   ☐ Use ExpressRoute   PREVIEW

NETWORK PREVIEW

| ⟨·⟩ Contoso | GATEWAY | ♀ New Local Network | ◉ DNS Servers |
| | VPN | | |

1   ← →   3   4

FIGURE 3-4 Site-to-site VPN can be used to create a private connection to a virtual network on Azure

---

EXAM TIP

Hybrid clouds and Azure are focal points in Windows Server 2012 and for Microsoft in general. Expect at least one question on connecting your corporate location to Azure using a site-to-site VPN.

Using the Connection Manager Administration Kit (CMAK) for VPN deployment configurations

The Connection Manager Administration Kit (CMAK) is a tool that allows an administrator to create a simplified method for users to create and initiate a VPN connection. By using CMAK, you can predefine the remote access server information, protocol options, and authentication method to be used. Even corporate branding and custom support numbers can be included. The result is a tool that can be made available to users to automate the VPN client configuration process.

CMAK is made available by installing the RAS Connection Manager Administration Kit (CMAK) feature in Windows Server 2012 and Windows 8. After it is installed, the Connection Manager Administration Kit Wizard (see Figure 3-5) guides you through the process of creating a Connection Manager profile. Options presented during the creation of a Connection Manager profile include configuring supported operating systems, naming for the profile and the executable, realm (domain) name, VPN connection types, proxy settings, and customization of graphics and support information.

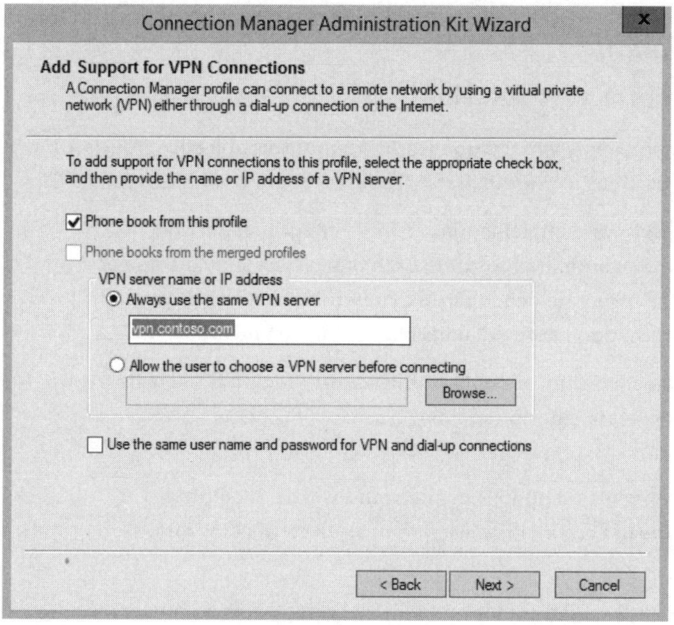

FIGURE 3-5 The Connection Manager Administration Kit Wizard is used to create a Connection Manager profile that users can use to configure their VPN connection

The end product of the Connection Manager Administration Kit Wizard is an executable file that automates the process of creating and configuring a connection profile for end users, requiring minimal user interaction and reducing the support workload. Distributing this executable file can be accomplished through Group Policy, physical media such as CD or USB storage, or through a corporate website. After the end user runs the executable, a VPN connection profile is created, as shown in Figure 3-6, allowing connection to the corporate network.

FIGURE 3-6 Users can easily create connection profiles using the executable created by CMAK

Thought experiment

Designing a corporate VPN solution

In this thought experiment, apply what you've learned about this objective. You can find answers to these questions in the "Answers" section at the end of this chapter.

Your company is working toward implementing a single integrated network throughout the nationwide corporate footprint. Each branch site should connect back to the datacenter at corporate headquarters. Answer the following questions regarding how your corporation's network unification goals can be achieved:

1. The first step of connecting sites throughout the country/region is to create a connection to the corporate datacenter. What type of VPN connection can be used for this scenario?

2. Your corporate network, including VPN connections, will be encrypted using IPsec. What type of CA should be used to provide certificates for IPsec authentication?

3. Remote clients with work-issued computers will use DirectAccess to connect to the corporate network. What firewall rules need to be configured to allow this traffic to the remote access server at corporate headquarters?

4. To increase flexibility, your CIO wants to explore the possibility of shifting some corporate application servers to the cloud. What capabilities are offered with Azure to enable cloud functionality while maintaining connectivity to on-premises resources and ensuring the security of your corporate data?

Objective summary

- Certificates are integral to securing VPN and remote access solutions, and can be used to authenticate users or computers with the remote access server. Depending on usage, either a public CA or an internal CA can be used.

- Some firewall configuration is required for VPN to allow the chosen protocol to reach the remote access server. Additional rules are required for 6to4 translation or use of public IPv6 addresses.

- VPNs can be created for either client-server or site-to-site communication, depending on the need. Windows Server 2012 R2 introduces the ability to support multitenant site-to-site VPNs for hosting providers to provide clients with secure access to their applications.

- Lack of necessary bandwidth to support the VPN workload can affect users and prevent access to corporate resources. Bandwidth should be considered during the design phase to determine which Internet connection to use and whether upgrades are needed.

- Each VPN protocol has different strengths and weaknesses related to security, compatibility, and performance. They should be considered when choosing the protocol to support.

- Workloads in Azure can be connected to on-premises networks through the use of VPN and Azure-based virtual networks.

- CMAK is used to create VPN connection profiles for end users, which enable simple configuration of the VPN client for end users.

Objective review

Answer the following questions to test your knowledge of the information in this objective. You can find the answers to these questions and explanations of why each answer choice is correct or incorrect in the "Answers" section at the end of this chapter.

1. What type of server is required to use IPsec authentication?

   A. Public CA

   B. Enterprise CA

   C. Stand-alone CA

   D. Remote access server

2. Which firewall ports must be opened to enable L2TP traffic?

   A. TCP 1701

   B. TCP 1723

   C. TCP 443

   D. TCP 80

3. What feature in Windows Server 2012 R2 enables the deployment of a remote access solution allowing clients to connect directly to their own virtual networks within your datacenter?

   A. Site-to-site VPN

   B. Multisite VPN

   C. Multitenant site-to-site

   D. Microsoft Azure Virtual Network

4. Which VPN solution supports 3DES encryption?

   A. PPTP

   B. L2TP/IPsec

   C. SSTP

   D. All of the above

5. Which VPN protocol supports smart cards for authentication?

   A. PPTP

   B. L2TP/IPsec

   C. SSTP

   D. All of the above

6. What is the primary advantage of SSTP over PPTP and L2TP/IPsec?

   A. NAT traversal

   B. Security

   C. Performance

   D. Client compatibility

7. Which is not part of the Azure virtual network creation process?

   A. Private DNS addresses

   B. On-premises IP address pool configuration

   C. Local IP subnet definition

   D. VPN server IP address

8. What is the purpose of CMAK?

   A. Manage VPN connection permissions for users

   B. Deploy and configure remote access servers

   C. Create preconfigured VPN profiles for end users

   D. Create a site-to-site VPN connection with an Azure virtual network

9. How is CMAK installed?

   A. The Windows feature must be installed.

   B. CMAK must be downloaded from the Microsoft website.

   C. CMAK is included on the Windows Server 2012 installation media.

   D. CMAK is installed by default on both Windows 8 and Windows Server 2012.

Objective 3.2: Design a DirectAccess solution

DirectAccess is a remote access solution for Windows clients that allows for automatic, always-on connections to the corporate network. Introduced in Windows Server 2008 R2, DirectAccess is an improved method of providing remote connectivity to domain-joined computers. Typically deployed in conjunction with a more traditional VPN option, DirectAccess supports only client operating systems using Windows 7 or later. In addition to providing clients the ability to remain connected to corporate resources while outside the scope of the company network,

DirectAccess provides the ability to join computers to the domain while outside the bounds of the physical network, and a means to manage computers while they are outside the corporate network.

A big aspect of DirectAccess has to do with requirements. DirectAccess in Windows Server 2012 R2 is extremely flexible, capable of being configured in multiple topologies, and offers several new features. Each of these configuration topologies and features comes with its own set of requirements, which you will need to know to effectively design a DirectAccess deployment.

This objective covers how to:

- Understand DirectAccess deployment topology
- Migrate from Forefront UAG
- Use One-Time Password (OTP)
- Use enterprise Certificate Authority (CA) certificates

Understanding deployment topology

A major limitation of DirectAccess in Windows Server 2008 R2 was the inability to use the same server for both DirectAccess and traditional VPN through the use of routing and remote access. Windows Server 2012 unifies these capabilities in the Routing and Remote Access Service (RRAS) role.

Several of the new features in Windows Server 2012 have to do with support for different deployment topologies for DirectAccess. Windows Server 2008 R2 DirectAccess servers were required to have two network connections: one to the public Internet and one to the private network. Windows Server 2012 supports placement of remote access servers behind a NAT device and removes the requirement for multiple network connections. This greatly increases the flexibility of your network topology when planning for placement of your remote access server. Figure 3-7 shows the difference between these two topologies and exemplifies the increased flexibility offered by placing the DirectAccess server behind a NAT device.

Topologies featuring connectivity to both internal and external networks are still supported, but they are no longer the only option. The network topology can be configured in the Remote Access Server Setup Wizard, shown in Figure 3-8. Windows Server 2012 also removes the requirement for multiple public IPv4 addresses. ISATAP for IPv6 to IPv4 address translation is not supported with DirectAccess.

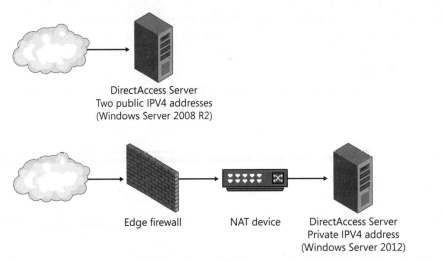

FIGURE 3-7 DirectAccess in Windows Server 2008 R2 required a direct connection to the Internet and at least two public IP addresses; Windows Server 2012 supports deployment behind a NAT device, adding much needed flexibility to the deployment topology

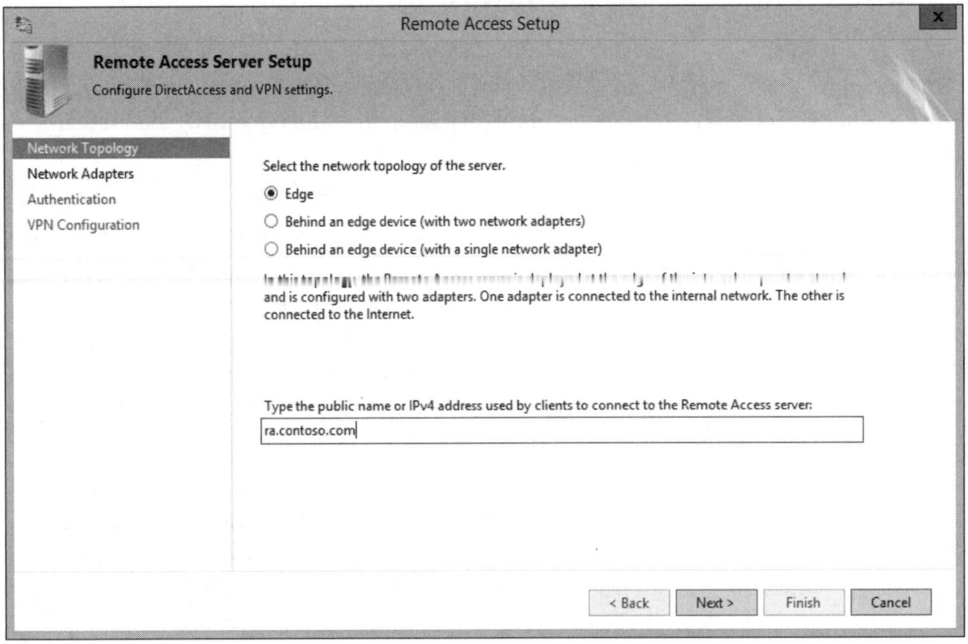

![Remote Access Setup dialog]

FIGURE 3-8 Windows Server 2012 supports placement of a remote access server behind a NAT device

Windows Server 2012 introduced support for Network Load Balancing (NLB) for remote access servers, which allows you to provide high availability in your remote access as well as improve scalability for large implementations.

In addition to the requirements for DirectAccess changing in Windows Server 2012, different topologies also have unique requirements. A single remote access server deployed using the Getting Started Wizard supports only clients running Windows 8 Enterprise or Windows 8.1 Enterprise. PKI is not required for a single remote access server deployed using the wizard, but two-factor authentication is not supported. DirectAccess clients cannot be configured in force tunnel mode (shown in Figure 3-9) when deployed using the Getting Started Wizard, resulting in only traffic destined for the corporate network being routed through the DirectAccess connection.

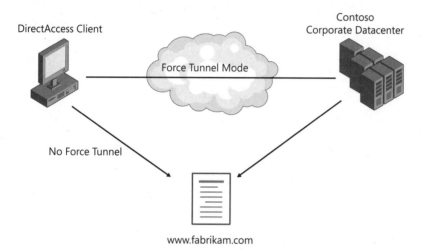

FIGURE 3-9 Force tunnel mode requires all traffic to go through the DirectAccess server and the associated corporate infrastructure; without force tunnel mode, only traffic destined for the corporate network goes through the DirectAccess connection

When a single remote access server is deployed using the Remote Access Setup Wizard, several requirements are different than when the Getting Started Wizard is used. (The two configuration options are shown in Figure 3-10.) Clients running Windows 7 or later are supported in this scenario, and a PKI is a requirement. Force tunnel mode is supported, but not when using KerbProxy authentication.

A multisite DirectAccess deployment enables automatic site selection for Windows 8–based VPN clients. However, Windows 7 clients can be configured to connect only to a single site. Multisite DirectAccess requires both IPv6 and a PKI.

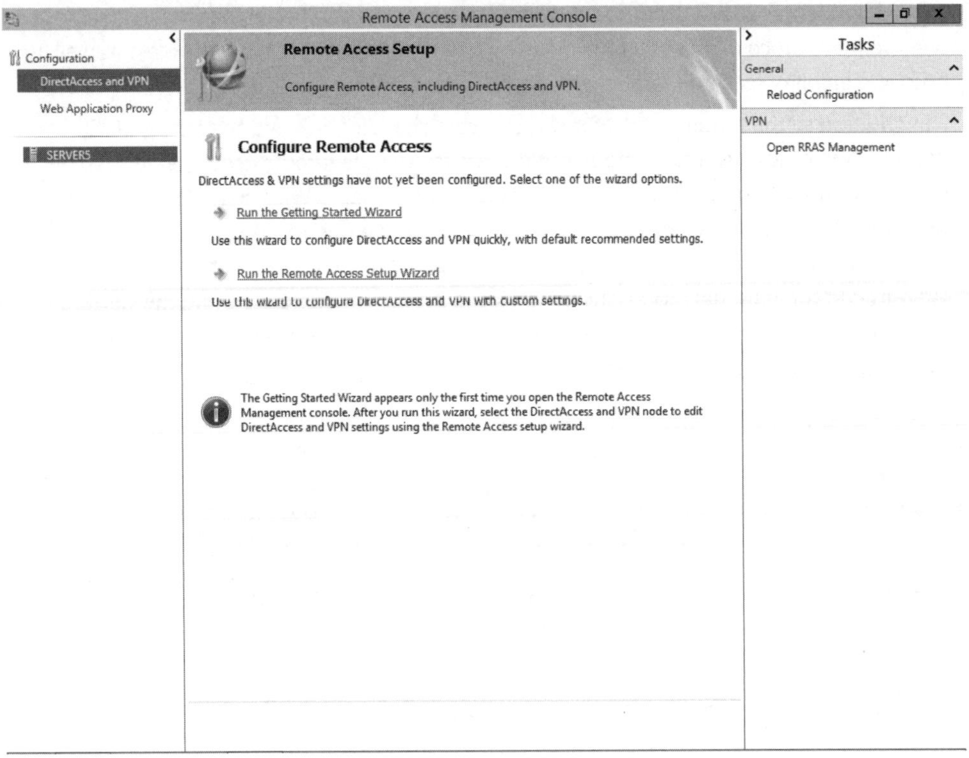

![Remote Access Management Console screenshot]

Remote Access Management Console

Configuration
　DirectAccess and VPN
　Web Application Proxy

SERVERS

Remote Access Setup

Configure Remote Access, including DirectAccess and VPN.

Configure Remote Access

DirectAccess & VPN settings have not yet been configured. Select one of the wizard options.

→ Run the Getting Started Wizard

Use this wizard to configure DirectAccess and VPN quickly, with default recommended settings.

→ Run the Remote Access Setup Wizard

Use this wizard to configure DirectAccess and VPN with custom settings.

ⓘ The Getting Started Wizard appears only the first time you open the Remote Access
Management console. After you run this wizard, select the DirectAccess and VPN node to edit
DirectAccess and VPN settings using the Remote Access setup wizard.

Tasks

General ⌃
　Reload Configuration

VPN ⌃
　Open RRAS Management

FIGURE 3-10 The two wizards presented in the Configure Remote Access page offer very different end results

EXAM TIP

The topology changes in DirectAccess are reason enough for many users to start implementing DirectAccess in their organizations. Support for a DirectAccess server behind a NAT device was introduced in Windows Server 2012, so make sure you understand the differences between the options.

Migrating from Forefront UAG

Migration from an existing Forefront Unified Access Gateway (UAG) DirectAccess server to a Windows Server 2012 R2 remote access server is supported, but there are several steps in the migration process that you should know. Two migration methods are supported: a side-by-side migration allows you to continue to serve clients throughout the migration process; an offline migration results in some downtime. Side-by-side migrations add complexity because some duplication of configuration options is required (such as fully qualified domain names [FQDNs] and IP addresses) because these settings must be unique to each server.

Prior to beginning the migration of your DirectAccess configuration, there are three prerequisites. First, the Forefront UAG server must be at SP1 before you can perform a migration. Also, ISATAP is not supported on the internal network, so it is recommended that native IPv6 be used. Finally, if the UAG server is also operating as a Network Policy Server (NPS) for Network Access Protection (NAP), this function cannot operate on the same server as the remote access server.

A side-by-side migration from Forefront UAG to a Windows Server 2012 remote access server involves exporting the DirectAccess settings using the Forefront UAG export feature, reconfiguring DirectAccess Group Policy Objects (GPOs), configuring new infrastructure and server settings, and deploying DirectAccess. Side-by-side migrations allow you to provide continuous DirectAccess service throughout the migration, which can be untenable for organizations requiring full-time availability from their DirectAccess servers. A side-by-side configuration adds complexity in the duplication required by supporting services and network configuration. FQDNs of the servers must be unique, as do IP addresses. Because both DirectAccess servers coexist for a time, these settings cannot be reused in a side-by-side migration, as shown in Figure 3-11. Due to the changes in the server's FQDN, certificates must be reissued for the new servers as well.

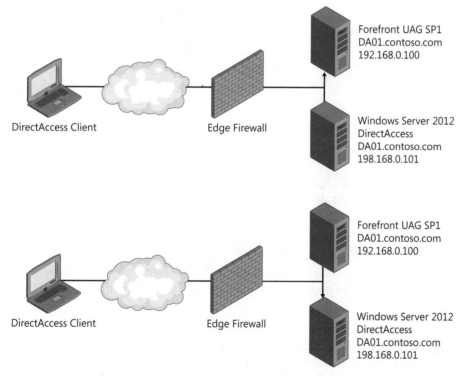

FIGURE 3-11 A side-by-side migration from Forefront UAG results in both the FQDN and IP address of the remote access server changing, which in turn requires that new certificates be issued

An offline migration involves configuring the new remote access server and reconfiguring the necessary GPOs. Offline migrations require some downtime because the new servers will typically reuse the same FQDN, IP address, and certificates, resulting in a trade-off between the procedural ease of the transition and the required downtime. Figure 3-12 shows an example of an offline migration, in which the Windows Server 2012 DirectAccess server is brought online and configured only after the Forefront UAG server is disconnected.

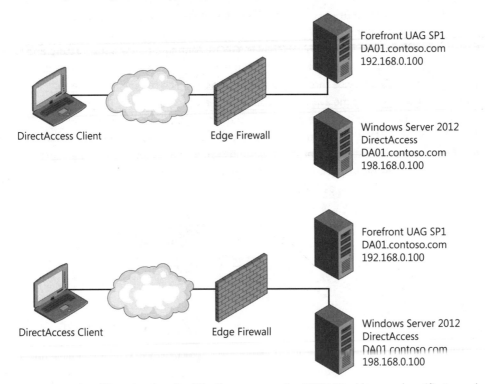

FIGURE 3-12 An offline migration simplifies the process as the FQDN, IP address, and certificate can be reused; downtime is required, however

> **MORE INFO**   **MIGRATING FROM FOREFRONT UAG**
>
> Migrating from Forefront UAG to Windows Server 2012 DirectAccess is a complex process. For complete instructions on the full process, go to *http://technet.microsoft.com/en-us/library/hh831658.aspx.*

Using One-Time Password (OTP)

DirectAccess in Windows Server 2012 supports One-Time Password (OTP) two-factor authentication, providing increased security for remote access connections. Two-factor authentication was supported in Windows Server 2008 R2, but only by using smart cards. Support for OTP vendor solutions such as RSA SecurID enables existing enterprise security systems to be used in conjunction with DirectAccess. DirectAccess also can be used with Trusted Platform Module (TPM)–based virtual smart cards to perform two-factor authentication. The option for OTP can be selected in the Authentication page of the Remote Access Server Setup Wizard, as shown in Figure 3-13. Windows 7 clients support DirectAccess with OTP authentication, but must use the DirectAccess Connectivity Assistant (DCA) 2.0.

To support OTP, an internal PKI must be available to issue certificates to DirectAccess clients. A Remote Authentication Dial-In User Service (RADIUS) server must also be configured to perform authentication. (RADIUS will be discussed in more detail in Objective 3.5).

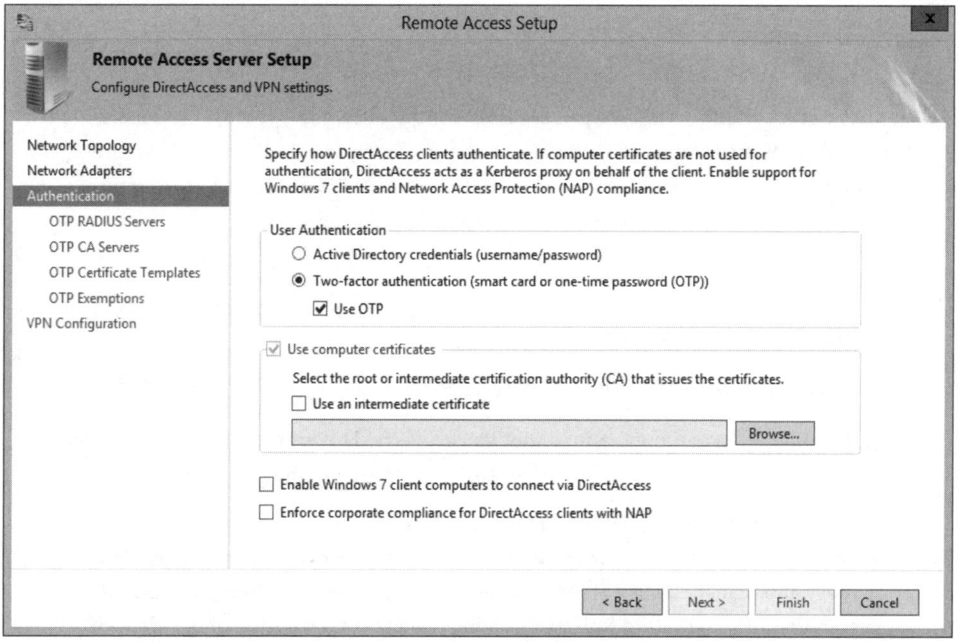

FIGURE 3-13 Two-factor authentication using OTP can be configured for remote access connections

> **MORE INFO** **PKI AND CERTIFICATE CONFIGURATION FOR OTP**
>
> For specifics on configuration of certificate templates, enrollment, and CA configuration for OTP, visit this page: *http://technet.microsoft.com/en-us/library/jj134161.aspx*.

Using enterprise Certificate Authority (CA) certificates

Certificates are central to several aspects of DirectAccess, and a PKI is required for some features such as OTP or smart card authentication. You must also have a PKI in place to support Windows 7 clients or to use a force tunnel configuration. Although many aspects of DirectAccess require certificates, it is no longer a requirement of DirectAccess as a whole in Windows Server 2012, which is a significant change from DirectAccess in Windows Server 2008 R2.

With DirectAccess, both the remote access server (IP-HTTPS) and the network location server require certificates. IP-HTTPS requires an HTTPS website certificate configured with the public IPv4 address or FQDN of the remote access server. The Certificate Revocation List (CRL) distribution point for the certificate issued for IP-HTTPS must be available to external clients, either by using a certificate issued by a public CA or by making the CRL from an internal CA available from outside the corporate network. The network location server also requires a website certificate, but because the network location server will be available only to clients already accessing the internal network, the CRL used to validate this certificate needs to be available only to the internal network.

MORE INFO   **DIRECTACCESS CERTIFICATE REQUIREMENTS**

For information on the certificate prerequisites for the different DirectAccess deployment topologies, visit: *http://technet.microsoft.com/en-us/library/dn464273.aspx*. For more detail on the certificate needs of individual servers in your DirectAccess infrastructure, visit: *http://technet.microsoft.com/en-us/library/jj134148.aspx*.

Thought experiment
Planning a DirectAccess deployment

In this thought experiment, apply what you've learned about this objective. You can find answers to these questions in the "Answers" section at the end of this chapter.

You have been tasked with briefing management on the options available for improving your corporate remote access solution. Of specific importance are the security and manageability of remote clients. Management also wants to know the best method for migrating from the existing DirectAccess solution on a Forefront UAG server.

1. One of the questions presented to you by corporate management has to do with the requirements for managing remote clients through DirectAccess. Can remote management through DirectAccess be enabled without permitting remote access to resources in the corporate network? How would you configure DirectAccess for only remote management?

2. A key requirement of any remote access solution is the ability to limit the clients that can connect remotely as well as the application servers that they can access remotely. Are these options configurable using DirectAccess in Windows Server 2012 R2?

3. What options are available for migrating from the Forefront UAG DirectAccess server? Are there any benefits of using one method over the other? What similarities are there in the two procedures?

Objective summary

- In addition to supporting both DirectAccess and traditional VPN solutions on the same server, Windows Server 2012 improves the flexibility of the network location of the remote access server. Deployment behind a NAT device is now fully supported in Windows Server 2012.

- Two methods of migration from a Forefront UAG–based DirectAccess deployment are supported. A side-by-side migration eliminates downtime due to the migration, but requires duplication of FQDNs and IP addresses; an offline migration provides a simplified deployment, but requires some downtime.

- OTP support allows third-party OTP solutions to be integrated with your remote access solution. Virtual smart cards enabled by TPM chips are also supported.

- Although DirectAccess does not require a PKI in Windows Server 2012, different topologies and features require that a PKI be implemented. Additionally, both IP-HTTPS and the network location server require website certificates to be validated by DirectAccess clients.

Objective review

Answer the following questions to test your knowledge of the information in this objective. You can find the answers to these questions and explanations of why each answer choice is correct or incorrect in the "Answers" section at the end of this chapter.

1. Which of the following remote access configuration options is used to enable placement of the DirectAccess server behind a NAT device? (Choose all that apply.)

   A. Edge topology

   B. Behind an edge device (with two network adapters)

   C. Behind an edge device (with one network adapter)

   D. DirectAccess for remote management only

2. Which options are not available when DirectAccess is configured using the Getting Started Wizard? (Choose all that apply.)

   A. Force tunnel mode

   B. Two-factor authentication

   C. Placement behind an edge device

   D. DirectAccess for remote management only

3. Which of the following is a newly supported method of authentication for DirectAccess in Windows Server 2012? (Choose all that apply.)

   A. OTP

   B. Smart card

   C. User name and password

   D. Virtual smart card

4. What prerequisite must be met before migrating from a Forefront UAG DirectAccess server to one based on Windows Server 2012?

   A. Public and private IPv6 support.

   B. Forefront UAG SP1 must be installed.

   C. A PKI must be deployed.

   D. Additional public IPv4 addresses must be available.

5. What benefit is provided by performing a side-by-side migration from Forefront UAG DirectAccess to Windows Server 2012?

   A. IP addresses and FQDNs can be reused.

   B. The migration process is automated.

   C. New certificates do not need to be issued.

   D. No downtime is required.

6. What requirement must be met for Windows 7 clients to use OTP for authentication to DirectAccess?

   A. PKI

   B. DCA 2.0

   C. RADIUS

   D. Windows 7 SP1

7. Which of the following certificate requirements is best served by a certificate issued from a public CA?

   A. Client computer certificate for IPsec

   B. Server computer certificate for IPsec

   C. SSL certificate for a network location server

   D. SSL certificate for an IP-HTTPS server

Objective 3.3: Design a Web Application Proxy solution

As cloud-based applications become more prolific, there is a need to provide similar flexibility with on-premises applications that reside within the corporate network. Although a solution such as DirectAccess provides simplified connectivity to internal network resources, DirectAccess is not a good fit when multiple device types or non-domain-joined computers are used.

Web Application Proxy is a new feature in Windows Server 2012 R2 that allows you to provide access to web applications within your internal corporate network through the use of a reverse proxy. Authentication requests can be passed from the Web Application Proxy to internal web applications to provide access to client devices that might not otherwise be able to gain access to resources on the corporate network.

The Web Application Proxy feature makes heavy use of Active Directory Federation Services (AD FS) and was previously known as AD FS 2.0 proxy. AD FS is covered in the 70-414 exam, as is the integration between Web Application Proxy and AD FS, but you need to know the basics for this exam as well.

> **This objective covers how to:**
> - Plan for applications
> - Use authentication and authorization
> - Use Workplace Join
> - Use devices
> - Use multifactor authentication
> - Use multifactor access control
> - Use Single Sign-On (SSO)
> - Use certificates
> - Plan access for internal and external clients

Planning for applications

The process of making web applications available through Web Application Proxy is known as publishing. Published applications can be accessed by remote clients using a number of different methods, including a standard web browser, Microsoft Office applications, or a Windows Store app. The device used does not require any additional software to access the application, and it does not have to be joined to the Active Directory domain.

A primary role of a Web Application Proxy is to facilitate authentication between the remote client and the application. Several forms of application authentication can be used through Web Application Proxy, including claims-based, integrated Windows authentication; Microsoft Office Forms Based Authentication (MS-OFBA); and OAuth 2.0 authentication from Windows Store apps. Some examples of applications that can be published through Web Application Proxy are Microsoft SharePoint Server, Microsoft Exchange Server, and Microsoft Lync Server.

Using authentication and authorization

Authentication, which is the primary functionality offered by Web Application Proxy, affects the publication process significantly. Web Application Proxy also provides an additional layer in the authentication and authorization process for external clients, allowing you to limit access to applications from outside the network to only clients meeting certain requirements.

Access to a web application through a Web Application Proxy is enabled using AD FS. The connection to an AD FS server is configured using the Web Application Proxy Configuration Wizard, as shown in Figure 3-14. Preauthentication occurs to prevent any unauthorized traffic from reaching the internal web application. Several security mechanisms can be used to provide authentication and authorization to published web applications, many of which are discussed throughout this chapter.

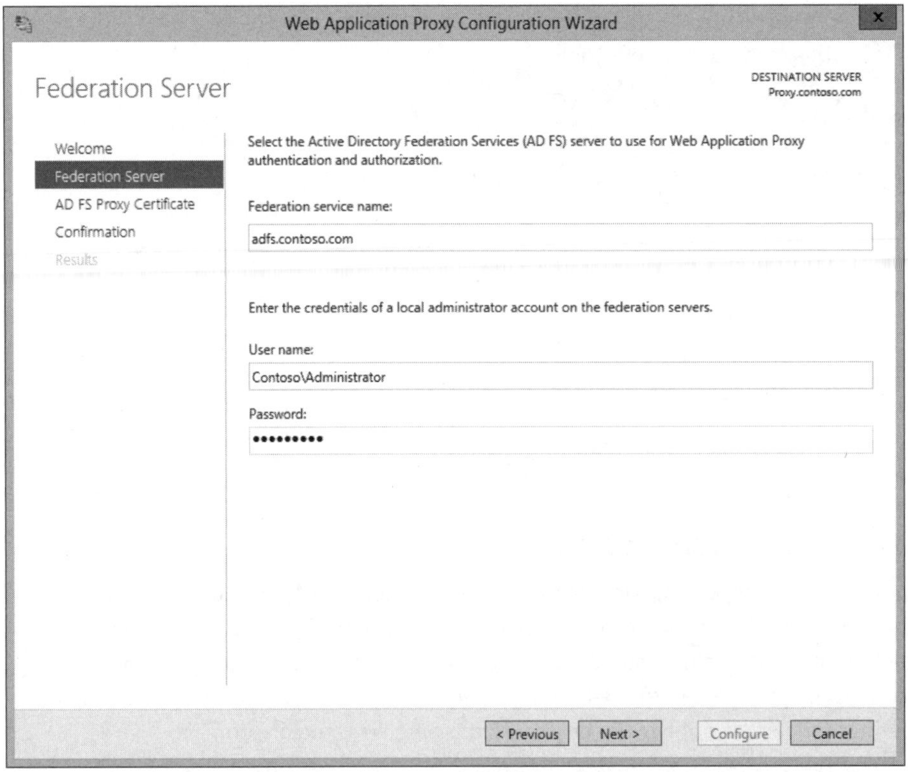

FIGURE 3-14 AD FS is used to perform the authentication process for Web Application Proxy

Preauthentication in Web Application Proxy comes in two forms: AD FS preauthentication and pass-through preauthentication. With AD FS preauthentication, a user is required to authenticate in some way prior to accessing the application, ensuring that only authorized users can reach the application. AD FS preauthentication is required for applications to make use of Workplace Join and multifactor authentication, both of which are discussed in this chapter.

Pass-through authentication does not require any user interaction before being directed to the application. In most cases, pass-through authentication is used only when the application performs authentication and authorization.

Using Workplace Join

A new feature in both Windows Server 2012 R2 and Windows 8.1, Workplace Join allows devices to be registered with the Active Directory Domain Services (AD DS) using the Device Registration Service (DRS) with AD FS. To support the DRS, the Active Directory Forest must be at the Windows Server 2012 R2 functional level, a process that extends the Active Directory schema to contain references to registered devices.

To enable the DRS, you must run the Initialize-ADDeviceRegistration command once for the forest from a federation server. The Enable-AdfsDeviceRegistration command must also be run once on each federation server. The DRS is automatically published to the Web Application Proxy when the proxy is deployed to make it available to external users. If the DRS is enabled after the Web Application Proxy has been deployed, you can run the Update-WebApplicationProxyDeviceRegistration command on the Web Application Proxy server to publish the DRS and make it available to external users.

Both Windows 8.1 and iOS devices can be connected using Workplace Join. By requiring registered users within AD FS (see Figure 3-15), device registration using Workplace Join can be configured as a requirement for accessing published applications.

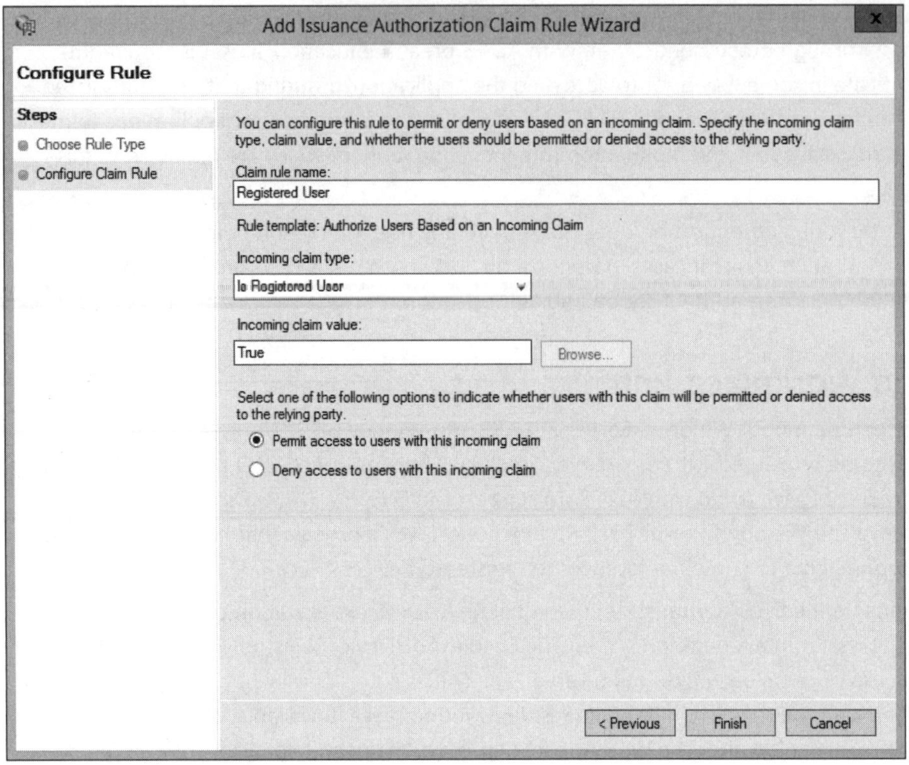

FIGURE 3-15 Configuring AD FS to require registration

Using devices

One of the major benefits of using Web Application Proxy is that it enables you to allow users to access internal web applications using whatever device they have available, whether it be a company-issued laptop or tablet, or even a personal device. The risk of allowing personal and unmanaged devices to connect to the corporate network is mitigated because an internal network connection is not required. As mentioned in the previous section, only Windows 8.1 and iOS devices currently support Workplace Join.

Using multifactor authentication

In addition to being able to limit access to applications to only those devices that are connected using Workplace Join, Web Application Proxy can require multifactor authentication through the use of certificates, smart cards, or OTP. Workplace Join is also a form of multifactor authentication because the device must be registered in addition to the user providing credentials.

Using multifactor access control

With AD FS preauthentication in Windows Server 2012 R2, access control can be managed using multiple factors such as user, device, location, or authentication data. Any of these claim types can be required to gain access to applications through the Web Application Proxy. For example, you could configure a multifactor access control policy to require members of certain Active Directory groups to perform authentication using a smart card before gaining access to an application through the Web Application Proxy.

Using Single Sign-On (SSO)

A Web Application Proxy can provide Single Sign-On (SSO) only if the Web Application Proxy is a member of an Active Directory domain. AD FS preauthentication is used to allow SSO to published applications. After a user authenticates to the Web Application Proxy, AD FS attaches an SSO cookie to further requests, ensuring that the user continues to have access to published applications.

EXAM TIP

There are many similarities between some of the different authentication types available for use with AD FS and Web Application Proxy. You should have a good understanding of the options and how they differ.

Using certificates

Web Application Proxy depends heavily on SSL certificates to secure traffic with remote clients. Because these clients are not required to be domain joined, the certificates used are usually issued by an external CA. Single-name certificates, subject alternative name (SAN) certificates, and wildcard certificates are supported. Multiple certificates might be required to support multiple published applications.

In addition to the Web Application Proxy server, AD FS relies on certificates for the services it provides. The certificates used for AD FS must also be from an external CA. AD FS requires a SAN certificate because both the <federation service name>.<domain suffix> and enterpriseregistration.<domain suffix> FQDNs must be supported.

Planning access for internal and external clients

The intent of deploying Web Application Proxy is to enable external clients to access internal web applications. Using FQDNs that resolve to the application internally and the Web Application Proxy externally enables users to access their applications without having to remember a unique external URL. Web Application Proxy can facilitate this process through the use of URL translation, shown in Figure 3-16, which is configured during the application publishing process.

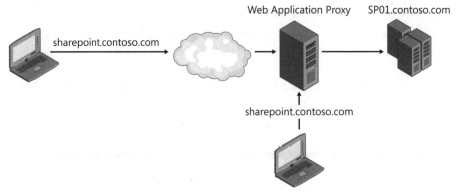

FIGURE 3-16 URL translation is used to allow users to access applications using the same URL from both internal and external clients

Thought experiment

Planning a Web Application Proxy deployment

In this thought experiment, apply what you've learned about this objective. You can find answers to these questions in the "Answers" section at the end of this chapter.

Your company is considering allowing users to access web applications hosted within the corporate network using devices they have available. Answer the following questions for the corporate management team regarding Web Application Proxy:

1. Is there a way to allow access to internal web applications from devices that are not domain joined, but still require a device registration process? What limitations should be in place if you implement such a solution?

2. Passwords and other authentication methods can be problematic and awkward on tablet devices. We certainly want users to authenticate to our web applications, but allowing them to authenticate once and then access any application they have access to would be the best solution. Are there capabilities to do this using Web Application Proxy? What requirements would have to be met for SSO?

3. What certificate needs are introduced by implementing Web Application Proxy? Can these needs be met using an internal CA?

Objective summary

- Web Application Proxy provides external clients with access to internal web applications enabled through the publishing process.
- AD FS is used to provide multiple authentication methods for Web Application Proxy.
- Applications published in Web Application Proxy are accessible through a standard web browser, Microsoft Office applications, or Windows Store apps.
- Web Application Proxy supports AD FS preauthentication, which allows you to ensure that clients are allowed to access an application prior to serving the application. AD FS preauthentication also allows you to use Workplace Join and multifactor authentication.
- Workplace Join can be used with Web Application Proxy to provide access only to devices that have completed the registration process.
- Any device with a web browser can access applications through the Web Application Proxy, although only Windows 8.1 and iOS devices support Workplace Join.
- Multifactor authentication can be used with AD FS preauthentication to require authentication by using certificates, smart cards, or OTP.
- Multifactor access control allows you to design policies to gain more control over the authentication process through a Web Application Proxy.
- Published applications can make use of SSO within Web Application Proxy.
- To secure communication with external clients, certificates from an external CA are required for the Web Application Proxy and AD FS servers.
- Web Application Proxy uses URL translation to allow both internal and external clients to access applications using a consistent FQDN.

Objective review

Answer the following questions to test your knowledge of the information in this objective. You can find the answers to these questions and explanations of why each answer choice is correct or incorrect in the "Answers" section at the end of this chapter.

1. Which service does Web Application Proxy interact with to perform authentication?

    A. AD FS

    B. AD DS

    C. AD CS

    D. AD FS Proxy

2. What is required of a device to access an application through a Web Application Proxy?

   A. Membership in an Active Directory domain

   B. Registration through Workplace Join

   C. Windows 8.1 operating system

   D. Web browser, Microsoft Office application, or compatible Windows 8.1 app

3. Which of the following relies exclusively on the application to authenticate users?

   A. AD FS preauthentication

   B. SSO

   C. Pass-through authentication

   D. Multifactor access control

4. What benefits are offered by using Workplace Join as an authentication method for a Web Application Proxy? (Choose all that apply.)

   A. It does not require devices to be domain members.

   B. It allows the use of any device with a web browser.

   C. It requires device registration.

   D. It ensures that devices meet corporate security requirements.

5. Which operating systems support Workplace Join? (Choose all that apply.)

   A. Windows 8

   B. iOS

   C. Windows 0.1

   D. UNIX

6. What allows you to require members of a specific group to authenticate using a smart card?

   A. SSO

   B. Workplace Join

   C. Multifactor authentication

   D. Multifactor access control

7. What are the requirements to use SSO with Web Application Proxy?

   A. The client must be connected using Workplace Join.

   B. The client must be joined to the domain.

   C. The Web Application Proxy server must be domain joined.

   D. The client must be using a Windows 8.1 or iOS device.

8. What aspect of Web Application Proxy allows both internal and external clients to access applications using the same URL?

   A. DNS CNAME records

   B. URL translation

   C. Pass-through authentication

   D. Workplace Join

Objective 3.4: Implement a scalable remote access solution

As businesses rely more extensively on remote access solutions, it is important to know the options available to increase scalability and fault tolerance for remote access. Whether you support traditional VPN services, site-to-site connectivity, DirectAccess, or Web Application Proxy, reliability and performance are critical. Fortunately, Windows Server 2012 R2 includes capabilities to support high availability and expansion of the remote access services throughout your enterprise.

> **This objective covers how to:**
> - Configure site-to-site VPNs
> - Configure packet filters
> - Implement packet tracing
> - Implement multisite remote access
> - Configure remote access clustered with Network Load Balancing (NLB)
> - Implement an advanced DirectAccess solution
> - Configure multiple RADIUS server groups and infrastructure
> - Configure Web Application Proxy for clustering

Configuring site-to-site VPNs

Site-to-site VPN meets many of the requirements formerly met only through dedicated network connectivity between corporate locations. Through site-to-site VPN connections, an enterprise can link multiple physical locations across the globe into a single logical network, which improves access to applications, shared resources, and services critical to the corporate infrastructure. As mentioned earlier in this chapter, site-to-site VPN connections can also be used to create a secure tunnel to cloud services such as Azure. Windows Server 2012 supports either the PPTP or L2TP/IPsec protocol for creation of site-to-site connections, with all the implications related to security and performance applying.

Site-to-site VPN can be enabled through the Remote Access Management Console by clicking the Enable Site-to-Site VPN link in the Tasks panel. After the configuration is complete, the RRAS has to be restarted.

Configuring packet filters

Packet filters are similar to network firewall rules in that they are used to restrict certain types of network traffic. The Routing and Remote Access console allows you to manage the types of network traffic allowed to traverse a network interface. Both inbound and outbound filters can be configured, and IPv4 and IPv6 traffic are both supported. Packet filters can be configured to pass or drop packets that meet the configured filters.

To configure packet filters, navigate to the General node under either IPv4 or IPv6 in the Routing and Remote Access console. Within the properties for a network interface are buttons labeled Inbound Filters and Outbound Filters. The Inbound Filters window is shown in Figure 3-17.

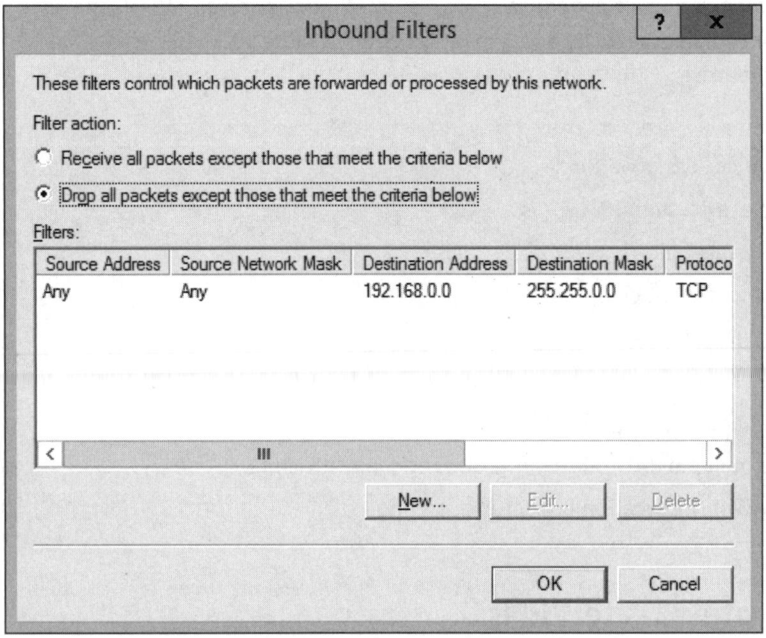

FIGURE 3-17 Inbound packet filters are used to control the flow of traffic through a remote access server

> **MORE INFO   PACKET FILTERING**
>
> For more detailed directions on configuring packet filters in the Routing and Remote Access console, visit: *http://technet.microsoft.com/en-us/library/dd469754(v=WS.10).aspx*.

Implementing packet tracing

Packet tracing enables troubleshooting of network connections by logging traffic, which can be monitored and analyzed to pinpoint configuration problems. Packet tracing can be enabled in the Dashboard section of the Remote Access Management Console by clicking the Start Tracing link in the Tasks panel, which displays the window shown in Figure 3-18. New logs can be created, existing logs can be appended to, and existing logs can be overwritten using circular logging. Packet tracing is useful for troubleshooting network or firewall problems, or for tracking security concerns.

Packet tracing is resource-intensive, using both processor and storage resources. The tracing feature should be enabled only for troubleshooting purposes and should be disabled after diagnostics are complete.

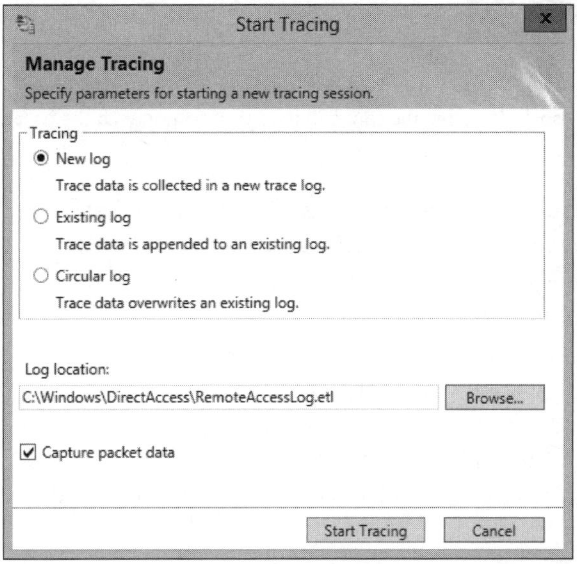

FIGURE 3-18 Packet tracing can be used to create log files detailing remote access traffic

Implementing multisite remote access

A multisite remote access deployment enables users to connect directly to any site containing a remote access server configured as an entry point. The decision about which site to connect to can be fully automatic for Windows 8 clients, it can be the site with the best possible connectivity (as shown in Figure 3-19), or the user can be allowed to decide which site to use. Even a global load balancer can be used for users to be automatically directed to another site if one site is unavailable. Windows 7 users are restricted to a single site, so if the remote access server at the predefined site is unavailable, they must wait until the remote access server returns to service.

Multisite remote access can be used to deploy endpoints to every corporate location or only those that serve as central hubs. In addition to providing optimal performance between remote users and the remote access server, consider the location of corporate resources being accessed through the remote access connection; it might affect your deployment of remote access endpoints through your corporate infrastructure.

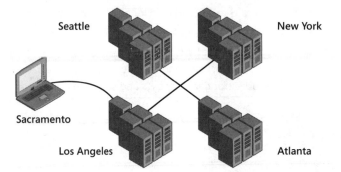

FIGURE 3-19 Multisite remote access makes possible automatic connection to the location with the best connectivity

There are a couple of requirements for multisite remote access. First, Web Application Proxy cannot be installed on the same remote access server. IPsec authentication must be configured for the remote access server, and both the network location server and the IP-HTTPS server must use certificates from a CA (they cannot be self-signed).

Two wizards govern the use of multisite remote access. The Enable Multisite Deployment Wizard is used to configure the initial multisite deployment, including the selection of the first entry point for the multisite deployment. During multisite deployment, you can configure global load balancing and support for Windows 7 clients. Additional entry points are created through the Add An Entry Point Wizard, which is run on the DirectAccess server being added.

Configuring remote access clustered with NLB

To provide high availability, remote access can be configured as an NLB cluster. Prior to configuring NLB for remote access, the NLB feature must be installed using the Add Roles And Features Wizard.

Executing the Enable Load Balancing Wizard allows you to specify IPv4 and IPv6 prefixes for use with the NLB cluster. Because each server in the NLB cluster must be able to authenticate as the IP-HTTPS server, the HTTPS certificate must be deployed to each server in the cluster.

MORE INFO **IMPLEMENTING NLB FOR DIRECTACCESS**

For complete details on deploying DirectAccess in an NLB cluster, visit *http://technet. microsoft.com/en-us/library/jj134175.aspx.*

Implementing an advanced DirectAccess solution

Upon initial deployment of a remote access server, you have the choice of running a Getting Started Wizard or the Remote Access Setup Wizard. Although the Getting Started Wizard helps you get DirectAccess up and running with minimal effort, it does not give you the options required to configure the more advanced aspects of DirectAccess and does not support implementing these options at a later date without completely reconfiguring DirectAccess.

If you plan to use OTP or smart cards for authentication immediately or in the future, you must use the Remote Access Setup Wizard because the CA must be configured as well as RADIUS and certificates for OTP. The same is true for multisite DirectAccess: If not configured, using the Remote Access Setup Wizard multisite is not supported, and the DirectAccess server must be reconfigured. Support for Windows 7 also requires configuration using the Remote Access Setup Wizard because support for Windows 7 clients also requires computer certificates issued by a root or intermediate CA. NAP enforcement and RADIUS authentication are also enabled with the Remote Access Setup Wizard.

Configuring multiple RADIUS server groups and infrastructure

Both DirectAccess and traditional VPN connections can be authenticated through a RADIUS server such as a Windows Server 2012 R2–based NPS. RADIUS gives you increased control over the authentication process through policies and centralized management, and it also allows you to use other authentication types such as OTP with Web Application Proxy.

Another benefit of using RADIUS for authentication is the ability to manage authentication traffic, distributing it across a RADIUS server group. The Remote Access Setup Wizard allows for RADIUS authentication on the VPN Configuration page. One or more RADIUS servers can be configured and prioritized in a list. RADIUS server groups can then be configured, as shown in Figure 3-20, to handle these authentication requests as they are routed to the RADIUS servers. (NPS and RADIUS are discussed in more detail in Objective 3.5.)

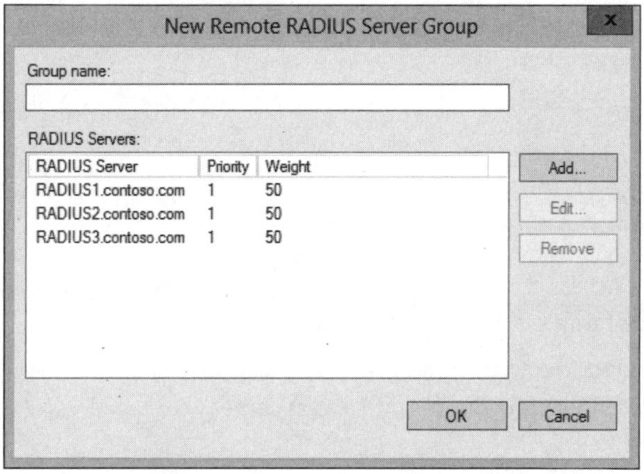

FIGURE 3-20 RADIUS server groups are used to load balance, prioritize, and provide high availability for RADIUS authentication

Configuring Web Application Proxy for clustering

To provide optimal performance and high availability, it might be necessary to deploy multiple Web Application Proxy servers. Configuration information for Web Application Proxy servers is stored within AD FS. Additional Web Application Proxy servers are configured automatically using this configuration information during deployment through the use of the Web Application Proxy Configuration Wizard.

> ## Thought experiment
> ### Configuring a scalable remote access implementation
>
> In this thought experiment, apply what you've learned about this objective. You can find answers to these questions in the "Answers" section at the end of this chapter.
>
> You have been tasked with implementing a modern remote access solution for your corporation, replacing the existing VPN solution. With the modernization of the internal corporate network and application infrastructure, the remote access solution must be able to provide seamless access to these applications.
>
> 1. Your company has begun to expand to other locations, and maintaining access to network resources regardless of corporate location is critical for users. What remote access tool allows you to link corporate locations into a single logical network?
>
> 2. In addition to linking corporate locations into a single network, a solution that allows users to automatically create a remote access connection to the closest corporate location has been requested. What option in Windows Server 2012 supports this functionality?
>
> 3. Is there any functionality in Windows Server 2012 R2 that allows you to create a high-availability solution to provide remote access to internal web applications? What configuration steps are required to implement this solution in a clustered environment?

Objective summary

- Site-to-site VPNs can be used to create a single logical network out of multiple physical locations.
- Using the Routing and Remote Access console, packet filters can be configured to allow or disallow certain types of traffic over a specific network interface.
- Packet tracing is a troubleshooting tool that allows you to log diagnostic information about network traffic as it passes through your remote access server.

- Multisite remote access in Windows Server 2012 can be used to automatically connect Windows 8 users to the site offering the best connectivity.
- Remote access servers can be made highly available and can distribute the workload across multiple servers using NLB clusters.
- Several features in remote access can be used only when they are configured using advanced settings: multiple servers, multisite, two-factor authentication, and force tunneling.
- RADIUS servers provide increased flexibility for authenticating remote access connections, including the capability to create RADIUS server groups to provide improved performance and fault tolerance.
- Web Application Proxy servers can be clustered to provide high availability and improve performance.

Objective review

Answer the following questions to test your knowledge of the information in this objective. You can find the answers to these questions and explanations of why each answer choice is correct or incorrect in the "Answers" section at the end of this chapter.

1. Your users can connect to your remote access server, but cannot access network resources. What might be the cause of this problem?

   A. Packet filtering on the Internet connection

   B. Packet filtering on the intranet connection

   C. Packet tracing is enabled

   D. Packet tracing is disabled

2. What is the minimum required client operating system supported for a user to automatically connect to the optimal remote access server?

   A. Windows Vista SP1

   B. Windows 7

   C. Windows 8

   D. Windows 8.1

3. Which of the following allows Windows 8 clients to automatically connect to the closest remote access server?

   A. DirectAccess

   B. Web Application Proxy cluster

   C. Site-to-site VPN

   D. Multisite remote access

4. What feature allows you to create a highly available remote access solution?

   A. Remote access cluster using NLB

   B. RADIUS server groups

   C. Web Application Proxy clusters

   D. Site-to-site VPN

5. What capabilities are provided by RADIUS server groups?

   A. Distribution of the authentication workload

   B. The ability to remotely access internal web applications using devices that are not domain joined

   C. Automatic connection to the nearest remote access entry point

   D. Enforcement of network policies prior to establishing a remote access connection

Objective 3.5: Design and implement a network protection solution

The NPS role includes features that allow you to authenticate clients attempting to connect to the network and enforce policies prior to allowing clients to fully access the corporate network. There are several aspects of implementing a network protection solution, including deploying NPS, managing network policies, creating a remediation network, choosing an enforcement method, and configuring network clients.

One aspect of network protection is NAP, a feature that allows clients to be evaluated for health before being allowed to connect to the network. NAP is deprecated in Windows Server 2012 R2, so the functionality is still fully supported for both Windows Server 2012 R2 and Windows 8.1, but will likely be removed in future product versions. Microsoft recommends using its System Center Configuration Manager to perform health policy enforcement and remediation going forward.

As with any security measure in your network, NPS can result in significant network issues if misconfigured, even to the point of lost network connectivity. Proper planning, testing, and a phased implementation are highly recommended.

Configuring NAP enforcement methods

NAP can be a powerful tool for network protection because it enables you to evaluate network clients based on health criteria such as antivirus definitions, software updates, and firewall configuration. Two things must be in place for this enforcement to occur: NAP client software on the client computer and an enforcement method used to refer network clients to the NPS.

The NAP client on Windows computers can be managed in several ways. The NAP Client Configuration MMC snap-in can be accessed by entering **NAPCLCFG.MSC** at the Run prompt. (The NAP Client Configuration window is shown in Figure 3-21.) NAP clients for domain member computers can also be configured using Group Policy, which is always the preferred method for multiple computers in an enterprise environment. Finally, the NETSH command-line tool allows you to configure NAP client enforcement using NETSH NAP CLIENT. Each enforcement method used on your network must be enabled within the NAP client, and the Network Access Protection Agent service must be started for NAP enforcement to perform correctly.

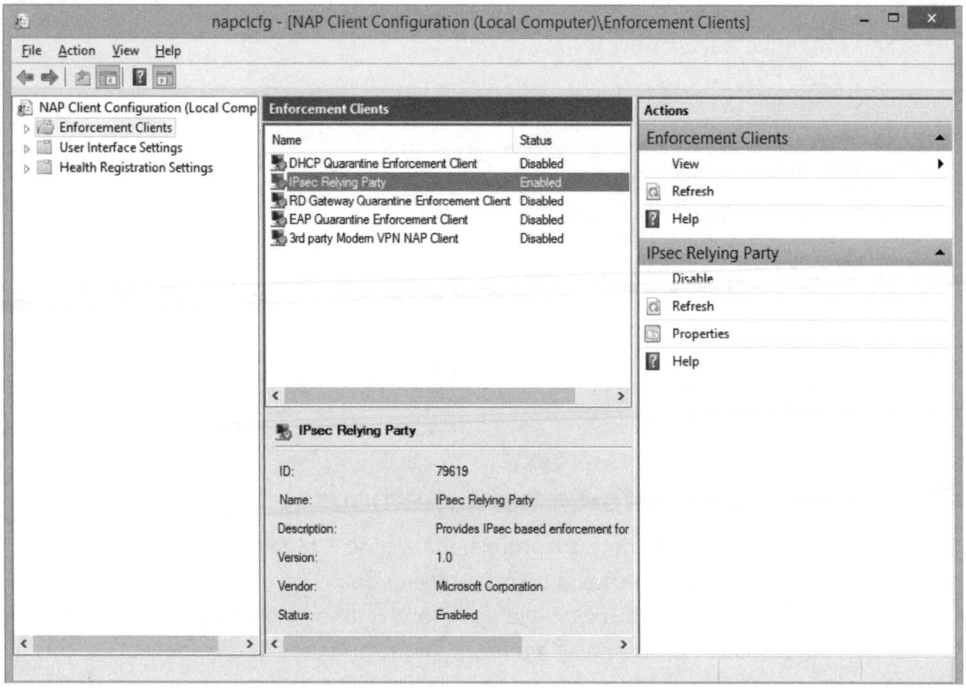

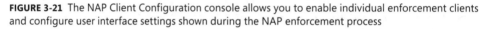

FIGURE 3-21 The NAP Client Configuration console allows you to enable individual enforcement clients and configure user interface settings shown during the NAP enforcement process

NAP policies are enforced by segregating clients that do not meet the health policies of the network, as well as those that cannot be validated, from computers that meet the health policies. Each enforcement method handles this segregation in a different way, but the common thread is that each method is capable of performing or facilitating a health evaluation prior to giving the client access to the network.

DHCP

DHCP servers using Windows Server can be used to provide NAP enforcement for DHCP clients if the server also performs the NPS role. The NPS role can either perform authentication locally or be configured as a RADIUS proxy to forward requests to the NPS performing the authentication. NAP enforcement can be enabled for individual DHCP scopes or for all scopes configured on the DHCP server.

DHCP is a weak NAP enforcement method because it can only prevent clients from gaining an IP address through DHCP. Network clients with a static IP address or an automatically configured IP address such as an automatic private IP address (APIPA) or IPv6 autoconfiguration can still access the network.

IPsec

IPsec, along with 802.1x, is one of the preferred methods of NAP enforcement of internal network clients. Enforcement occurs by configuring computer certificate issuance so that only computers that meet the requirements of the network policy receive a computer certificate, which enables communication with other computers on the network. When used as a NAP enforcement method, the IPsec client configuration must be configured to require IPsec for all network traffic. Only computers placed in the remediation network should be allowed to communicate to clients without using IPsec. As with NAP client enforcement, Group Policy can be used to configure IPsec policies on domain-joined computers.

NAP enforcement using IPsec requires heavy use of Active Directory Certificate Services (AD CS), including the capability to automatically issue computer certificates. The IPsec enforcement method also uses the Health Registration Authority (HRA), which is installed as a feature. The HRA must also be an NPS, either performing authentication or forwarding requests to an authenticating NPS.

VPN

Remote access clients can be evaluated by NAP and NPS when initiating a remote access connection to the corporate network. The NPS role must be installed on the remote access server and can be configured to operate as a RADIUS proxy or to handle authentication requests locally. When using the VPN NAP enforcement, the Extensible Authentication Protocol (EAP) enforcement method must be enabled on the NAP client.

NAP enforcement of VPN clients can be configured in conjunction with a corporate PKI using Protected Extensible Authentication Protocol-Transport Layer Security (PEAP-TLS) or EAP-TLS with AD CS.

802.1x

Unlike other NAP enforcement methods, 802.1x relies on physical networking hardware such as switches and wireless access points to initiate RADIUS authentication and health evaluation. These network hardware devices are configured as RADIUS clients during policy configuration. The result is that having 802.1x-capable networking hardware is a require-ment for using this enforcement method. In the 802.1x enforcement method, noncompliant network clients are segregated from healthy computers, either through IP filtering or VLANs. Similar to VPN-based enforcement, NAP clients must be configured to use the EAP enforce-ment method. 802.1x enforcement can also work with your corporate PKI using EAP-TLS, or PEAP-TLS and AD CS.

EXAM TIP

Even though NAP is deprecated in Windows Server 2012 R2, it is still covered on the exam. At a minimum, you need to know the enforcement methods, what they require, and how they segregate compliant from noncompliant computers.

Designing an NPS infrastructure

The design of your NPS infrastructure is critical for high availability and performance reasons. Authentication traffic can be routed through your network using RADIUS proxies, and high availability for authentication can be managed using RADIUS server groups. The NAP infrastructure must include remediation of noncompliant computers, ideally offering a path to update antivirus signatures or to acquire system updates.

Planning capacity

There are several aspects of your NPS infrastructure that should be evaluated and monitored for performance problems. Each step in the health evaluation and authentication process should be assessed to ensure optimal performance.

Enforcement servers for the DHCP, IPsec, and VPN enforcement methods should be analyzed to ensure that the additional workload from NAP enforcement does not affect their capability to respond to client requests. In the case of DHCP and VPN, high-availability options for those services can be used to distribute the workload across additional resources. In the case of IPsec enforcement, the HRA server should be monitored to ensure that it can respond to health certificate requests in a timely manner. Enforcement servers can be configured to perform validation or forward the authentication request to a RADIUS server group (see Figure 3-22).

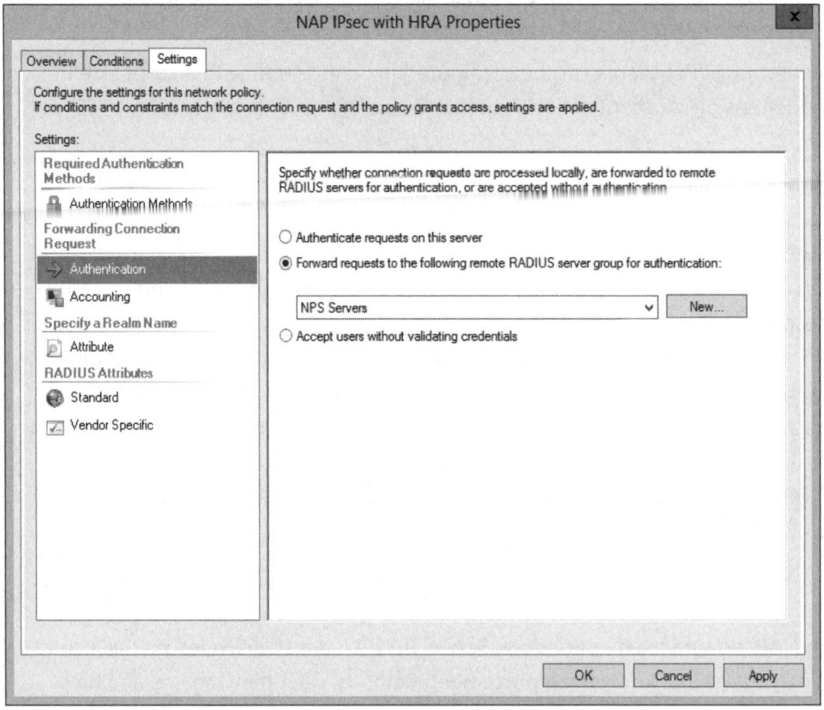

FIGURE 3-22 By configuring the network policy on a NAP enforcement server, you can forward authentication requests to a RADIUS server group of your choosing

NAP health policy servers can be load balanced using RADIUS server groups, as shown in Figure 3-23, which allows you to distribute RADIUS authentication requests to multiple NPS servers on your network. Load balancing allows you to set priority and weight values to manage the distribution of the authentication workload and to configure the circumstances under which a RADIUS server should be considered unavailable.

Capacity should be a consideration for remediation servers such as Windows Server Update Servers (WSUS). Many criteria determine the load for remediation servers, including the number of clients, the level of enforcement, and whether the same servers are used to update compliant and noncompliant computers.

Planning for server placement

Regardless of the NAP enforcement method, some network services must be available to both compliant and noncompliant computers. Health policy servers must be able to accept authentication requests from clients, but must also be able to authenticate users and computers to an Active Directory domain controller.

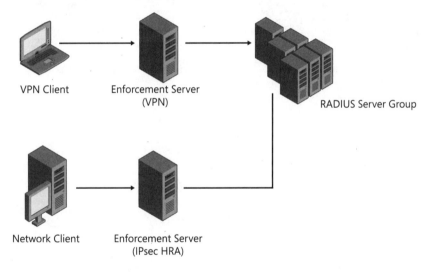

VPN Client   Enforcement Server
              (VPN)   RADIUS Server Group

Network Client   Enforcement Server
                  (IPsec HRA)

FIGURE 3-23 RADIUS server groups can be used to provide improved performance and fault tolerance for authentication traffic

Enforcement servers such as DHCP, VPN, or HRA servers must be able to communicate with all clients, regardless of policy compliance. Servers used for remediation are not required to be able to communicate across compliance levels, but having separate update mechanisms adds unnecessary complexity to your network.

Understanding firewall considerations

The Windows Firewall should automatically create exceptions for ports used by NPS and RADIUS traffic, including User Datagram Protocol (UDP) ports 1812, 1813, 1645, and 1646.

Other firewalls external to NPS servers have to be configured to allow these ports through to the server for authentication to occur.

Deploying a Network Policy Server (NPS)

The primary piece in a network protection infrastructure is one or more NPS servers, which forward RADIUS authentication requests, analyze authentication requests for compliance, and manage the policies used to determine compliance. NPS policies and enforcement can be initiated using the Configure NAP Wizard. Each of the three policy types can also be created or modified manually by editing the properties of individual policies, as shown in Figure 3-24.

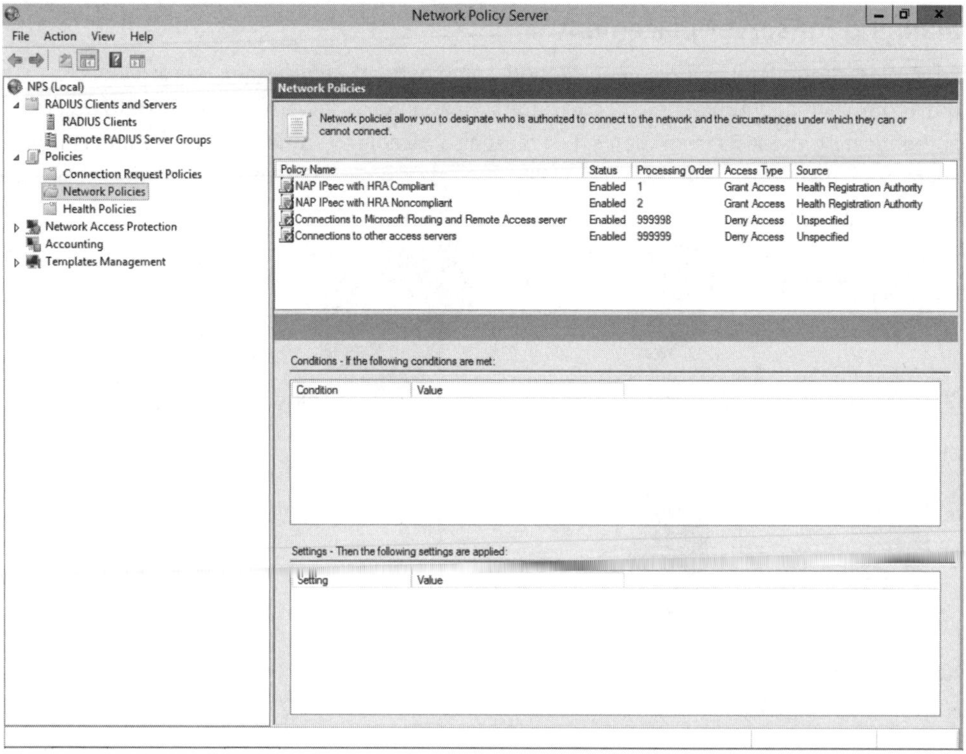

FIGURE 3-24 Policies can be manually edited by modifying their properties in the Network Policy Server management console

Connection Request Policies allow you to identify and route incoming authentication traffic, choose the enforcement method and other criteria such as time or IP address range, and then either forward to another RADIUS server to perform the authentication or handle it internally.

Network Policies determine whether clients meet the requirements to be authenticated and allowed into the network. NAP clients are evaluated by their health, resulting in the client being allowed or denied network access.

The final policy type configured on the NPS is the Health Policy, which is used to refer to one or more system health validators (SHVs). Only the default Windows SHV (shown in Figure 3-25) is included with NPS in Windows Server 2012, but third-party SHVs can be integrated and enforced. The Windows SHV allows you to evaluate configuration and status of Windows updates, antimalware protection, and the Windows Firewall.

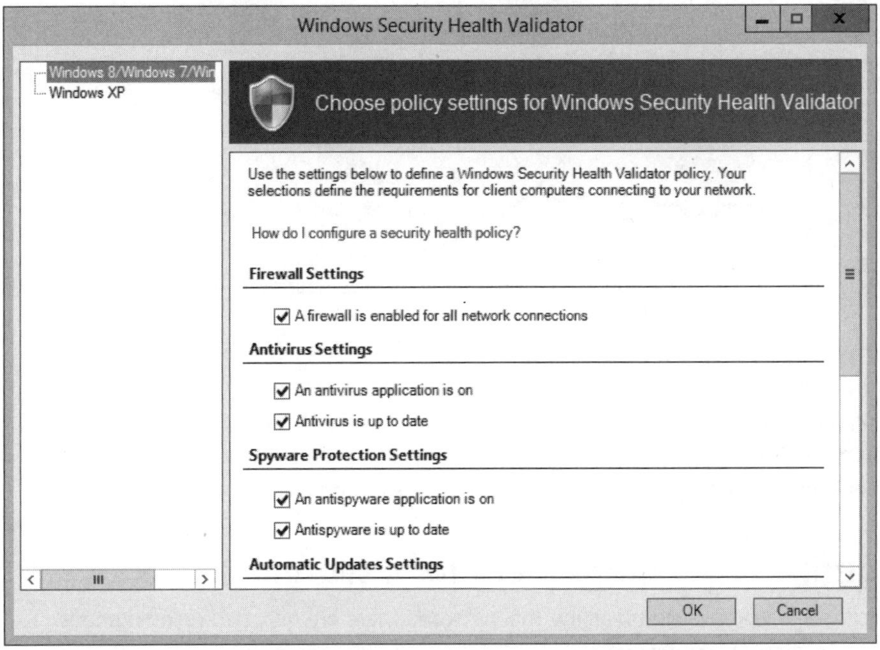

FIGURE 3-25 The Windows Security Health Validator is the only SHV provided by default

Creating a remediation network

With NAP and NPS, you can provide limited network connectivity to noncompliant network clients. This connectivity can be used to prevent access to sensitive systems and healthy clients, or as a remediation network to provide a way to become compliant with network policies (see Figure 3-26).

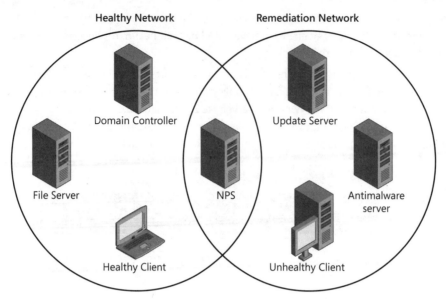

Healthy Network · Remediation Network

Domain Controller · Update Server · File Server · NPS · Antimalware server · Healthy Client · Unhealthy Client

FIGURE 3-26 A remediation network provides a way for unhealthy computers to join the healthy network

To allow noncompliant computers to access servers offering system or antivirus updates, some additional configuration of these servers is needed to prevent network traffic from being blocked. The method to enable this network traffic through depends on the enforcement method used, but it can be as easy as assigning a static IP address (for DHCP enforcement) or configuring less-restrictive IPsec policies using a GPO.

Configuring NAP enforcement for IPsec and 802.1x

For enforcing NAP compliance on an internal network, there are only two recommended enforcement options. IPsec enforces compliance through the use of IPsec policies that require computer certificates to authenticate network communication. 802.1x enforces NAP at the network hardware level, assigning computers to different VLANs based on client health. Both of these solutions are strong options for protecting your network, but the configuration of each option is quite different.

Enforcing IPsec

The core of the IPsec enforcement method includes configuring computer certificate autoenrollment and IPsec policies using Group Policy. The next step is to configure the NPS server with the appropriate policies. The NAP policies configured within the NPS determine which clients are issued certificates. Figure 3-27 shows a healthy client requesting a certificate from a CA, which is also the HRA. In this scenario, the HRA forwards the authentication request to another NPS, which validates the client's health, and the HRA issues the certificate. After the client receives the certificate, it can then communicate with the file server using IPsec authenticated using the computer certificate.

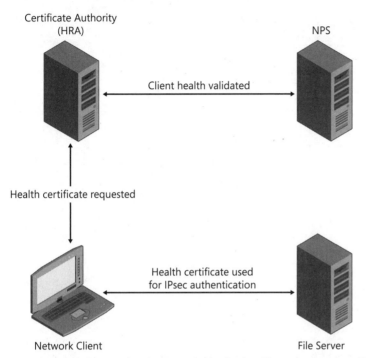

FIGURE 3-27 The IPsec enforcement method relies heavily on computer certificates that are used to facilitate IPsec authentication between healthy computers; computers that cannot be validated do not receive certificates and cannot communicate with healthy computers

To configure IPsec enforcement on your NPS, launch the Configure NAP Wizard and choose the IPsec With Health Registration Authority (HRA) option. The next page allows you to identify remote HRA servers as RADIUS clients. If the same server is performing both HRA and NPS roles, you can skip this step. The Configure Machine Groups page allows you to specify security groups containing computers to which the policy will apply. To enforce NAP on all computers, leave the Machine Groups list empty. The final step of enforcing NAP policies using IPsec is to choose the SHVs to use for enforcement and determine whether clients are automatically remediated when possible. Figure 3-28 shows a fully configured network policy, enforcing NAP using IPsec.

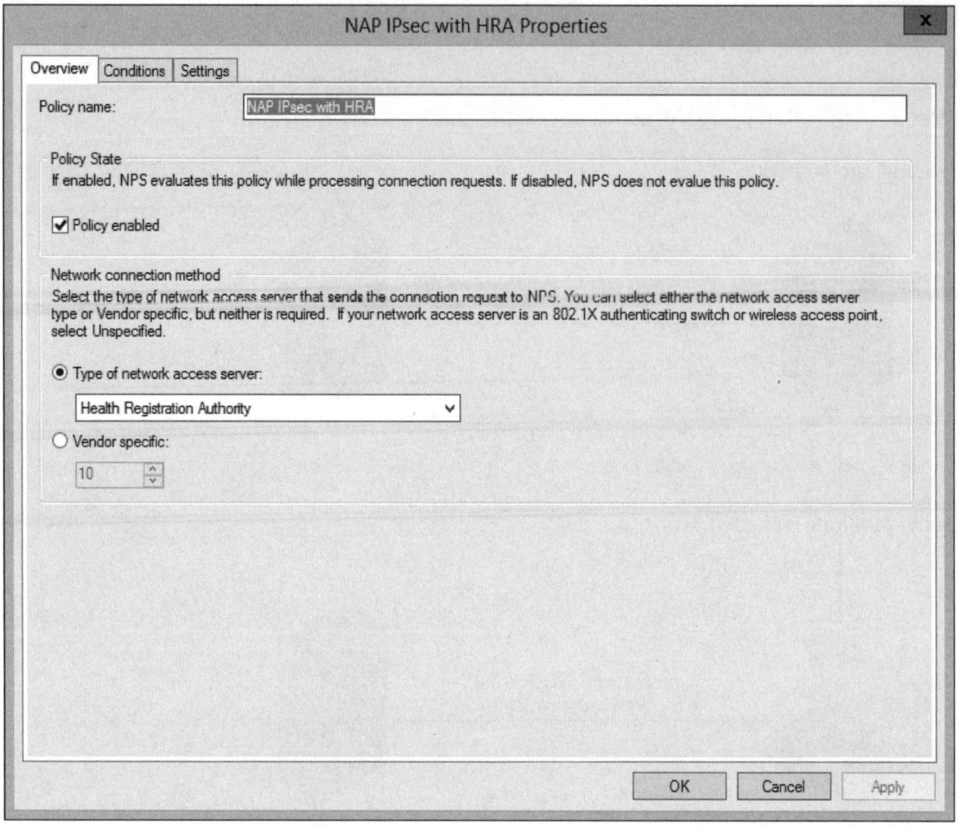

FIGURE 3-28 The IPsec enforcement method uses the Health Registration Authority network access server

Enforcing 802.1x

For NAP enforcement, 802.1x wired and wireless enforcement are configured separately. The Configure NAP Wizard allows you to choose one type of 802.1x client to configure before continuing with the wizard (see Figure 3-29). Regardless of the network connection, the remainder of the wizard is the same for both wired and wireless clients.

The second page of the Configure NAP Wizard requires you to identify RADIUS clients. For wired 802.1x configuration, this list should include 802.1x authenticating switches; for wireless networks, you have to list 802.1x wireless access points. On the Configure User Groups And Machine Groups page, you can identify groups of users or computers that should be authenticated using 802.1x. NAP enforcement using 802.1x uses PEAP for authentication, which can be configured by choosing a server certificate and EAP type in the Configure An Authentication Model page.

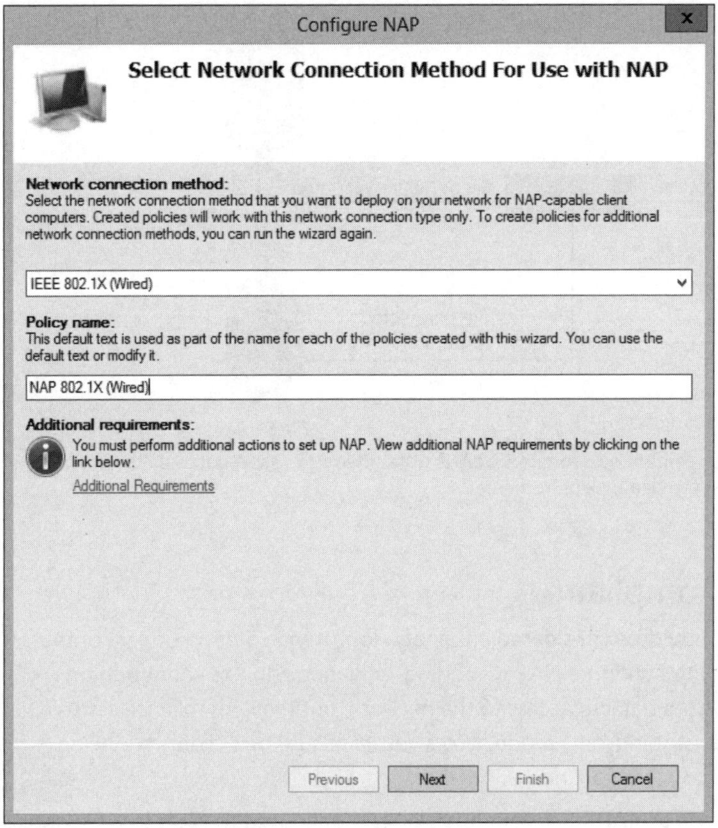

FIGURE 3-29 802.1x enforcement of NAP must be configured individually for wired and wireless clients

Traffic controls are used by 802.1x to segregate traffic between compliant and noncompliant systems. There are several options that can be used for traffic control, some of which are dependent on the vendor of your networking hardware. Finally, you can configure the SHVs to be used to determine compliance with the corporate health policy. You can also configure how to handle clients that do not support NAP, either by allowing them full access to the network or restricting them to a restricted network.

Figure 3-30 shows the 802.1x authentication process at work. When the network client first makes a physical connection to the 802.1x switch, an authentication request is passed to the NPS. After the client health is validated, the switch places the network client on the corporate VLAN, allowing it to communicate to the file server.

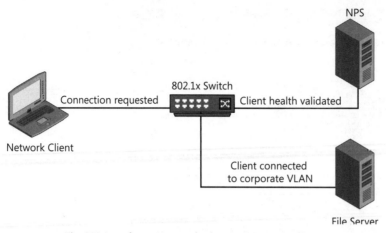

FIGURE 3-30 The 802.1x enforcement method uses VLANs or IP filtering to segregate healthy computers from those that do not meet the health requirements

Monitoring for compliance

One aspect of NAP that should be considered either as a long-term solution or part of the testing phase is the ability to configure NAP in logging-only mode. In this configuration, clients are not restricted from gaining access to the network, but their compliance status is monitored and logged. Logging-only mode allows you to ensure that clients are being validated properly prior to fully enforcing NAP policies.

NAP logging, also known as RADIUS accounting, can be configured to write to a file on the local hard drive or to a Microsoft SQL Server database (which can be configured in the Accounting options). Another vital configuration step is to determine what action should be performed if the NPS cannot write to a log file, specifically whether incoming connection requests should be discarded or allowed.

Objective summary

- NPS supports four enforcement methods, DHCP, IPsec, VPN, and 802.1x.
- RADIUS, a standard protocol used for network authentication, is used with NPS to enforce authentication policies, including client health.
- Because DHCP enforcement can be easily bypassed through the use of a static IP address, it is not recommended for use in secure environments.
- IPsec enforcement uses policies requiring certificate-based authentication to prevent noncompliant computers from connecting with compliant systems.
- VPN connections can use network protection to ensure that remote computers meet local network policies.
- The 802.1x enforcement method uses techniques such as IP filtering or VLANs to segregate network traffic.
- RADIUS proxy and RADIUS server groups can be used to manage the authentication workload by spreading requests across multiple servers.

- NPS servers should be placed in network locations that perform NAP enforcement, specifically VPN servers or an HRA.
- Network and host-based firewalls must be configured to allow RADIUS authentication traffic to pass.
- The NPS server functions as a RADIUS server, authenticating clients and performing policy validation.
- A remediation network can be implemented to assist clients in taking the corrective actions necessary to achieve full connectivity to the network.
- IPsec and 802.1x enforcement are the preferred options for internal corporate networks. IPsec uses computer certificate–based authentication to segregate network traffic. The 802.1x enforcement method uses network infrastructure devices to route authentication traffic to a RADIUS server for validation, and separates clients using VLANs or IP filtering.

Objective review

Answer the following questions to test your knowledge of the information in this objective. You can find the answers to these questions and explanations of why each answer choice is correct or incorrect in the "Answers" section at the end of this chapter.

1. Which is the weakest NAP enforcement method?
   A. DHCP
   B. IPsec
   C. VPN
   D. 802.1x

2. What authentication standard is performed by an NPS?
   A. 802.1x
   B. RADIUS
   C. IPsec
   D. VPN

3. What enforcement method uses compatible networking hardware?
   A. DHCP
   B. IPsec
   C. VPN
   D. 802.1x

4. What enforcement method uses computer certificates to restrict network communication between clients?

   A. DHCP

   B. IPsec

   C. VPN

   D. 802.1x

5. What types of servers would typically be contained in a remediation network? (Choose all that apply.)

   A. Windows Server Update Server

   B. Active Directory domain controller

   C. Corporate file server

   D. Antimalware update server

6. What type of enforcement server is specifically used with the IPsec enforcement method?

   A. HRA

   B. RADIUS

   C. DHCP

   D. NPS

Answers

This section contains the solutions to the thought experiments and answers to the lesson review questions in this chapter.

Objective 3.1: Thought experiment

1. Site-to-site VPN connections allow you to connect remote locations to the same logical network.

2. An internal enterprise CA is used to allow automatic enrollment for computer certificates to facilitate IPsec authentication on a network.

3. The required firewall rules depend on the infrastructure and its configuration. DirectAccess uses IP-HTTPS on port 443, the 6to4 protocol uses port 41, the network location server uses port 62000, and IPv6 uses TCP port 50 and UDP port 500.

4. Web Application Proxy enables you to allow remote clients to connect to web applications on the internal network. Web Application Proxy makes use of AD FS and supports PKI, OTP, and multifactor authentication.

Objective 3.1: Review

1. **Correct answer:** B

   A. **Incorrect:** Public CAs provide certificates for public-facing applications, not internal computers.

   B. **Correct:** An enterprise CA enables you to configure your certificates to allow computers to automatically enroll, making possible the process of configuring IPsec using computer certificates.

   C. **Incorrect:** A stand-alone CA lets you create certificates for use on the internal network, but does not allow you to use autoenrollment of computer certificates.

   D. **Incorrect:** Remote access servers are not required to use IPsec authentication.

2. **Correct answer:** A

   A. **Correct:** Port 1701 is used by L2TP traffic.

   B. **Incorrect:** PPTP uses port 1723.

   C. **Incorrect:** HTTPS traffic uses TCP port 443.

   D. **Incorrect:** Port 80 is used by standard HTTP traffic.

3. Correct answer: C

    A. Incorrect: Site-to-site VPN allows disparate locations to connect into a single logical network.

    B. Incorrect: Multisite VPN allows Windows 8 clients to connect to the optimal remote access server in your organization.

    C. Correct: Multitenant site-to-site VPN allows hosting providers to create virtual networks for individual clients, ensuring that they are connected only to the network segment containing their applications.

    D. Incorrect: Azure virtual networks offer similar functionality to multitenant site-to-site VPNs, but not on-premises datacenters.

4. Correct answer: B

    A. Incorrect: PPTP uses MPPE.

    B. Correct: 3DES is supported only by L2TP/IPsec.

    C. Incorrect: SSTP uses SSL to encrypt its tunnel.

    D. Incorrect: Only L2TP/IPsec supports 3DES.

5. Correct answer: C

    A. Incorrect: PPTP supports certificate-based authentication, but not smart cards.

    B. Incorrect: L2TP/IPsec also uses certificates for authentication, but smart cards are not supported for authentication.

    C. Correct: Smart card authentication is supported using SSTP.

    D. Incorrect: Of the traditional VPN protocols supported in Windows Server 2012, only SSTP supports authentication with smart cards.

6. Correct answer: A

    A. Correct: Because SSTP uses port 443, which is rarely blocked by network firewalls, it is the best solution for traversing NAT devices.

    B. Incorrect: SSTP provides strong security for both authentication and encryption, as does L2TP/IPSec.

    C. Incorrect: PPTP provides the best performance of the traditional VPN protocols.

    D. Incorrect: SSTP requires Windows 7 clients or later, whereas both PPTP and L2TP/IPsec support older client operating systems.

7. **Correct answer:** A

   A. **Correct:** Local DNS servers are not part of the Azure virtual network creation process, but they can be used by resources contained within the Azure virtual network.

   B. **Incorrect:** On-premises IP address pools are one aspect of the Azure virtual network creation process.

   C. **Incorrect:** Azure virtual networks allow you to define subnets within your local network.

   D. **Incorrect:** The VPN server IP address is part of the site-to-site VPN creation process.

8. **Correct answer:** C

   A. **Incorrect:** CMAK does not affect user permissions for VPN.

   B. **Incorrect:** Remote access servers are deployed using the Add Roles And Features Wizard and the Remote Access Management Console.

   C. **Correct:** CMAK is used to create VPN profiles that are easy for end users to deploy on their own computers.

   D. **Incorrect:** Site-to-site VPN connections with Azure are created using the new virtual network creation wizards in Azure.

9. **Correct answer:** A

   A. **Correct:** CMAK is installed through the RAS Connection Manager Administration Kit (CMAK) feature.

   B. **Incorrect:** CMAK does not need to be downloaded from the Microsoft website.

   C. **Incorrect:** The Windows Server 2012 installation media do not contain the CMAK setup files.

   D. **Incorrect:** CMAK is not installed by default on either Windows 8 or Windows Server 2012.

Objective 3.2: Thought experiment

1. DirectAccess can be configured for remote access and remote management, or just for remote management.

2. The DirectAccess Client Setup Wizard allows you to select security groups containing users that should be allowed to connect remotely, whereas the DirectAccess Application Server Setup page is used to select security groups containing application servers to which these users should be allowed to connect.

3. Migration from Forefront UAG DirectAccess to Windows Server 2012 DirectAccess can be accomplished side-by-side or in offline mode. A side-by-side migration allows you to continue to service DirectAccess clients throughout the process, but requires some duplication of DNS records and IP addresses during the migration. Both methods require configuration of the new remote access server and relevant GPOs.

Objective 3.2: Review

1. **Correct answers:** B, C

   A. **Incorrect:** An edge topology is used when the remote access server has a direct connection to the Internet.

   B. **Correct:** The option for behind an edge device (with two network adapters) can be used when a NAT device is used on the network.

   C. **Correct:** When a NAT device is providing address translation, the option for behind an edge device (with one network adapter) can be used.

   D. **Incorrect:** NAT has no relation to DirectAccess for remote management.

2. **Correct answers:** A, B

   A. **Correct:** Force tunnel mode requires configuration using the Remote Access Setup Wizard.

   B. **Correct:** Two-factor authentication is not supported when DirectAccess is configured using the Getting Started Wizard.

   C. **Incorrect:** The wizard used to configure DirectAccess has no impact on the placement of the DirectAccess server.

   D. **Incorrect:** Either configuration option supports DirectAccess for remote management only.

3. **Correct answers:** A, D

   A. **Correct:** OTP is a new feature for authentication in DirectAccess on Windows Server 2012.

   B. **Incorrect:** Smart card authentication was supported in previous versions of DirectAccess.

   C. **Incorrect:** Authentication using a user name and password have always been supported for remote access.

   D. **Correct:** Using Trusted Platform Modules, Virtual Smart Cards are a new feature in DirectAccess for Windows Server 2012.

4. **Correct answer:** B

   A. **Incorrect:** IPv6 support is not required for migration of DirectAccess from Forefront UAG to Windows Server 2012.

   B. **Correct:** Forefront UAG SP1 must be installed before migration of DirectAccess can occur.

   C. **Incorrect:** A PKI is not a requirement for migration of DirectAccess from Forefront UAG to Windows Server 2012.

   D. **Incorrect:** Because Windows Server 2012 does not require public IPv4 addresses, additional public addresses are not required.

5. **Correct answer:** D

   A. **Incorrect:** In a side-by-side migration of DirectAccess, IP addresses and FQDNs cannot be reused because both DirectAccess servers must be connected to the network at the same time.

   B. **Incorrect:** Side-by-side migration and offline migration do not support automated migration.

   C. **Incorrect:** New certificates must be issued in a side-by-side migration because the FQDN of the DirectAccess server changes.

   D. **Correct:** No downtime is required in a side-by-side DirectAccess migration from Forefront UAG to Windows Server 2012.

6. **Correct answer:** B

   A. **Incorrect:** A PKI is required for Windows 7 clients to connect to DirectAccess, but it does not enable support for OTP.

   B. **Correct:** The DirectAccess Connectivity Assistant 2.0 is required for Windows 7 clients to use OTP for DirectAccess authentication.

   C. **Incorrect:** A RADIUS server is required to support the use of OTP, but it does not enable support for Windows 7 clients.

   D. **Incorrect:** Windows 7 SP1 does not bring OTP support to Windows 7 DirectAccess clients.

7. **Correct answer:** D

   A. **Incorrect:** Using certificates from a public CA is not practical for client computer certificates.

   B. **Incorrect:** Computer certificates, even for servers, are best served by an internal enterprise CA.

   C. **Incorrect:** The network location can use a certificate from a public CA, but an internal CA is supported, provided that the CRL is accessible.

   D. **Correct:** It is recommended to use an SSL certificate from a public CA for the IP-HTTPS server because some remote access clients might not be domain joined.

Objective 3.3: Thought experiment

1. Workplace Join allows you to support Web Application Proxy while still requiring a device registration process. Workplace Join is supported only on Windows 8.1 and iOS devices at this time.

2. Although SSO is supported with Web Application Proxy, it requires AD FS.

3. Certificates from a public CA are required for both the Web Application Proxy and AD FS.

Objective 3.3: Review

1. **Correct answer:** A

    A. **Correct:** Web Application Proxy requires an AD FS server, and uses AD FS heavily for authentication and authorization.

    B. **Incorrect:** Although ultimately AD DS contains the security principals used to authenticate users and computers, AD FS is the service that performs the authentication requests against AD DS for the Web Application Proxy.

    C. **Incorrect:** Certificates are used extensively with Web Application Proxy, but AD CS does not perform authentication.

    D. **Incorrect:** AD FS Proxy is the precursor to Web Application Proxy.

2. **Correct answer:** D

    A. **Incorrect:** Domain membership is not a requirement for client access through a Web Application Proxy.

    B. **Incorrect:** Workplace Join can be configured as an authentication requirement for access to applications through a Web Application Proxy, but it is not mandatory.

    C. **Incorrect:** Windows 8.1 is one of the supported operating systems for Workplace Join, but is not required to use Web Application Proxy.

    D. **Correct:** Web Application Proxy supports clients that have a web browser, Microsoft Office application, or compatible Windows 8.1 app.

3. **Correct answer:** C

    A. **Incorrect:** AD FS preauthentication requires authentication prior to the client being referred to the application.

    B. **Incorrect:** SSO is used by Web Application Proxy to allow users to authenticate once, but this is still handled by the Web Application Proxy, not the application.

    C. **Correct:** Pass-through authentication forwards users to the application they have requested without performing any authentication at the Web Application Proxy level.

    D. **Incorrect:** Multifactor access control is performed at the Web Application Proxy level.

4. **Correct answers:** A, C

   A. **Correct:** Workplace Join allows supported nondomain devices to be registered with the AD DS using the DRS within AD FS.

   B. **Incorrect:** Workplace Join does not support all device types; only Windows 8.1 and iOS devices are supported.

   C. **Correct:** Registration with AD DS is required for Workplace Join.

   D. **Incorrect:** Workplace Join cannot be used to verify that clients meet network security policies.

5. **Correct answers:** B, C

   A. **Incorrect:** Windows 8 does not support Workplace Join.

   B. **Correct:** Devices using iOS support Workplace Join.

   C. **Correct:** Windows 8.1 clients can be registered using Workplace Join.

   D. **Incorrect:** Registration of UNIX devices using Workplace Join is not supported.

6. **Correct answer:** D

   A. **Incorrect:** SSO allows users to maintain a session after authenticating once.

   B. **Incorrect:** Workplace Join does not allow you to conditionally require smart cards for authentication.

   C. **Incorrect:** Multifactor authentication can be configured for all users, but not conditionally without using multifactor access control.

   D. **Correct:** Multifactor access control allows you to create rules for authentication, including the ability to require smart cards for certain groups of users.

7. **Correct answer:** C

   A. **Incorrect:** SSO is supported for any device that can use Web Application Proxy.

   B. **Incorrect:** Client computers do not have to be domain joined to use SSO.

   C. **Correct:** The Web Application Proxy must be domain joined to support SSO.

   D. **Incorrect:** Client devices do not have to be running Windows 8.1 or iOS to support SSO.

8. **Correct answer:** B

    A. **Incorrect:** DNS CNAME records can be created to make the same FQDN resolve to the same host for both internal and external clients, but this is not a function of Web Application Proxy.

    B. **Correct:** URL translation, which is part of the application publishing process in Web Application Proxy, allows both internal and external clients to use the same URL to access applications.

    C. **Incorrect:** Pass-through authentication bypasses authentication at the Web Application Proxy level, but does not affect the URL used to access the application.

    D. **Incorrect:** Workplace Join has no bearing on the URL used to reach a published application.

Objective 3.4: Thought experiment

1. A site-to-site VPN connects multiple corporate locations into the same logical network.

2. Multisite remote access supports clients automatically, discovering the best entry point to connect to remotely.

3. Web Application Proxy can run in a multiserver environment. All configuration information for Web Application Proxy is contained within AD FS, so installing additional servers automatically configures them for this scenario.

Objective 3.4: Review

1. **Correct answer:** B

    A. **Incorrect:** Misconfigured packet filtering on the Internet connection would probably prevent clients from connecting to the remote access server.

    B. **Correct:** Packet filtering on an intranet connection would constrain traffic from the remote access server to internal network resources.

    C. **Incorrect:** Packet tracing only monitors network traffic; it does not restrict network traffic.

    D. **Incorrect:** Packet tracing being disabled would have no effect on remote access.

2. **Correct answer:** C

   A. **Incorrect:** Windows Vista clients cannot use automatic server selection in a multisite DirectAccess.

   B. **Incorrect:** Windows 7 does not support the automatic selection of a DirectAccess server in a multisite deployment.

   C. **Correct:** Windows 8 clients can automatically choose the optimal DirectAccess server with which to connect in a multisite configuration.

   D. **Incorrect:** Windows 8.1 clients fully support multisite DirectAccess autoconfiguration, but it is not the minimum.

3. **Correct answer:** D

   A. **Incorrect:** DirectAccess is the remote access protocol used, but it does not allow this by default.

   B. **Incorrect:** Web Application Proxy in a cluster provides high availability and is not a full remote access solution.

   C. **Incorrect:** Site-to-site VPN allows two or more locations to communicate with each other and does not support client failover.

   D. **Correct:** Windows 8 clients can automatically connect to the best DirectAccess server in a multisite deployment.

4. **Correct answer:** A

   A. **Correct:** NLB allows you to create a highly available remote access solution.

   B. **Incorrect:** RADIUS server groups provide high availability for RADIUS authentication, but not remote access.

   C. **Incorrect:** Web Application Proxy is not a full remote access solution.

   D. **Incorrect:** Site-to-site VPN is used to connect multiple network locations to the same logical network.

5. **Correct answer:** A

   A. **Correct:** RADIUS server groups are used to distribute authentication workload, providing high availability and scalability.

   B. **Incorrect:** Remote access to internal web applications is best served by Web Application Proxy.

   C. **Incorrect:** Automatic connection to the optimal remote access entry point is a function of multisite remote access.

   D. **Incorrect:** Network policy enforcement is a function of NPS and NAP.

Objective 3.5: Thought experiment

1. Enforcement decisions need to be made by determining what enforcement methods are needed and what options are already available. If VPN or DirectAccess are used, the VPN enforcement method is probably needed. The decision between 802.1x and IPsec for the internal network would probably come down to which is easier to manage: the enterprise CA and computer certificates or the 802.1x configuration for network switches and wireless access points.

2. RADIUS server groups can be used to add scale and high availability to your NPS deployment.

3. A remediation network is the best way to provide noncompliant computers the capability to meet the network policies.

Objective 3.5: Review

1. **Correct answer:** A

   A. **Correct:** DHCP enforcement of NAP can be bypassed by configuring a static IP address, making it the weakest enforcement method by far.

   B. **Incorrect:** IPsec is a strong enforcement method that uses computer certificates to authenticate network communication.

   C. **Incorrect:** VPN connections can be enforced effectively by using NPS in conjunction with the remote access server.

   D. **Incorrect:** The 802.1x enforcement method is a strong enforcement method, effectively segregating network clients into separate logical networks.

2. **Correct answer:** B

   A. **Incorrect:** 802.1x uses RADIUS authentication provided by the NPS, but does not perform the authentication.

   B. **Correct:** RADIUS authentication is a standard for network authentication and is performed by the NPS server.

   C. **Incorrect:** IPsec is not an authentication method.

   D. **Incorrect:** VPN is not an authentication method.

3. **Correct answer:** D

   A. **Incorrect:** DHCP enforcement uses DHCP request negotiation to segregate computers.

   B. **Incorrect:** IPsec uses computer certificates and IPsec policies to prevent noncompliant computers from communicating with compliant computers.

   C. **Incorrect:** VPN enforcement is done at the remote access server.

   D. **Correct:** 802.1x compatible network hardware can be used to enforce NAP policies.

4. **Correct answer:** B

   A. **Incorrect:** DHCP enforcement provides IP leases so that noncompliant computers cannot communicate with those that are compliant.

   B. **Correct:** IPsec enforcement of NAP uses computer certificates to authenticate compliant computers, allowing them to communicate.

   C. **Incorrect:** NAP enforcement of VPN connections segregates noncompliant computers into their own logical network.

   D. **Incorrect:** Enforcement using 802.1x uses hardware-level networking features such as VLANs or IP filtering.

5. **Correct answers:** A, D

   A. **Correct:** A Windows Server Update Server is typically included on a remediation network to provide system updates to noncompliant computers.

   B. **Incorrect:** An Active Directory domain controller should be protected from vulnerable computers and should not be included in a remediation network.

   C. **Incorrect:** Corporate file servers can contain protected information and should be left on a protected network segment.

   D. **Correct:** Antivirus and other antimalware updates should be provided on the remediation network when possible.

6. **Correct answer:** A

   A. **Correct:** An HRA is the NPS role used to request client health certificates for the IPsec enforcement method.

   B. **Incorrect:** RADIUS servers and the RADIUS authentication protocol are used throughout NAP enforcement, regardless of the method used.

   C. **Incorrect:** The DHCP enforcement method uses DHCP servers to forward authentication requests to the NPS.

   D. **Incorrect:** NPS servers function as RADIUS servers and are used in each enforcement method.

CHAPTER 4

Design and implement an Active Directory infrastructure (logical)

Active Directory, which is a critical piece of most modern corporate networks, provides authentication and authorization for every aspect of your network, including email, file shares, and corporate websites. Active Directory is also one of those services that people notice only when something malfunctions. One observation that can be made regarding Active Directory in Windows Server 2012 is that several of the processes that used to be critical skills for certification candidates can now be handled automatically. Preparing the Active Directory schema used to be a required first step performed when introducing a domain controller with a newer version of Windows Server. This step is handled automatically if not accomplished before adding a Windows Server 2012 domain controller to an Active Directory Forest.

This chapter focuses on the objects in Active Directory that define the logical structure, including forests and domains, as well as management tools such as Group Policy and controlling permissions on Active Directory objects. A consistent theme throughout this chapter is making design decisions consistent with the corporate structure and using this organizational hierarchy within Active Directory to simplify management of users and computers. These concepts hold true throughout the logical structure of Active Directory as forests, domains, and even the use of organizational units (OUs) facilitate deployment of Group Policy and provide a basis for an administrative permission model and delegation of control.

Objectives in this chapter:

- Objective 4.1: Design a forest and domain infrastructure
- Objective 4.2: Implement a forest and domain infrastructure
- Objective 4.3: Design a Group Policy strategy
- Objective 4.4: Design an Active Directory permission model

Objective 4.1: Design a forest and domain infrastructure

Unlike some other services discussed in this book, Active Directory Forests often maintain their logical structure for years with minimal changes due to the dependence that other services and applications have on the directory structure. Although the tools and process for altering the logical structure within Active Directory have improved greatly in Windows Server 2012, the design process is critical to the long-term success of your corporate infrastructure.

When you think of a design phase, you typically think of building something that does not yet exist. As you progress through this section of the book, you learn that this is not always true. Although it is certainly true that new Active Directory Forests should be carefully planned prior to implementation, most of this topic is dedicated to altering the existing structure of one or more forests into something that matches the needs of a corporation. The lesson to be learned is that any changes to the structure of Active Directory should be carefully planned to prevent degradation or complete loss of service.

> **This objective covers how to:**
> - Build a multiforest architecture and manage trust relationships
> - Manage functional levels and domain upgrades
> - Perform domain migration and alter the forest structure
> - Implement hybrid cloud services, including Microsoft Azure Active Directory and DirSync

Building multiforest structures and trust relationships

Many Active Directory implementations are configured using a single forest because it is most efficient for authentication, replication, and management. Occasionally, a multiforest architecture is used either out of necessity, such as when two companies merge; or by design, such as when dealing with regulatory requirements or business needs. Some enterprises might even make a design decision to implement Active Directory in multiple forests for reasons of scope. Although Active Directory can handle the requirements of a large organization in a single forest, breaking large corporate branches into separate forests can often make them easier to manage. The most common reason for multiple forests within an organization is to create a test forest, providing a safe environment for testing changes to the enterprise prior to implementing them in the production forest. Test forests are highly recommended for any operation that has the potential to affect a large number of users, particularly those without a clean rollback capability. You learn more about test forests in Objective 4.2.

When multiple forests are implemented as a design choice or out of necessity, trust relationships can be used to retain a level of cohesion between the two forests, or even between specific domains within these forests. Trusts enable you to provide for authentication and authorization between forests while maintaining separate organizational and management structures. Without trust relationships, organizations using multiple forests cannot perform authentication or share resources without users having accounts in both forests (which can be the desired effect in some cases).

Multiforest architecture

An *Active Directory forest* refers to all domains within a contiguous namespace, such as microsoft.com; a *multiforest* architecture refers to an implementation using noncontiguous namespaces such as contoso.com and contosowest.com, as shown in Figure 4-1. These two forests have separate domain controllers, groups, and users. Although this level of segregation seems counterintuitive for a system typically used to provide enterprise-wide authentication and authorization, it can be useful for corporations requiring this level of separation. Although the words "separation" and "segregation" are often used to describe a multiforest architecture, this separation is often logical, not physical. Many scenarios of multiforest implementation feature forests operating side-by-side, even on the same physical network segment.

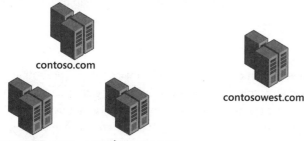

FIGURE 4-1 A simple multiforest implementation

In a single-forest Active Directory architecture, members of certain administrative groups have control over aspects of the entire forest. A multiforest architecture enables you to limit control over a portion of your infrastructure to only administrators within that segment of your organization. Although Active Directory provides numerous methods and techniques for managing group membership and restricting control over different domains or OUs, a single-forest architecture does not provide the same level of administrative segregation that can be achieved by implementing multiple forests.

Another reason to deploy multiple Active Directory forests involves the use of applications that extend the default Active Directory schema. For performance or security reasons, a decision can be made to create a separate forest to contain one or more of these applications, limiting these schema changes to the forest that is custom-built for this purpose.

To further understand how a multiforest implementation of Active Directory can be used in a corporate environment, consider the following scenario. Hospitals and other medical facilities must meet regulatory requirements specific to the health and medical industry. These same organizations have both traditional computing requirements, such as email and productivity tools, and expensive and sensitive equipment that can be computer operated. To facilitate the potentially drastic management needs for these two types of systems, separate forests could be implemented. These two forests would have separate administrative groups, different policies and security requirements, and even separate sets of users.

Another organization that can benefit from separate forests is a university. Most college campuses have a corporate network for faculty to communicate, track grades, or perform research. Allowing students to access this university network (or, more specifically, the faculty forest) could prove problematic from a security standpoint. Multiple Active Directory forests could provide a solution that would allow students to access network and university resources without introducing security weaknesses into the faculty forest.

A multiforest architecture relies heavily on a Domain Name System (DNS). Because authentication requests are routed to domain controllers using SRV records in DNS zones, DNS must be properly configured for users to be properly authenticated. Multiple Active Directory forests increase the level of complexity required to provide for authentication to both domains. Although multiforest architecture is possible even on the same physical network segment, the DNS complexities required for this configuration should be part of the Active Directory design process.

Trust relationships

Active Directory forests contain built-in relationships between domains that enable authentication and authorization to be handled automatically throughout the forest. In a multiforest architecture, these relationships must be created manually through the use of trusts. After a trust is established between two forests, authentication traffic is passed between domain controllers to enable users to log on to a trusting domain. After authentication, a user receives access to resources based on their group membership and established permissions.

Trust relationships are created using Active Directory domains and trusts within the domain properties. Several types of trusts are available, and each provides a different function (see Table 4-1). A key aspect of a trust is its transitivity, which determines whether the trust relationship is extended to other domains within the same forest as the trusted domain.

TABLE 4-1 Trust types

Trust type	Transitivity	Description
External	Nontransitive	Provides access to a single domain in a separate forest
Forest	Transitive	Creates a relationship with another forest
Realm	Transitive	Creates a trust relationship with a non–Windows Kerberos realm
Shortcut	Transitive	Improves interdomain authentication performance within the same forest

Although this table provides a solid description of each of the available trust types, sometimes use cases or examples are a better way to understand when a particular option should be implemented or used. Each of the different trust types is designed to meet specific organizational or technological needs, and understanding these differences simplifies the process of determining which is best for a specific situation.

External trusts are used to create a trust relationship between individual domains in separate forests, as shown in Figure 4-2. Because external trusts are nontransitive, the trust relationship does not extend to users or groups from other domains in either forest. Because they are limited to a single domain in each forest, external trusts are best used in scenarios in which restricting the scope of the trust is required. One example of an external trust that meets needs is a partnership between two universities collaborating on a shared resource project. Suppose that one or both universities want to restrict the scope of this trust to a specific department or office. If each department had its own domain, an external trust could be used to prevent resources from other domains in the forest being made available to the trusted domain.

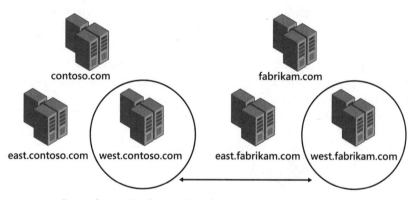

FIGURE 4-2 External trusts involve two domains in separate forests

Forest trusts, such as the one illustrated in Figure 4-3, encompass the entire scope of an Active Directory forest. Although this level of trust can be disconcerting, it is also a convenient way for two organizations to enable their users to authenticate while on the other's network and access resources from a partner. Use cases for forest trusts include corporate mergers, acquisitions, spinoffs, and any other corporate event that involves aspects of one company moving to another. In many cases, a forest trust is a temporary solution until the two forests (and the organizations they support) can be fully merged.

Realm trusts have a specific function, which is to facilitate trust relationships between an Active Directory forest and a Kerberos realm, typically in UNIX environments. Use cases for realm trusts are straightforward because they are used only when communication with a Kerberos realm is required.

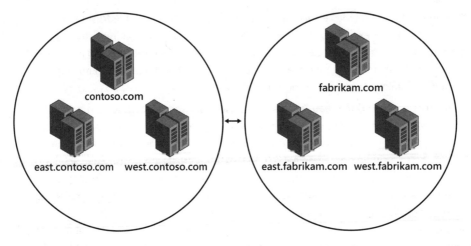

FIGURE 4-3 Forest trusts are transitive, encompassing the entirety of both forests

Shortcut trusts differ slightly from other trust types in that they create trust relationships between two domains on a single forest, such as the one shown in Figure 4-4. Users in different domains in a single Active Directory forest can authenticate and receive authorization by default without the need for trust relationships. In large forests, performance can suffer for these authentication requests due to the amount of time required to route the traffic through the forest. Shortcut trusts can link domains to bypass much of the authentication routing process, thus improving performance.

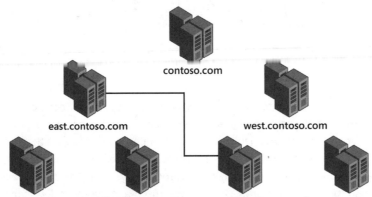

FIGURE 4-4 A shortcut trust is created between two domains in the same forest to improve authentication between the two domains

Each of these trust types can be one- or two-way trusts. *Two-way trusts* refer to those in which each side of the trust relationship trusts the other. A *one-way trust* is used when only one entity trusts the other. Terminology is key to understanding trust direction. A trusting domain enables users from another (trusted) domain to access its resources. Trust relationships are often defined or diagrammed using the trust direction, which goes from the trusting domain to the trusted domain.

In addition to enabling cross-forest authentication and authorization, trusts are also used extensively when the structure of a forest is altered through domain migration or domain rename (both topics are discussed later in this chapter).

Managing functional levels and domain upgrades

Domain and forest functional levels directly affect the feature set available in Active Directory. It is important to know which features become available at different domain and forest functional levels and what limitations you might encounter when moving between functional levels.

Functional levels

Each generation of Windows Server introduces new domain and forest functional levels, which typically bring new features. Domain functional levels are limited by the domain controllers within the domain because the minimum domain controller operating system determines the maximum functional level of which the domain is capable. Likewise, forest functional levels are dependent on domain functional levels. A forest functional level cannot be raised until each of the domains within the forest is raised to the corresponding level. The example shown in Figure 4-5 can support a Windows Server 2008 forest functional level because the east.contoso.com domain is still at the Windows Server 2008 domain functional level.

contoso.com
(Windows Server 2012 R2)

east.contoso.com   **central.contoso.com**   **west.contoso.com**
(Windows Server 2008)   **(Windows Server 2008 R2)**   **(Windows Server 2012)**

FIGURE 4-5 A forest shows domain functional levels; the forest functional level is limited to the lowest domain functional level (in this case, Windows Server 2008)

A Windows Server 2003 forest functional level must be achieved before a Windows Server 2012 domain controller can be used. So each domain controller in the forest must use Windows Server 2003 at a minimum, and each domain within the forest must be up to the Windows Server 2003 domain functional level.

The Windows Server 2008 domain functional level added Distributed File System Replication (DFSR) support for SYSVOL, adds information about a user's last interactive logon, and enables fine-grained password policies. Additionally, Advanced Encryption Standard (AES) support was added to the Kerberos protocol. No new features are added at the Windows Server 2008 forest functional level, but any additional domains added to the forest are automatically introduced at the Windows Server 2008 domain functional level.

Windows Server 2008 R2 domains add authentication mechanism assurance to a user's Kerberos token, providing support for Active Directory Federation Services (AD FS)–enabled applications and the ability to authorize user access attempts based on logon method (user name and password or smart card). Automated service principal name (SPN) management for services is provided when operating using Managed Service Accounts (MSAs), enabling name changes to be handled automatically when the host name or DNS name of the computer is altered. At the forest, the Windows Server 2008 R2 functional level adds support for the Active Directory Recycle Bin.

The Windows Server 2012 domain functional level provides additional features for Kerberos authentication, specifically Key Distribution Center (KDC) support for claims, compound authentication, and Kerberos armoring. Forests using the Windows Server 2012 functional level receive no additional features over the Windows Server 2008 R2 level.

Windows Server 2012 R2 domains now support additional security for Active Directory objects with membership in Protected Users, a new domain-level security group introduced in Windows Server 2012 R2. Members of this group are prevented from using NTLM authentication, DES or RC4 ciphers in Kerberos preauthentication, delegation, or user ticket renewal beyond the four-hour lifetime. These restrictions for members of the Protected Users group are applied only if a Windows 8.1 client authenticates to a Windows Server 2012 R2 domain controller. Authentication policies are introduced in Windows Server 2012 R2 domains, providing control over the hosts an account can use to sign on and to provide additional access control for authenticating to services running as an account. No additional features are gained by using the Windows Server 2012 R2 forest functional level.

EXAM TIP

You will probably get a question or two about domain and forest functional levels on the exam. Have a solid understanding of the requirements necessary to raise functional levels. Also try to commit to memory the different features enabled at each domain and forest functional level.

Domain upgrades

Because domain and forest functional levels are dependent on which Windows Server version the domain controllers are running, it is critical to take these limitations into account when you plan and design changes to an Active Directory implementation. For example, if you want to implement Windows Server 2012 domain controllers in your forest, you must first upgrade or replace any remaining Windows Server 2000 domain controllers, raise the functional level of all domains to at least the Windows Server 2003 level, and then raise the forest functional level.

The domain upgrade process occurs prior to the functional level being raised. When the first domain controller running a newer version of Windows Server is introduced, whether it is an in-place upgrade of an existing domain controller or the addition of a new domain controller, the Active Directory schema is modified, adding new object types and attributes. This process is illustrated in Figure 4-6. Windows Server 2012 makes this a more seamless process than previous versions by bringing the Active Directory preparation step into the domain controller deployment process. Rather than running adprep manually, the wizard automatically performs the preparation step (discussed in more detail in Objective 4.2).

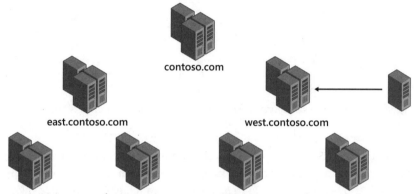

FIGURE 4-6 When a domain controller with a new version of Windows Server is introduced, the domain, forest, and schema go through an upgrade process

Altering the forest structure

In the past, modifying an existing Active Directory forest was almost impossible. Over the years, however, Microsoft has added support for altering a forest and even moving objects between forests or domains. As tasks that were previously considered to be critical skills for enterprise administrators working with Active Directory become simplified through wizards and integral system capabilities, administrators must become comfortable with making alterations to the shape and structure of Active Directory.

Domain migration

The Active Directory Migration Tool (ADMT) enables you to migrate objects between domains or restructure your forest by moving a domain within the forest—or even into a new forest. Domain migrations are commonly used to integrate two corporations into one, as shown in Figure 4-7, or divide one business into two. Objects being moved between domains retain a security identifier (SID) history that can be used to maintain existing permissions throughout the migration process. The ADMT can be used through the ADMT console by using command-line options or within a script.

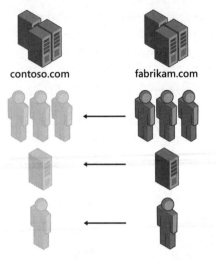

FIGURE 4-7 A domain migration can be used to move group, computer, and user objects between domains or forests

A big benefit of incorporating ADMT when you alter your forest structure is that it enables you to take a phased approach. Although certain steps in the domain rename process require mass changes to Active Directory in a single step, domain migration enables you to deploy a new domain and then migrate objects when convenient. Through SID history, existing permissions to corporate resources are retained throughout the migration process. Finally, most object types are retained in the source domain during migration, making recovery from a failed domain migration relatively painless.

Forest restructure

 An Active Directory forest gains its structure from the hierarchy within the namespace. By renaming domains within your forest with the domain rename tool (rendom.exe), you can alter the structure of your Active Directory forest. Domains can even be moved to their own forest by using domain rename, as shown in Figure 4-8.

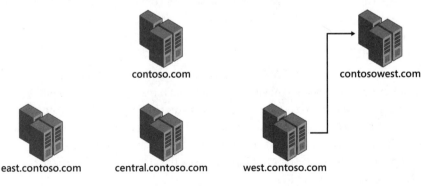

FIGURE 4-8 A forest restructure using domain rename

Although restructuring an Active Directory forest is possible using domain rename, it is a complex, multistep process that should not be undertaken lightly. To perform a domain rename, the forest must be frozen, prepped, and renamed; then cleanup efforts can begin. During the domain rename process, each domain controller in the forest must be reconfigured with the new structure of the forest. Remember that each computer within a domain is configured to specifically use that domain; during a domain rename, this configuration must be altered on each computer associated with that domain. The cleanup process includes removing obsolete domain names and restoring GPOs.

Implementing hybrid cloud services, including Microsoft Azure Active Directory and DirSync

Many businesses are considering services in the cloud as a way to gain efficiency and agility. Active Directory can be used in conjunction with cloud-based applications such as Microsoft Office 365 to provide password synchronization and Single Sign-On (SSO) capabilities. When you design an Active Directory implementation, remember the benefits offered by a hybrid cloud solution.

The number of scenarios in which a hybrid cloud approach can benefit a business are far too numerous to list here, but businesses need to make their own decisions on what areas make sense being moved to the cloud and what areas need to remain on-premises. For many businesses, hybrid scenarios make a lot of sense because they offer many of the benefits of using the cloud without loss of control over critical enterprise systems. As you evaluate use cases for the cloud, consider factors such as scalability, reliability, security, cost, maintenance, and user impact.

Azure Active Directory

Azure encompasses a large portion of the Microsoft cloud offerings for business. Part of this family of services is Azure Active Directory (Azure AD). Intended to serve as a bridge between on-premises Active Directory implementations and Microsoft cloud services such as Office 365 and Windows Intune, Azure AD also enables SSO with third-party cloud applications that support this feature.

Azure AD is available in two editions: Active Directory Free (AD Free) and Active Directory Premium (AD Premium). Azure AD Free supports up to 500,000 objects and supports synchronization with your on-premises Active Directory instance. Azure AD Premium allows for an unlimited number of objects and supports Forefront Identity Manager (FIM) for more robust synchronization between Azure AD and your on-premises Active Directory forest. Additional features in Azure AD Premium include high availability backed by a Service Level Agreement (SLA), group-based management for access to applications, custom branding with corporate logos and colors, and more robust self-service and reporting tools.

DirSync

The Azure AD directory synchronization (DirSync) tool, shown in Figure 4-9, enables synchronization of appropriate objects from within your corporate Active Directory to Azure AD. DirSync enables you to perform object synchronization on a schedule, mirroring objects contained in your on-premises Active Directory environment in Azure AD. Synchronized objects are used not only to provide users the ability to authenticate to cloud services but also for applications such as Office 365 to enable integration with an existing on-premises Microsoft Exchange Server environment, including mail-enabled groups and the global address list (GAL). DirSync and Azure AD offer two methods of handling authentication: password synchronization and SSO.

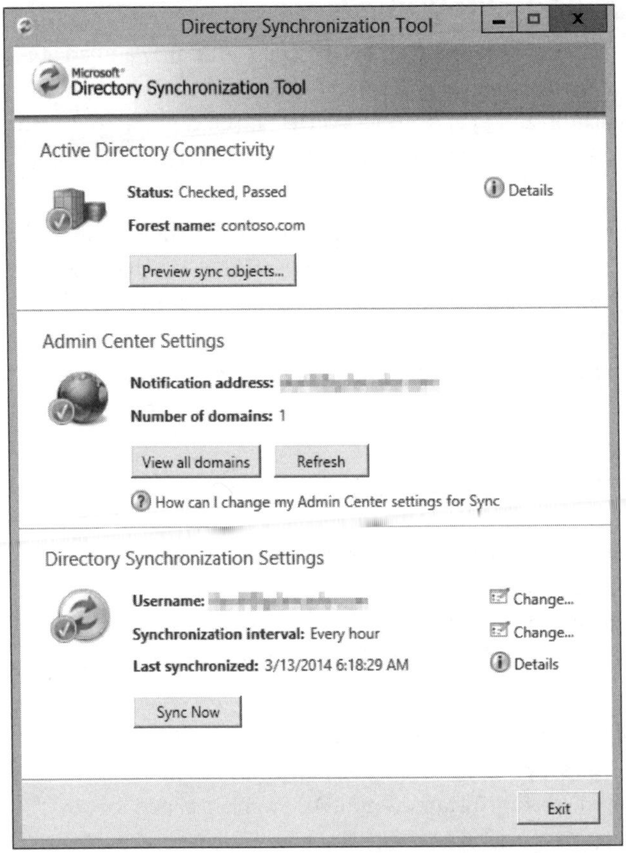

FIGURE 4-9 DirSync enables you to synchronize objects between the corporate Active Directory forest and Azure AD

Password synchronization is supported in DirSync version 6382.0000 and later, enabling users to authenticate to cloud services using the same user name and password as their on-premises Active Directory account. Passwords are synchronized in their hash form, maintaining security in transit, and ensuring that your corporate Active Directory will not be compromised in the event that synchronization traffic is somehow captured. If password synchronization is enabled after the initial implementation of Azure AD the initial synchronization process will overwrite existing cloud password, the cloud-based password will be set to never expire, and the corporate complexity policy will be enforced.

SSO support also uses DirSync, but it requires the use of a security token service (STS) such as AD FS, Shibboleth Identity Provider, or another third-party identity provider. Through the Azure AD authentication system and the STS, users are authenticated automatically to third-party cloud services without being required to provide credentials, a process that is shown in Figure 4-10. In addition to simplifying authentication for users, SSO provides several other benefits to your organization. All policies remain controlled through Active Directory, removing the need to manage security controls in the cloud. Access control can be managed within the STS, providing control over how users are authenticated through AD FS. Finally, SSO through AD FS enables you to use two-factor authentication such as smart cards.

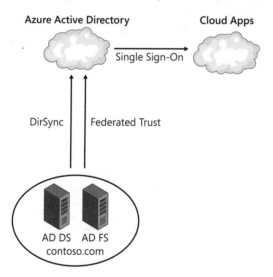

FIGURE 4-10 With DirSync and AD FS, users can authenticate to cloud applications without providing credentials a second time

---

MORE INFO **AZURE AD**

Because it is a relatively new offering, Azure AD will likely see numerous improvements and changes as the platform matures. More information can be found here: *http://technet. microsoft.com/en-us/library/hh967611.aspx.*

Thought experiment
Planning for corporate changes in Active Directory

In this thought experiment, apply what you've learned about this objective. You can find answers to these questions in the "Answers" section at the end of this chapter.

You are the lead network engineer for your corporation, and one of your primary jobs is to ensure that changes to the network structure are seamless and transparent to users.

Your forest currently matches the geographical structure of your company, with the forest root domain hosted at the corporate headquarters and domains representing each of the cities in which a corporate presence exists. Each of your domain controllers has already been upgraded to Windows Server 2012, as have the domain and forest functional levels.

Your company recently acquired a competitor that also has a presence in cities across the country/region. By coincidence, the Active Directory structure used by this competitor is remarkably similar to your own because its domains are determined by the cities in which its corporate branches are located.

Given this scenario, answer the following questions:

1. How could you quickly enable resource sharing between the two corporate entities?

2. What method could you use to incorporate users from cities in which both companies have an existing presence?

3. What steps should you take to integrate the domains in cities in which your company did not previously have a branch?

4. While planning to bring these existing domains into your forest, you discover that domain controllers within your competitor's forest are using everything from Windows Server 2003 to Windows Server 2012. How could this affect your plan to incorporate these domains into your forest?

Objective summary

- Forests enable your Active Directory infrastructure to match that of your business.
- Many corporate Active Directory implementations use a single forest, but multiple forests can also be used for design reasons.
- Trusts can be used to enable authentication and authorization between domains or forests.

- A trust's transitivity refers to whether the trust extends to other domains in the forest.
- Domain and forest functional levels provide additional features as the domain or forest is upgraded.
- A domain functional level can be only as high as its oldest domain controller.
- A forest functional level is limited by those of the domains it contains.
- Active Directory objects can be moved between domains and forests with the ADMT.
- Forest structures can be modified by renaming domains so they fit in an alternate location in the namespace.
- Active Directory can be integrated with cloud-based services in a hybrid cloud scenario, offering features such as SSO to popular web services such as Office 365.

Objective review

Answer the following questions to test your knowledge of the information in this objective. You can find the answers to these questions and explanations of why each answer choice is correct or incorrect in the "Answers" section at the end of this chapter.

1. Which business needs would cause you to consider a multiple forest architecture for your Active Directory design? (Choose all that apply.)
   A. Required segregation of administration responsibilities
   B. Corporate merger
   C. Third-party applications that modify the Active Directory schema
   D. Corporate locations in different parts of the country/region

2. What type of trust should be used to enable users between two forests to authenticate and access resources within the other forest?
   A. Forest trust
   B. Realm trust
   C. External trust
   D. Shortcut trust

3. What is the minimum forest functional level that supports the Active Directory Recycle Bin?
   A. Windows Server 2003
   B. Windows Server 2008
   C. Windows Server 2008 R2
   D. Windows Server 2012

4. Which domain functional levels cannot be used with a Windows Server 2012 forest functional level? (Choose all that apply.)

    A. Windows Server 2003

    B. Windows Server 2008

    C. Windows Server 2008 R2

    D. Windows Server 2012

5. What are the minimum requirements for users with membership in the Protected Users group to have their authentication traffic protected? (Choose all that apply.)

    A. Windows 8 client

    B. Windows 8.1 client

    C. Windows Server 2012 domain controller

    D. Windows Server 2012 R2 domain controller

6. A recent corporate merger has necessitated the incorporation of users, groups, and computers from another Active Directory forest. What tool enables you to bring these objects into your forest while maintaining existing access to resources?

    A. Domain migration

    B. Forest trust

    C. External trust

    D. Domain rename

7. Your organization is undergoing a major restructure, requiring changes to your forest and domain design. What action enables you to move domains within a forest?

    A. Domain upgrade

    B. Domain migration

    C. Forest trust

    D. Domain rename

8. You need to provide access to web services without the need to manage additional credentials for your users. What tool enables this process?

    A. Windows Server 2012 forest functional level

    B. Forest trust

    C. Realm trust

    D. Hybrid cloud

9. Which of the following is *not* a feature of Azure AD Premium?

   A. Support for two-factor authentication

   B. Unlimited Active Directory objects

   C. Support for FIM

   D. SLA-backed high availability

10. What requirements must be met to provide SSO capability for cloud applications? (Choose all that apply.)

    A. Azure AD Premium

    B. Security token service

    C. Azure AD DirSync tool

    D. Windows Server 2012 forest functional level

Objective 4.2: Implement a forest and domain infrastructure

After your forest and domain implementation has been carefully planned and designed, the implementation phase begins. Creating or restructuring an Active Directory forest and creating trust relationships are among the more complex tasks of managing Active Directory. It is important to have an understanding of the processes used to make these sorts of changes and to be able to predict any potential problems you might encounter during these tasks.

Domain rename is used not only for managing the Active Directory namespace but it also enables you to significantly alter the structure of your Active Directory forest. Although comprehensive changes can be made using domain rename, it is an extremely complex, multistep process. Changes to DNS, Certificate Authorities (CAs), Group Policy, and several other aspects of your infrastructure are required when performing a domain rename.

Windows Server 2012 simplifies the domain upgrade process by removing the manual Active Directory preparation process entirely. When the first Windows Server 2012 domain controller is introduced to the forest, either through an operating system upgrade or installation of the Active Directory Domain Services (AD DS) role, schema preparation occurs, and the domain is upgraded.

Domain migration provides a means to move Active Directory objects between domains in a forest or between forests, even without causing problems with users accessing network resources. Performing domain migrations are somewhat less intensive than domain rename because the structure of the forest is not directly affected by the migration. The domain migration process is often used in conjunction with the deployment of new domains in the forest to effect changes to the overall forest structure.

Configuring domain rename

Performing a domain rename requires a series of multistep processes, each of which requires prior planning for both the implementation and recovery if the process fails. Because of the complexity involved, domain rename is intended to be used as a last option and is no substitute for a well-designed Active Directory architecture.

Caveats aside, sometimes performing a domain rename is the only option to preserve the objects, configuration, and security associated with an Active Directory domain. Corporate reorganization is a fact of life in large organizations, and often cannot be planned for ahead of time. For this reason, it is important to know the steps to perform a domain rename, the tools and components involved, and the requirements for each step to be successful.

Preparing for domain rename

There are several preparation steps that must be completed before you begin a domain rename. The first step is fairly straightforward because a domain rename requires a forest functional level of Windows Server 2003 and above. If your forest does not meet this requirement, you need to upgrade your domains and forest, or else you simply cannot continue with the domain rename.

The second step deals with situations in which you are restructuring your forest by using this process. If a domain is being moved in the forest, specifically if it will have a different parent domain after the domain rename, you must first create a shortcut trust between the domain being renamed and its future parent domain, as shown in Figure 4-11. During the domain rename process, this shortcut trust becomes a parent-child trust relationship that preserves the transitive trust relationship among all domains in the forest. This step is critical for maintaining users' ability to authenticate and receive access to domain resources.

Step 3 of preparing for a domain rename involves configuring a DNS zone for your re-named domain. Each of the SRV records and structure needed to support the current Active Directory domain must be duplicated in a new DNS zone that matches the new namespace. Because DNS is critical to the ability of clients to perform authentication to Active Directory, it must be properly configured prior to a domain rename. Additionally, the domain rename process alters the fully qualified domain name (FQDN) of all domain controllers, servers, and computers within the affected domains. For the domain rename process to complete properly, DNS must be properly configured for both the source and target domains.

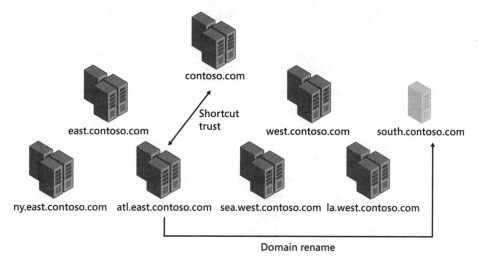

FIGURE 4-11 The shortcut trust being created in preparation for domain rename

The fourth preparation step for a domain rename is to relocate folder redirection or roaming user profiles. If you use either of these methods to centralize user data, changing the domain name might invalidate the path to these files. Distributed File System (DFS) is often used to handle folder redirection and roaming user profiles. When domain-based DFS namespaces are used, the domain rename process might invalidate these folder paths, resulting in users being unable to log on until the paths are resolved. Domain-based DFS namespaces support both NetBIOS and FQDNs for name resolution. If the NetBIOS name is used and remains unchanged throughout the domain rename process, users should be unaffected. If the DFS namespace becomes invalid during domain rename, steps must be taken to ensure that users can access the appropriate folders. Migrating to a new domain–based DFS namespace is the recommended solution, and Group Policy can be used to configure the new network paths.

Configuring member computers for the domain name change is step 5. Although member computers can be configured to automatically handle the DNS name change by modifying their DNS suffix, it could potentially result in excessive network traffic due to Active Directory and DNS replication as computers are moved to the new domain. Group Policy can be used to ensure that the proper domain name is applied to each computer by configuring the Primary DNS Suffix prior to executing the domain rename. To limit concurrent network traffic, it is recommended to perform Primary DNS Suffix changes using Group Policy in stages.

Configuration of CAs is step 6. This step involves ensuring that your CAs are not also domain controllers because that will cause issues after the domain rename. Prior to the domain rename, ensure that the Certificate Revocation Lists (CRLs) and CA certificates will not expire soon. Some certificates might need to be reissued following the domain rename.

The final preparation step involves domains that use Microsoft Exchange Server 2003 SP1. There is an Exchange Domain Rename Fix-up Tool that must be used to prepare these servers for the rename.

> **MORE INFO DOMAIN RENAME PREPARATION**
>
> Proper planning and preparation for domain rename is absolutely critical. For more detailed instructions, visit *http://technet.microsoft.com/en-us/library/cc794919.aspx*.

Performing domain rename

After you are properly prepared, you can begin the domain rename process. The first step is to set up a control station, which should be a member server within the domain being renamed. This control station should not be a domain controller and should have the domain rename tools installed as part of the Remote Server Administration Tools (RSAT). In Windows Server 2012 and Windows Server 2012 R2, the tools used for domain rename (Rendom.exe, Repadmin.exe, Dfsutil.exe, and Gpfixup.exe) are located in the System32 directory. Best practice dictates that you copy these files to their own directory (something like C:\domren) for the duration of this process (see Figure 4-12).

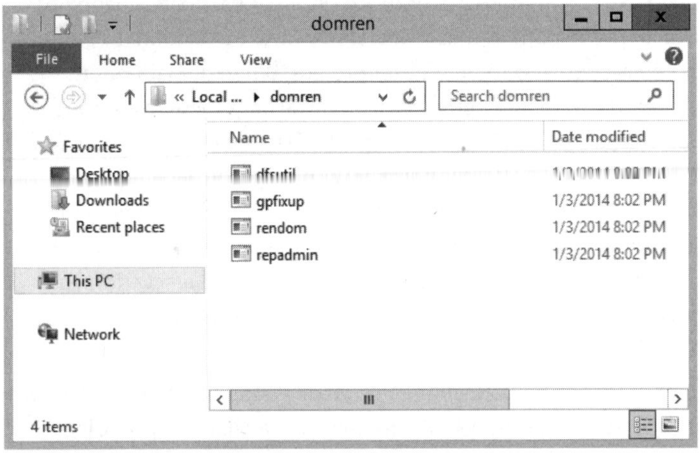

FIGURE 4-12 An example of the working folder to be created during a domain rename

Next, you must freeze the forest configuration, which prevents the addition or removal of other domains in the forest, application directory partitions, or shortcut trusts. It also prevents changes to the partial attribute set, which is the set of attributes that replicates to the global catalog. The forest configuration will be unfrozen at a later step. Due to the limitations placed on Active Directory by a frozen configuration, it is important to complete the remainder of this process in a timely manner.

The third step is to back up each domain controller in the forest by using a full system state backup. This is a critical step for being able to recover if something catastrophic happens.

Step 4 uses the domain rename tools, specifically rendom.exe, to generate a forest description file using the following command:

```
rendom /list
```

This command creates a Domainlist.xml file to contain a description of the current forest structure. You should create a backup copy of this file prior to proceeding to the next step. A sample of a domain entry from the Domainlist.xml file is shown here:

```
<Domain>
  <Guid>89cf8ae3-f4a3-453b-ac5c-cb05a76bfa40</Guid>
  <DNSname>research.contoso.com</DNSname>
  <NetBiosName>RESEARCH</NetBiosName>
 <DcName></DcName>
</Domain>
```

The fifth step is to edit the Domainlist.xml file, modifying the DNSname attribute, the NetBiosName attribute, or both. These names should match the location within the domain infrastructure in which you want this domain to be moved, as shown in the following example, which changes the research.contoso.com domain into the contosoresearch.com forest root domain. The Guid is used to identify each domain in the forest and cannot be altered. Application partitions also appear as unique domain entries, and their naming should be edited to match the rest of the forest.

```
<Domain>
  <Guid>89cf8ae3-f4a3-453b-ac5c-cb05a76bfa40</Guid>
  <DNSname>contosoresearch.com</DNSname>
  <NetBiosName>CONTOSORESEARCH</NetBiosName>
  <DcName></DcName>
</Domain>
```

After the domain description file has been modified, you must generate domain rename instructions and upload them to the domain controller operating as the domain-naming master by using the following command:

```
rendom /upload
```

This command creates a Dclist.xml file that contains a listing of each domain controller in the forest.

Finally, you can push the instruction set to each domain controller in the forest by using the following repadmin command:

```
repadmin /syncall /d /e /P /q DomainNamingMaster
```

In most forests, these instructions are not immediately synchronized to all domain controllers, so you can use the following command to check the readiness of domain controllers throughout the forest:

```
rendom /prepare
```

This command updates the Dclist.xml file that was created earlier, so you can track the status of the preparation step and monitor the process for errors. This XML file can be analyzed to determine domain controller readiness. When each domain controller achieves the Prepared state, you are ready to move to the next step.

After each domain controller is prepared for the domain rename, you can issue the rename using this command:

```
rendom /execute
```

Examine the Dclist.xml file again; if any domain controllers still show a status of Prepared, you must repeat the command. Repeat executing the domain rename until each domain controller shows a state of Done or Error. You can force the command to make another attempt on domain controllers showing an Error state by placing the word *yes* inside the Retry attribute under that domain controller and then rerunning the execute command.

After the domain rename execution is complete, there is an additional step for domains containing Exchange servers. The Exchange Domain Rename Fix-up Tool must be used to make necessary changes to your Exchange servers, after which you must restart each Exchange server twice.

At this point, you can unfreeze the forest configuration with this command:

```
rendom /end
```

After the forest configuration is unfrozen, reestablish any forest or external trusts. The domain rename process invalidates these trusts.

Finally, you must repair the GPOs within the domain by using the following:

```
gpfixup /olddns:OldDomainDnsName
        /newdns:NewDomainDNSName
        /oldnb:OldDomainNetBIOSName
        /newnb:NewDomainNetBIOSName
        /dc:DcDnsName 2>&1 >gpfixup.log
```

This command should appear on one line, and the oldnb and newnb parameters are needed only if the NetBIOS name of the domain has changed. These changes need to be replicated to other domain controllers within the domain by using this command:

```
repadmin /syncall /d /e /P /q DcDnsName NewDomainDN
```

Each renamed domain must have its GPOs repaired by using these steps.

> **MORE INFO**   **PERFORMING DOMAIN RENAME**
>
> Executing a domain rename is a complex process; for complete details on each of the steps involved, visit *http://technet.microsoft.com/en-us/library/cc794793.aspx*.

Completing a domain rename

After the domain rename is issued on each of your domain controllers, several more steps must be completed to ensure that all the parts of your directory function properly.

For CRLs to function properly after a domain rename, CNAME records should be created in DNS for the original FQDN of the certificate authority to resolve to the new FQDN. This CNAME record should be retained until all existing certificates have been renewed. If the URLs in your certificates use Lightweight Directory Access Protocol (LDAP) exclusively, this process does not work, and the entire certificate hierarchy has to be renewed.

Several miscellaneous cleanup steps should occur after a domain rename, some of which are applicable only if certain steps were taken in preparation for the domain rename:

- After the domain rename process, in which the structure of the forest has changed, redundant shortcut trusts can be safely removed using Active Directory Domains And Trusts.
- If Group Policy was used to configure the primary DNS suffix of member computers, the applicable GPO can be reconfigured or removed.
- DNS zones that no longer match the directory structure are now extraneous and can be removed.
- Member computers should be restarted twice to ensure that the computer and its applications and services are all made aware of the domain change.

After the domain rename is complete, a system state backup of all domain controllers should be performed one final time because restoring to a previous backup would result in the domain rename process having to be run again. If GPOs were backed up using the Group Policy Management Console (GPMC), these backups will be invalid due to the domain rename. It is recommended that you do a fresh backup of your GPOs as well.

Certain attributes within Active Directory, specifically the nsDS-DnsRootAlias and msDS-UpdateScript attributes, must be altered after the domain rename is complete. This step can be accomplished using rendom.exe with the /clean switch.

Finally, domain controllers must be renamed to match the new domain structure. Domain controllers are not automatically renamed during the domain rename process, so they must be reconfigured after the domain rename process has completed. Domain controllers can be renamed through the system properties, as shown in Figure 4-13.

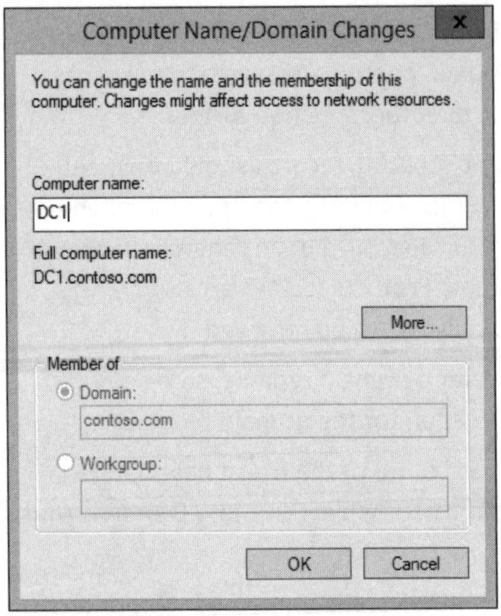

FIGURE 4-13 Renaming a domain controller

The host name of a domain controller can also be configured from the command line using the following process.

1. Add a new computer name:

   ```
   netdom computername <CurrentComputerName> /add:<NewComputerName>
   ```

2. Specify the new computer name as the primary name:

   ```
   netdom computername <CurrentComputerName> /makeprimary:<NewComputerName>
   ```

3. Restart the domain controller

4. Remove the old computer name:

   ```
   netdom computername <NewComputerName> /remove:<OldComputerName>
   ```

> **MORE INFO COMPLETING A DOMAIN RENAME**
>
> For complete details on the steps involved in completing a domain rename, visit
> *http://technet.microsoft.com/en-us/library/cc794825.aspx.*

EXAM TIP

Domain rename will probably be included in the exam. Be confident in your understanding of the general process steps as well as the command-line tools and switches used to initiate each step.

Configuring Kerberos realm trusts

Kerberos realm trusts are used to create a trust relationship between an Active Directory domain and a Kerberos realm running UNIX. Realm trusts are created with the New Trust Wizard found in Active Directory Domains And Trusts (see Figure 4-14). Using the New Trust Wizard, you can configure the transitivity and direction of the trust, the name of the Kerberos realm, and the trust password. You can also configure the realm trust to use AES encryption.

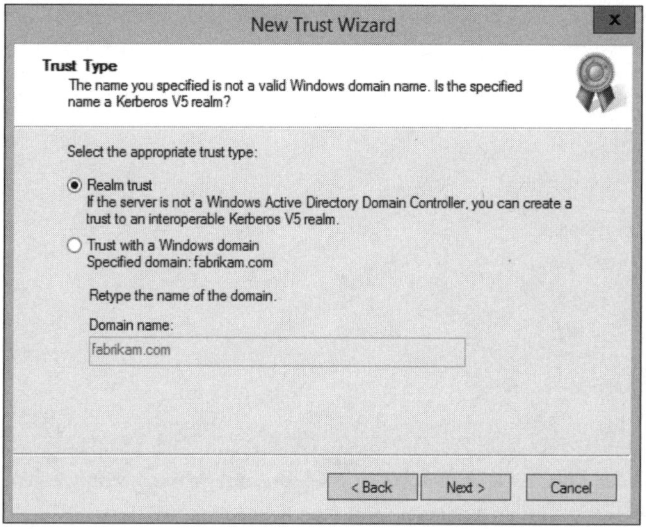

FIGURE 4-14 The New Trust Wizard is used to create a Kerberos realm trust

Implementing a domain upgrade

In previous versions of Windows Server, the domain-upgrade process had to be completed using adprep. Windows Server 2012 integrates the domain upgrade process into the Active Directory Domain Services Configuration Wizard when domain and forest preparation have not yet been performed.

When you add the first Windows Server 2012 domain controller to an existing forest, an additional step appears in the wizard, notifying you that the forest, schema, and domain must be prepped for the domain controller. An example of this preparation step is shown in Figure 4-15.

Although the domain and forest preparation steps have been integrated into the Active Directory Domain Services Configuration Wizard, in many cases this step is best performed manually in advance of deploying the first domain controller. By manually extending the schema prior to deploying your first Windows Server 2012 or Windows Server 2012 R2 domain controller, you allow time for schema replication to occur throughout the forest.

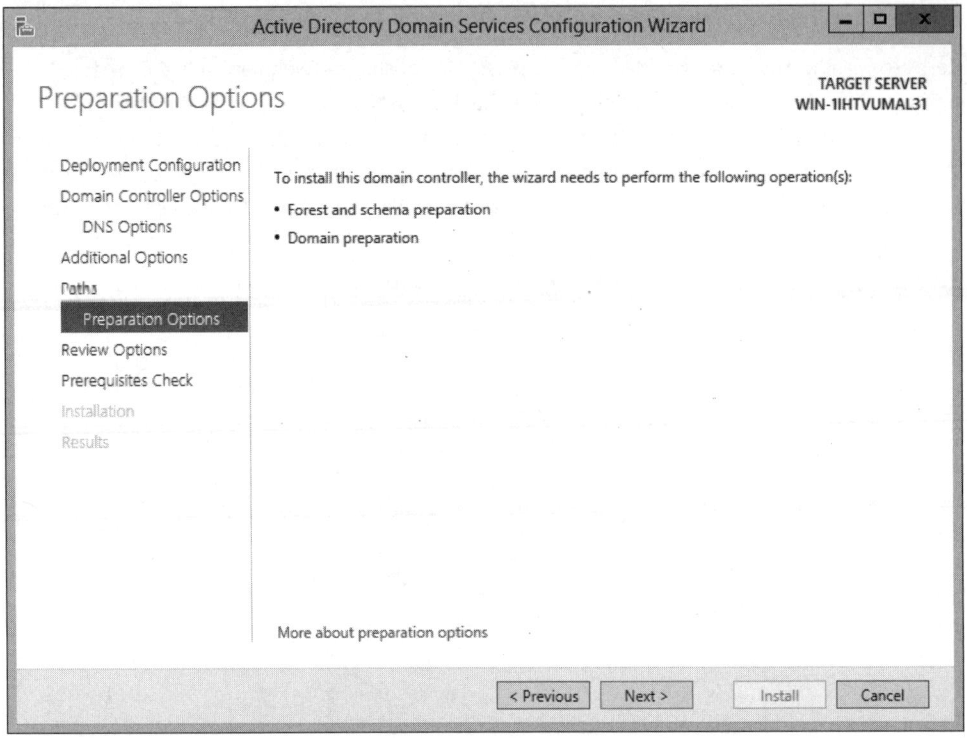

FIGURE 4-15 Upgrading a forest and domain during a domain controller deployment

In Windows Server 2012 and Windows Server 2012 R2, adprep is contained in the \Support\Adprep folder of the installation media.

Manual forest preparation is performed using the adprep /forestprep command. This step should be accomplished by a member of the Enterprise Admins, Schema Admins, and Domain Admins groups on the domain controller running the schema master Flexible Single Master Operations (FSMO) role. Forest preparation is performed once for the entire forest.

Preparation of each domain is accomplished using the adprep /domainprep command. Domain preparation should be performed on the domain controller performing the infrastructure master role by a member of the Domain Admins group.

Implementing a domain migration

Besides renaming domains and altering a forest structure, the migration of objects between domains and forests can also assist with modifying Active Directory to meet the changing needs of your business. The process of moving objects and performing the security translation associated with the movement of these objects is known as *domain migration*.

The ADMT is provided as a means to assist with domain migrations. There are several versions of the ADMT, each corresponding to a specific version of Windows Server. At the time of this writing, the latest version of the ADMT is 3.2, which must be installed on a

Windows Server 2008 R2 server. The ADMT is a flexible tool in that it supports both wizard-based and scripted usage, making it simple to migrate a small number of objects—or even entire domains.

An *intraforest* domain migration is one in which the source and target domains are within the same forest. Some characteristics of an intraforest domain migration are important to understand because they differ from an interforest migration, which is discussed in the next section. Specifically, user and group objects are moved in an intraforest migration, whereas computers and MSAs are copied and the originals remain enabled in the source domain. Passwords are always retained in an intraforest migration. SID history is required for user, group, and computer accounts, although not so for MSAs.

Prior to running the ADMT to perform your migration, you must enable the File And Printer Sharing exception in Windows Firewall on member computers or servers. You should also have a rollback plan for disaster recovery, including periodic backups of domain controllers in both target and source domains. Testing the domain migration process is highly recommended, not only for familiarization with the process but also to find potential trouble areas prior to performing the migration on production Active Directory domains.

As with any complex process, there are several best practices concerning domain migration:

- Users who have encrypted files using Encrypting File System (EFS) cannot decrypt this data after a domain migration. Ensure that users decrypt these files prior to the migration.

- Performing regular backups of domain controllers throughout the domain migration process is recommended.

- Migrating objects in batches of 100 is recommended to better manage the process.

- Administration of user and group objects should occur in the source domain throughout the migration for changes to be reflected in both domains.

- User profiles must be managed differently depending on the type of user profiles being used.

- Roaming profiles can be translated using the Translate Roaming Profiles option in the User Options page of the User Account Migration Wizard.

- Local profiles should be translated in a separate step after user migration occurs. The Security Translation Wizard can be used to perform local profile translation using the User profiles option on the Translate Objects page.

- Member computers should be restarted after migration.

Unlike the domain rename process, a domain migration is selective, so you must specifically migrate objects individually or in groups. A key aspect of the process is to migrate objects in the proper order. For example, groups should be migrated prior to the users they contain. Likewise, service accounts and MSAs should be migrated before the workstations or member servers with which they are associated.

Each phase of a domain migration can be initiated by using the appropriate ADMT wizard or by using a command-line version such as admt group, admt computer, or admt user. The admt security option corresponds to the Security Translation Wizard, which enables the translation of local user profiles from the old user object to the new user object in the target domain.

> **MORE INFO**   **INTRAFOREST DOMAIN MIGRATION**
>
> The intraforest domain migration process is discussed more extensively here: *http://technet.microsoft.com/en-us/library/cc974371.aspx.*

Implementing a forest restructure

Between domain rename and domain migration, you are given a lot of flexibility in reshaping the structure of your forest, and many scenarios can make use of either tool. When ADMT is to be used as a strategy for restructuring an Active Directory forest, the domain structure must first be modified, typically by deploying new domains in the forest (see Figure 4-16). This process places less stress on the forest because a phased approach can be taken to incorporate changes to the domain structure, and mass changes that must be replicated to all domain controllers and member computers are avoided.

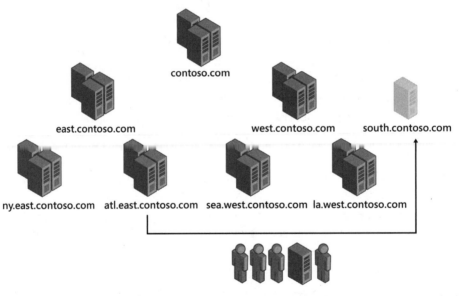

FIGURE 4-16 A forest restructure using domain migration

The domain rename process does not change drastically between a simple rename and a forest restructure with the domain moving somewhere else within the forest. There are some significant changes, though, with an Active Directory domain migration between forests—also called an interforest migration.

In an interforest domain migration, objects are cloned rather than moved; the original objects remain in the source domain. Although SID history and passwords can be retained, these settings are optional in an interforest migration.

A trust relationship, either external or forest, one- or two-way, should be used to create an initial relationship between Active Directory domains prior to attempting an interforest migration. This trust relationship can be removed after the migration is complete.

> **MORE INFO**   **FOREST RESTRUCTURE USING DOMAIN MIGRATION**
>
> More information on interforest Active Directory domain restructuring can be found at *http://technet.microsoft.com/en-us/library/cc974335.aspx*.

Deploying and managing a test forest

For many scenarios, it is beneficial to have a test instance of the Active Directory forest. Being able to validate changes to Group Policy and ensure proper policy application, test new automation methods such as scripts, or test third-party applications that integrate with Active Directory are critical steps that should be accomplished prior to implementation in a production forest. Any task with the potential to significantly affect the forest—such as domain upgrades, domain controller operating system upgrades, functional level changes, domain rename, and domain migration—should be tested prior to implementation in production.

Ideally, a test forest is a close match to your production forest to most effectively simulate the actions you are testing and identify any problems prior to the production implementation. As shown in Figure 4-17, synchronization of objects from your production forest to your test forest should be part of the test scenario.

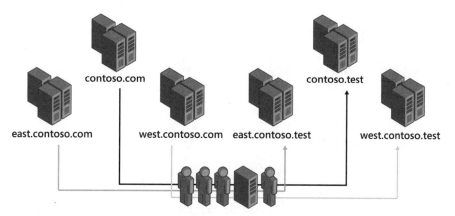

FIGURE 4-17 Synchronizing objects from a production Active Directory forest to a test forest

Microsoft Forefront Identity Manager 2012 R2 (FIM 2012 R2) provides a new level of user management for the enterprise. FIM offers self-service management for users such as password resets, enforcement of security policies, and increased audit capabilities and reporting.

FIM also provides the tools needed to synchronize user identities between forests or to Azure AD, as mentioned previously.

FIM supports both inbound and outbound synchronization, workflows, and rule-based synchronization. Rules can be used to synchronize users from certain domains within the forest, users within certain groups, or users that meet a defined set of criteria. In some testing scenarios, it can be useful to reintegrate users from the test environment at some point; this can be accomplished by using inbound synchronization.

> ### Thought experiment
> #### Restructuring Active Directory
>
> In this thought experiment, apply what you've learned about this objective. You can find answers to these questions in the "Answers" section at the end of this chapter.
>
> Your company has been hired to consult for an international corporation. Your client currently uses a single Active Directory forest with child domains representing each country/region in which the corporation has a presence.
>
> Rather than continue to operate in a single forest, your client wants to move to a multiple forest architecture. Each domain representing a country/region has to be transitioned into its own forest root domain. Some large countries/regions will be further broken down to represent geographical areas of the countries/regions they represent.
>
> Given this scenario, answer the following questions:
>
> 1. What process should you use to convert the current domains to their own forest root domains?
>
> 2. How can you create and populate regional domains within the large countries/regions?
>
> 3. What features will be lost by moving to the multiforest architecture? Is there anything that can be done to mitigate or restore these lost features?

Objective summary

- Domain rename enables you to restructure an Active Directory forest by altering the structure of the namespace.
- Windows Server 2012 simplifies the process of upgrading a domain by performing schema extension within the Active Directory Domain Services Configuration Wizard.
- Domain migration enables you to move objects between domains or forests while preserving passwords and SID history.

- The ADMT enables you to perform domain migration using a wizard-based interface or the command line.

Objective review

Answer the following questions to test your knowledge of the information in this objective. You can find the answers to these questions and explanations of why each answer choice is correct or incorrect in the "Answers" section at the end of this chapter.

1. Which files are used to perform a domain rename? (Choose all that apply.)

   A. Rendom.exe

   B. Admt.exe

   C. Repadmin.exe

   D. Gpfixup.exe

2. What command is used to provide the domain rename script to each domain controller in the forest?

   A. rendom /upload

   B. rendom /prepare

   C. rendom /execute

   D. repadmin /syncall

3. Which fields in the Domainlist.xml should be modified to effect a domain rename? (Choose two.)

   A. Guid

   B. DNSname

   C. NetBiosName

   D. DcName

4. What steps should be taken after a domain is renamed? (Choose all that apply.)

   A. Delete redundant shortcut trusts

   B. Force user password resets

   C. Migrate user and computer objects

   D. Rename domain controllers

5. What aspects of a domain upgrade are integrated into the Active Directory Domain Services Configuration Wizard and automatically handled? (Choose all that apply.)

   A. Domain preparation

   B. Forest preparation

   C. Domain functional level upgrade

   D. Forest functional level upgrade

6. How do migrated Active Directory objects retain their existing permissions when changing domains?

    A. Shortcut trusts

    B. Forest trusts

    C. SID history

    D. Password retention

7. What objects are moved (not copied) in an intraforest domain migration? (Choose all that apply.)

    A. MSAs

    B. Users

    C. Computers

    D. Groups

8. Which ADMT option configures local user profiles to work with migrated user accounts?

    A. admt user

    B. admt computer

    C. admt security

    D. admt profile

9. What should be used to synchronize user objects with a test Active Directory forest?

    A. Domain migration

    B. FIM

    C. Domain rename

    D. Active Directory replication

10. What options are available when using FIM to synchronize objects between forests? (Choose all that apply.)

    A. Inbound synchronization

    B. Outbound synchronization

    C. User profile migration

    D. Rule-based configuration

Objective 4.3: Design a Group Policy strategy

Group Policy, which is one of the most powerful aspects of Active Directory, is often a factor in the design strategy of the entire domain structure. The capability to apply a standard configuration to literally millions of computers across the globe is a major reason why so many large corporations use Active Directory and Windows Server.

Designing a Group Policy implementation involves applying the proper policies to users and computers in the most efficient way possible. Performance issues due to the application of a large number of policies must be balanced against the need to apply different policies to different sets of users or computers. Precedence is a key aspect of controlling the application of GPOs, as are the filtering methods available through Windows Management Instrumentation (WMI) and security groups.

Your Group Policy strategy should include the process for testing GPO application to ensure that clients are properly configured and for troubleshooting problems related to misconfiguration. Several tools are available to determine what policies are applied to a client or what policies would be applied to clients meeting certain criteria. Other tools facilitate advanced management of Group Policy, including staging, reporting, and backup capabilities. You should know what tools are available to manage and troubleshoot Group Policy and how they are used throughout the Group Policy life cycle.

> **This objective covers how to:**
>
> - Control GPO application through inheritance blocking, enforced policies, loopback processing, security filtering, and Windows Management Instrumentation (WMI) filtering
> - Manage GPO assignment, including site-linked GPOs, slow-link processing, group strategies, and organizational unit (OU) hierarchies
> - Use Advanced Group Policy Management (AGPM)
> - Cache Group Policy

Controlling GPO application

The most complex aspect of dealing with Group Policy is managing precedence and ensuring that the correct policies are applied to computers without accidentally applying something to the wrong computers. Understanding the different options available to alter the priority in which GPOs get applied is the most important part of understanding how Group Policy works. A properly configured Group Policy design enables you to configure the computers in your network without experiencing performance issues that result from the use of dozens of GPOs at each level of the domain. In some scenarios, GPO application can be as simple as linking a GPO to one or more OUs; in others, blocked inheritance and enforced policies are needed.

Minimizing the number of GPOs in use within your domain is beneficial for performance reasons, but sometimes additional policies must be created to target the necessary users or computers. Finding this balance should be a priority for the Group Policy design process and is a critical skill for you to develop.

EXAM TIP

Although it isn't called out specifically in the exam objectives, be sure you understand what tools are available to troubleshoot the application of GPOs and how they differ. Group Policy Modeling (GPM) and Gpresult.exe are critical tools to know and understand.

Inheritance blocking

By default, GPOs applied to an object in Active Directory are automatically inherited and applied to all objects below that object in the hierarchy. This default behavior can be modified by configuring a child OU to block inheritance, as shown in Figure 4-18.

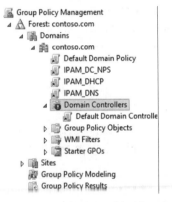

FIGURE 4-18 Inheritance blocking on the Domain Controllers OU

OUs that are specifically for servers often use inheritance blocking. Although you might want to use Group Policy to configure your servers, it is often a good idea to prevent unexpected changes to critical systems by blocking inheritance and applying GPOs directly to the OU.

In many cases, inheritance blocking is unnecessary because of the order in which GPOs are applied. By default, GPOs applied at a higher level in the hierarchy are processed first. When GPOs have conflicting settings, the GPO being applied at a lower level receives precedence.

Enforced policies

Although inheritance blocking changes the default inheritance in Group Policy, it can be overridden by an administrator choosing to enforce a GPO at a higher level in the OU hierarchy. Enforced GPOs are typically used to configure policies that are required regardless of a system's purpose or criticality. They are indicated by a padlock icon added to the linked GPO, as shown in Figure 4-19.

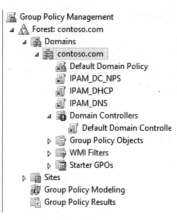

FIGURE 4-19 The GPO enforcement of the Default Domain Policy

Not only do enforced GPOs override inheritance blocking but they are also applied in reverse order. A GPO enforced at a lower level is applied before one at a higher level, resulting in conflicting settings being configured using the GPO at the higher level.

Because enforced GPOs at higher levels of the OU hierarchy receive precedence over all GPOs applied below them, these GPOs should be handled with extreme care because they can affect computers and users throughout the domain. The importance of testing GPO application corresponds directly to the number of users and computers that might be affected.

Loopback processing

When a computer retrieves GPOs from Active Directory, it typically does so for itself and the current user. A computer sometimes needs to receive a specific configuration regardless of the user (a computer left in a public area or used as a kiosk is a common example).

Unlike the other methods discussed in this section, loopback processing is configured within a GPO under Computer Configuration\Policies\Administrative Templates\System\Group Policy. Two modes are offered for loopback processing: merge mode and replace mode. *Merge mode* uses both the user and computer configuration, but any conflicting settings are configured with the computer setting. *Replace mode* ignores the user's configuration completely, using only those settings gathered for the computer.

Security filtering

One of the most common ways to fine-tune GPO application is to use security group filters. Each GPO is configured by default to target the Authenticated Users group, which results in the GPO always being applied. By removing the Authenticated Users group and specifying a more restrictive group, you can apply the GPO to only those users or computers that are members of that group. This technique enables you to provide a specific configuration to different classes of users, such as system administrators or corporate executives. Likewise, if a GPO should target only a certain group of computers, such as servers, security filtering can be used.

Security filtering can become increasingly powerful when used in conjunction with other GPO application strategies such as enforcement or loopback processing. By using multiple application methods, you can more strategically target specific groups of computers or users for GPO application.

Windows Management Instrumentation (WMI) filtering

The second type of filter that can be applied to a GPO uses WMI, a system that enables you to query for detailed information about a computer—such as manufacturer, processor architecture, or installed applications. WMI filters can be used to apply firewall settings to computers with a specific application installed or to enable certain services based on the hardware available to a computer. The example shown in Figure 4-20 even enables you to target Hyper-V virtual machines (VMs) with a GPO.

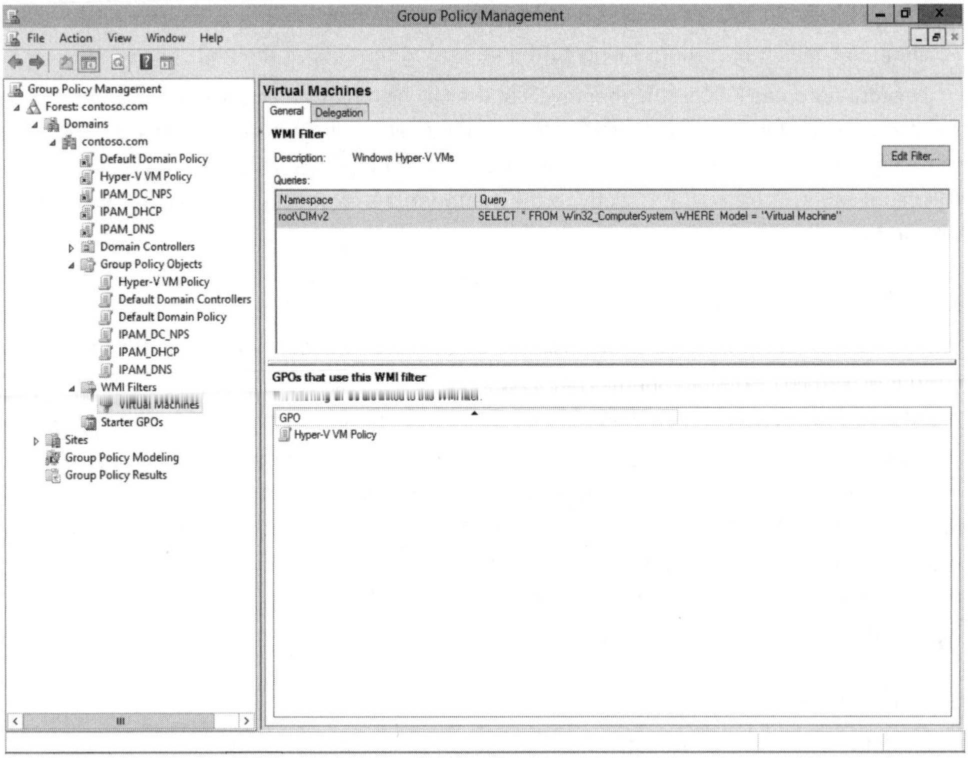

FIGURE 4-20 Using a WMI filter to apply a specific GPO to Hyper-V VMs

Managing GPO assignment

GPOs are assigned to a domain or OU because they typically have the most flexibility in applying specific policies and configurations based on the logical organizational structure of the company. Several other techniques and strategies can be used to assign GPOs for scenarios that don't necessarily fit the rigid structure built in to many Active Directory domains.

Many organizations have no need for GPO assignment methods other than directly to a domain or OU. However, knowing that these options are available can be particularly helpful for managing GPO assignment to specific sites or to mobile users.

Site-linked GPOs

As with domains and OUs, GPOs can be linked to Active Directory sites, part of the physical structure of Active Directory (discussed in more detail in Chapter 5, "Design and implement an active directory infrastructure [physical]"). Site-linked GPOs can be used in several scenarios, including the use of a local Windows Server Update Services (WSUS) server, a proxy server, or anything specific to the client's physical location. Figure 4-21 shows a GPO linked to the LosAngeles site.

FIGURE 4-21 Site-linked GPOs enable you to assign location-specific settings based on a user's current site

Slow-link processing

The application of GPOs can take a toll on performance, particularly on networks with slow connectivity to a domain controller. When a slow link is detected, only certain aspects of a GPO are applied to a client computer. By default, the threshold by which a slow link is judged is 500 kilobits per second (Kbps), but it can be modified by editing the Group Policy Slow Link Detection setting in Policies\Administrative Templates\System\Group Policy under both the User Configuration and Computer Configuration sections. You can also disable slow-link processing by configuring the Do Not Detect Slow Network Connections setting.

The default setting categories processed over slow links are listed in Table 4-2. Many of these settings can be modified using the Allow Processing Across A Slow Network Connection setting, although Administrative Templates And Security is always processed.

TABLE 4-2 Settings processed over slow links

Setting	Processed
802.3 Group Policy	Yes
Administrative Templates	Yes
Deployed Printer Connections	No
Disk Quotas	No
EFS	Yes
Folder Redirection	No
Group Policy Preferences	Yes
IE Maintenance	Yes
Internet Explorer Zone Mapping	Yes
IP Security	Yes
Microsoft Offline Files	Yes
QoS Packet Scheduler	Yes
Scripts	No
Security	Yes
Software Installation	No
Software Restriction Policies	Yes
Windows Search	Yes
Wireless	Yes

Group strategies

Security filtering adds quite a bit of flexibility to Group Policy. Rather than having to manage GPOs at multiple levels in a domain, you can assign them at the domain root and filter the GPO to one or more groups of users or computers. These groups could then be managed by lower-level administrators, a help desk, or even by script or other forms of automation. This technique provides some level of control over GPO application to administrators who do not have direct control over Group Policy.

Using security filtering exclusively to target users or computers for policy application can have a negative effect on performance. When Group Policy is applied, both the user and computer must go through an evaluation process to determine which GPOs should be applied and in what order. If GPOs are assigned in the OU hierarchy, they are evaluated to determine whether they should be applied. This evaluation process becomes more complex and intensive as more GPOs are added in the OU hierarchy.

Organizational unit (OU) hierarchies

Many of the strategies discussed earlier, such as inheritance and enforcement, are typically implemented against the OU hierarchy. Understanding how GPOs are applied and managed should have an impact on the OU structure and where certain objects fall within that structure. Precedence, the order in which GPOs are applied, determines which settings are applied to a computer when the GPO application process is completed.

By default, precedence occurs from top to bottom, so GPOs applied to the OU containing the user or computer are used to apply settings that conflicted with GPOs linked directly to the domain. Besides bypassing blocked inheritance, enforced GPOs also alter precedence. If two enforced GPOs are applied, one to an OU and the other to the domain, the GPO applied higher in the OU structure receives precedence.

Figure 4-22 shows an example of how GPOs could be applied to an OU structure. Two GPOs are assigned to the domain level, but only one is enforced to enable settings configured in the Contoso Corporate Standard GPO to be blocked at the Domain Controllers, Servers, and Admin OUs.

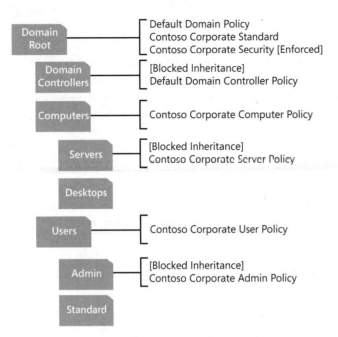

FIGURE 4-22 An example of how GPOs can be applied to an OU structure

GPO enforcement is sometimes unnecessary to achieve the desired result. A single GPO can be linked to more than one location in the OU structure. If a policy is being overridden within an OU, consider applying the GPO directly to the OU.

Applying GPOs properly and efficiently can become quite complex. Using the Group Policy Modeling Wizard can help to determine precedence and troubleshooting issues related to GPO application.

Using Advanced Group Policy Management (AGPM)

A Group Policy tool that is not provided by default is Advanced Group Policy Management (AGPM). Part of the Microsoft Desktop Optimization Pack (MDOP), which is available to Software Assurance customers, AGPM provides numerous benefits to Group Policy administrators. AGPM integrates directly with the GPMC, adding new features and capabilities (see Figure 4-23).

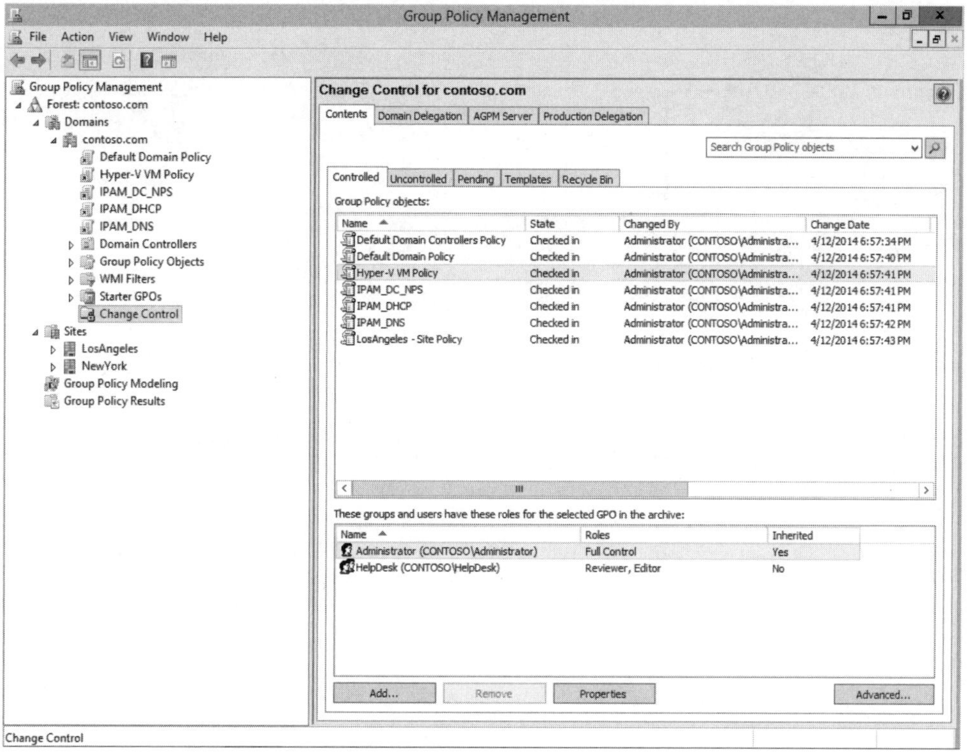

FIGURE 4-23 AGPM is integrated directly into the GPMC

Offline development and editing of GPOs is offered through the use of the AGPM archive. Administrators can design and build GPOs in an environment safe from accidental deployment by deploying the GPOs only when fully configured. If a problem occurs after a GPO is deployed, the GPO and its associated configuration can be quickly rolled back to the previous state.

Change control enables you to track GPOs as they go through the design and development process. Combined with role-based delegation, change control enables you to enable lower-level administrators to design and create GPOs without allowing them to deploy the GPO to production. After the GPO has been reviewed and approved for deployment, an administrator with the appropriate permissions can perform the deployment step. An example of the change control and role delegation process is shown in Figure 4-24.

Organizations with complex Group Policy implementations make heavy use of the search and filter capabilities provided in AGPM. The search functionality enables you to look for GPOs edited by a specific user, saved on a certain date, using a filter, or numerous other criteria.

Finally, AGPM enables you to manage Group Policy across multiple forests by importing and exporting GPOs, as shown in Figure 4-25. Cross-forest management can be used for multiple production forests and for moving GPOs between test and production environments.

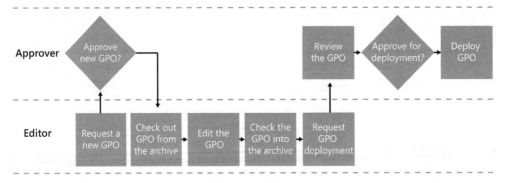

FIGURE 4-24 The change control and role delegation in AGPM

Export the GPO to a file

« Documents ▸ GPOs   Search GPOs

Organize ▾   New folder

★ Favorites   Name   Date modified   Type
   ▦ Desktop
   ▦ Downloads   No items match your search.
   ▦ Recent places

▦ This PC

▦ Network

File name: Hyper-V VM Policy

Save as type: Cabinet file

Hide Folders   Export   Cancel

FIGURE 4-25 AGPM provides a means for GPOs to be exported and migrated to another forest

Group Policy caching

A new feature in Windows Server 2012 R2 and Windows 8.1, Group Policy caching enables
faster processing of GPOs running in synchronous mode (in which policies are being enforced
prior to the user seeing a logon screen). By default, caching is disabled in Windows Server
2012 R2, but it can be enabled by editing the Computer Configuration\Policies\Administrative
Templates\System\Group Policy\Enable Group Policy Caching For Servers setting.

Group Policy caching is particularly useful for branch office scenarios in which network
connectivity to domain controllers might not be optimal. Instead of the computer's boot process being delayed while GPOs are downloaded, a cached copy can be used to apply policies.

Thought experiment

Optimizing Group Policy

In this thought experiment, apply what you've learned about this objective. You can find answers to these questions in the "Answers" section at the end of this chapter.

You have been tasked with improving the performance and efficiency of the Group Policy implementation used by your company. The organization has multiple Active Directory sites in a single domain. Each site has Active Directory users and computers in its own OUs to facilitate delegated administration by local administrators.

Given this scenario, answer the following questions:

1. You want to ensure that a set of default configuration settings is applied to computers throughout the organization without the possibility of being overridden. What is the most efficient way to accomplish this?

2. Each location has certain configuration requirements that differ from any other location. Also, users moving between locations should receive the configuration for the location in which they connect their computer. What is the best way to manage this requirement?

3. Some locations occasionally have connectivity issues that result in performance issues. What causes this and how could you mitigate this issue?

4. You have configured a GPO for server configuration that is applied synchronously. It is causing performance issues for servers at remote locations due to network latency. How could you remedy this problem?

5. Local administrators at each corporate location have requested the ability to create GPOs to be applied to their local sites. How might you facilitate this request while still maintaining control over what GPOs are actually applied to Active Directory?

Objective summary

- GPO precedence can be altered using inheritance blocking and enforced policies.
- Loopback processing can be used to enforce the computer configuration over that of the user.
- Security filtering can be used to target specific groups of users or computers, whereas WMI filtering can focus on computers with certain attributes or configurations.
- GPOs linked to an Active Directory site can be helpful for location-specific settings such as WSUS or web proxy servers.

- Slow-link processing configures how GPOs are applied over links to a domain controller without the required bandwidth.

- AGPM, which is part of the MDOP, adds several features to Group Policy such as role-based access control, GPO staging, and change management.

- Group Policy caching is a new feature in Windows Server 2012 R2 that enables cached GPOs to be used when running in synchronous mode.

Objective review

Answer the following questions to test your knowledge of the information in this objective. You can find the answers to these questions and explanations of why each answer choice is correct or incorrect in the "Answers" section at the end of this chapter.

1. What technique can be used to prevent GPOs from higher levels in the domain hierarchy from being applied to computers within an OU?

   A. Inheritance blocking

   B. Enforced policies

   C. Security filtering

   D. WMI filtering

2. Which option enables you to ensure that a GPO is applied to lower levels of the domain hierarchy?

   A. Inheritance blocking

   B. Enforced policies

   C. Security filtering

   D. WMI filtering

3. Which GPO would receive precedence and be applied to computers in an OU with blocked inheritance?

   A. GPO applied to domain level

   B. GPO applied to OU

   C. Enforced GPO applied to domain level

   D. Enforced GPO applied to OU

4. How can you ensure that a specific configuration is applied to a computer, regardless of the current user?

   A. Enforced policies

   B. Loopback processing

   C. WMI filtering

   D. Security filtering

5. What feature enables you to target a GPO for computers with a specific processor type?

   A. Loopback processing

   B. Enforced policies

   C. WMI filtering

   D. Security filtering

6. What is the best way to target a GPO for users or computers in a specific location?

   A. Security filtering

   B. Enforced policies

   C. Site-linked GPOs

   D. Loopback processing

7. What features are provided by AGPM? (Choose all that apply.)

   A. Role-based delegation

   B. Group Policy caching

   C. Change control

   D. Policy rollback

8. Which AGPM feature allows for policy rollback?

   A. AGPM archive

   B. Change control

   C. Role-based delegation

   D. Import and export

9. What features does Group Policy offer to improve performance over slow network connections? (Choose all that apply.)

   A. Site-linked GPOs

   B. Slow-link processing

   C. Loopback processing

   D. Group Policy caching

10. When are cached GPOs used?

    A. Loopback processing

    B. Slow-link processing

    C. Synchronous mode

    D. Enforced policies

Objective 4.4: Design an Active Directory permission model

For many reasons, delegating permissions is critical in a modern corporate environment. Many industries require a separation of duties to prevent unauthorized use and provide checks and balances. Others require the workload to be distributed for the system to be managed efficiently. Whatever the reason, Active Directory is fully capable of providing the appropriate level of access to administrators throughout an organization.

In addition to GPO application, planning for permissions delegation should determine the structure of your OU hierarchy. Permissions in Active Directory are applied to domains or OUs and their children: objects or additional OUs. To be properly restrictive, administrators should be delegated access to perform only the functions within the scope of their job and only over the areas they manage.

In addition to controlling delegation and permissions, areas of administrative control can be used to monitor administrative users and ensure that their privileges are not being abused. Active Directory quotas can be configured to prevent individual users from creating large numbers of objects. The adminSDHolder attribute and the Protected Users security group can also be used to provide additional protections for administrative users and other sensitive accounts in Active Directory.

> **This objective covers how to:**
>
> - Design and implement Active Directory object security
> - Manage quotas in Active Directory
> - Add custom items to the Delegation 0f Control Wizard
> - Deploy administration tools
> - Delegate permissions on administrative users (AdminSDHolder)
> - Plan for Kerberos delegation

Designing and implementing Active Directory object security

Similar to files or registry keys, objects within Active Directory have access control lists (ACLs) that determine which users or groups can read or make changes. Managing an object's ACL is done through the Security tab in the object's properties (see Figure 4-26).

Active Directory permissions do not always have to be configured manually with the Security tab; the Delegation of Control Wizard can be used as well. Launched through the context menu for an Active Directory container or OU, the Delegation of Control Wizard enables you to choose one or more user or security group objects and select tasks to delegate (see Figure 4-27). Custom tasks can also be managed using the Delegation of Control Wizard, including the ability to specify specific object types to manage and the level of control given over those objects.

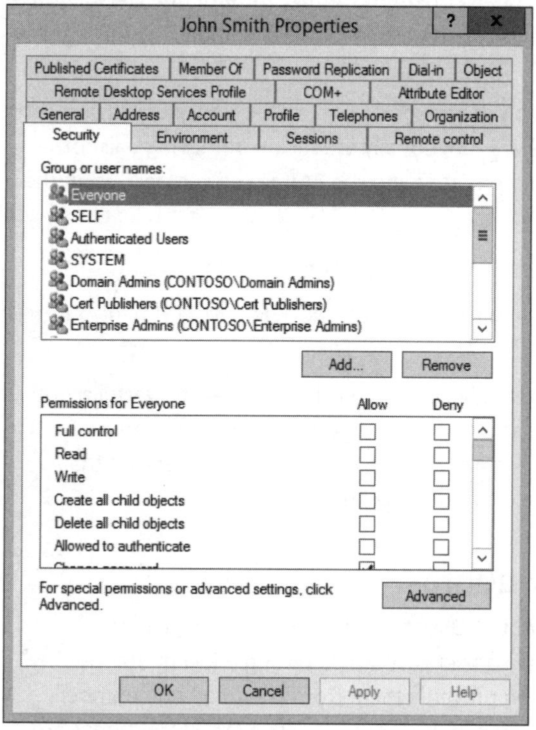

FIGURE 4-26 The Security tab for a user object

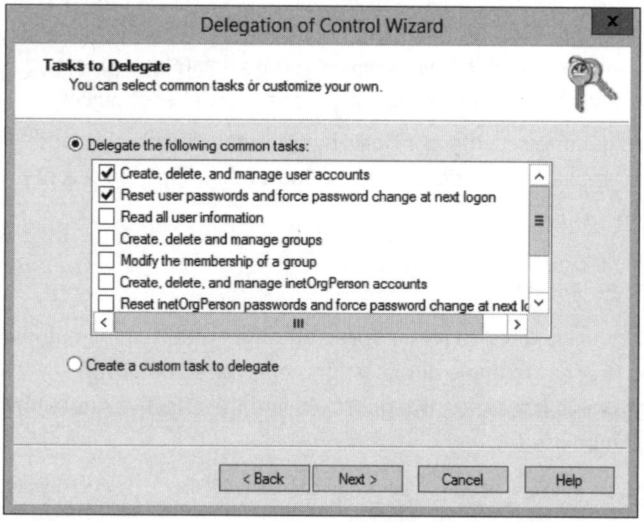

FIGURE 4-27 Choosing tasks to delegate using the Delegation of Control Wizard

As with files and folders, Active Directory object security can be inherited. For this reason, it is common for security to be managed at an OU and be applied to all objects within the scope of that OU. After an object's ACL has been configured, either through the Delegation of Control Wizard or the Security tab, removal of these permissions is accomplished through the Security tab.

PowerShell offers several methods to analyze and modify Active Directory object security. The following two lines of PowerShell code are functionally identical—retrieving a list of objects from the Computers container and then retrieving the ACL for each object using the DistinguishedName from the original query:

```
Get-ChildItem 'AD:\CN=Computers,DC=contoso,DC=com' | % {Get-ACL ("AD:\" +
$_.DistinguishedName)}
Get-ADObject -SearchBase 'CN=Computers,DC=contoso,DC=com' -SearchScope OneLevel -Filter
* | % {Get-ACL ("AD:\" + $_.DistinguishedName)}
```

With some simple modifications, these bits of code can be changed into powerful scripts. The flexibility offered by PowerShell enables you to create automated processes to perform deep analysis, even to the point of monitoring administrative user objects to ensure that administrators cannot make changes to their own user accounts.

Managing Active Directory quotas

Quotas manage the number of objects in Active Directory that are owned by a user, preventing the creation of more objects than a user is allowed. Setting a low quota for administrative users in a less-trusted position prevents them from creating large numbers of Active Directory objects, protecting against potential denial. Active Directory quotas are managed in two ways: default quotas and quotas assigned to a security principal.

Default quotas can be set for all users in the domain by configuring the msDS-DefaultQuota attribute on the NTDS Quotas container in ADSI Edit (see Figure 4-28). If the msDS-DefaultQuota attribute is not set (the default configuration) or if it has a value of -1, no default quotas are enforced, and users with the proper permissions can create an unlimited number of objects.

Quotas can be created and assigned to security principals by using the dsadd command-line tool. The following example can be used to add a quota of 500 to the HelpDesk security group in the contoso.com domain:

```
dsadd quota -part dc=contoso,dc=com -qlimit 500 -acct
cn=HelpDesk,ou=Users,dc=contoso,dc=com
```

Sometimes multiple quotas can be assigned to a user based on his membership in multiple groups with quotas assigned. If a user has multiple quota assignments based on group membership, the maximum quota value is the effective quota. To find the effective quota for a user, the following command can be used:

```
dsget user cn=johnmith,ou=Users,dc=contoso,dc=com -part dc=contoso,dc=com -qlimit -qused
```

A couple of aspects of quota management can cause issues for legitimate administrative actions. When performing an automated administrative process such as a domain migration or when creating objects using a script, large numbers of objects can be attributed to a single user. Be especially wary of quotas when you perform mass object creation using automated methods.

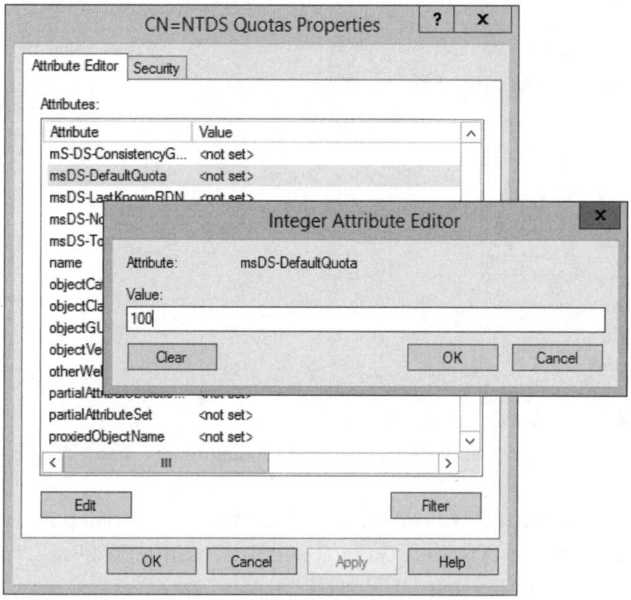

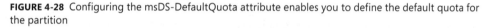

FIGURE 4-28 Configuring the msDS-DefaultQuota attribute enables you to define the default quota for the partition

Also interesting is the impact that deleted objects, also known as tombstone objects, have on quotas. By default, a deleted object counts fully against a user's quota, which can be managed by editing the msDS-TombstoneQuotaFactor attribute on the NTDS Quotas container. This attribute is configured as a percentage, which means that the default value of 100 results in a deleted object that counts the same as one that hasn't been deleted.

Creating custom tasks using the Delegation of Control Wizard

The Delegation of Control Wizard enables you to quickly assign permissions to a user or group by using a predefined set of common access levels, several of which are shown in Figure 4-29. When common access levels do not meet the requirements of the tasks to be delegated, you can choose the Create A Custom Task To Delegate option that enables you to customize the types of objects, attributes, and actions that can be viewed and modified by the assigned users.

Creating a custom task with the Delegation of Control Wizard involves two steps. The first step is to choose the types of Active Directory objects to be delegated. Although the typical object types (users, groups, and computers) are listed here, so are more than 100 other object types. The object type screen also enables you to choose whether to allow delegated users to create or delete objects of the selected types in the folder.

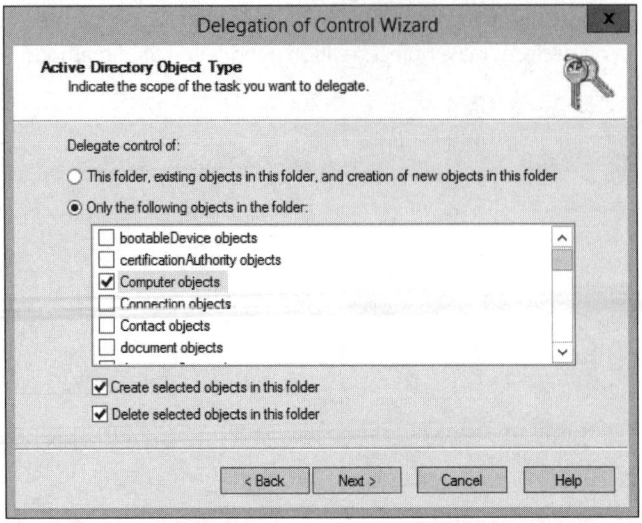

FIGURE 4-29 Choosing Active Directory object types to delegate using the Delegation of Control Wizard

The second step of delegating custom tasks is to choose the action types to be delegated (see Figure 4-30). Three permission types are provided. General permissions include a list of permission types that are familiar to most administrators: Full Control; Read; Write; and several others, such as Change Password and Reset Password. With property-specific permissions, you can perform fine-grained delegation to enable administration of specific object attributes. Finally, creating and deleting specific child objects can be managed, although these options are rarely used.

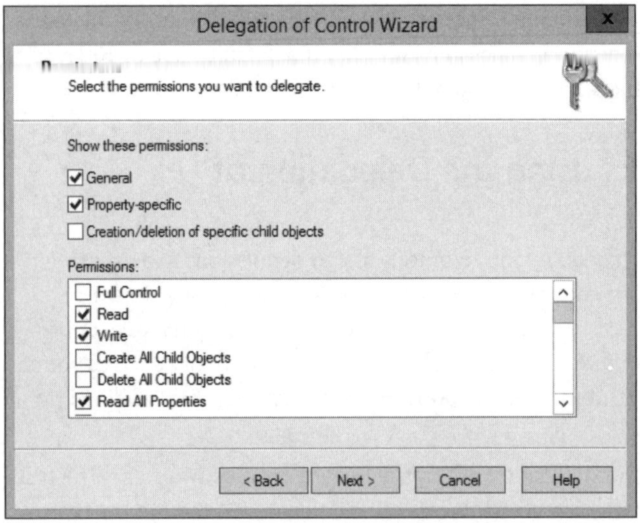

FIGURE 4-30 Configuring permissions to delegate using the Delegation of Control Wizard

Deploying administration tools

The tools used to manage Windows Server 2012 from a Windows 8 or Windows 8.1 computer are contained in the RSAT provided as a free download. The RSAT downloads for Windows 8 and Windows 8.1 are distinct and work only on the designated platform. PowerShell cmdlets and modules that correspond to the RSAT tools are also part of this installation. These tools do not need to be downloaded on Windows Server 2012 because the RSAT tools can be enabled by using the Add Roles and Features Wizard.

Unlike previous versions of RSAT, the installation consists of running the Windows Update Standalone Installer file; there is no need to enable features following installation.

Delegating permissions on administrative users (AdminSDHolder)

Active Directory has a special process for protecting certain objects that are considered critical, such as the Enterprise Admins group. Rather than allowing permissions on these objects to be configured directly, Active Directory resets the object permissions once per hour (by default) to those assigned to the AdminSDHolder object. To permanently configure permissions on these objects, you must edit the permissions on the AdminSDHolder object.

To configure permissions on the AdminSDHolder object, open ADSI Edit, choose the Default naming context, and navigate to the CN=System node under the domain in which you should find CN=AdminSDHolder. The Security tab in the object's properties, shown in Figure 4-31, shows that few groups within the domain have permissions to edit administrative objects.

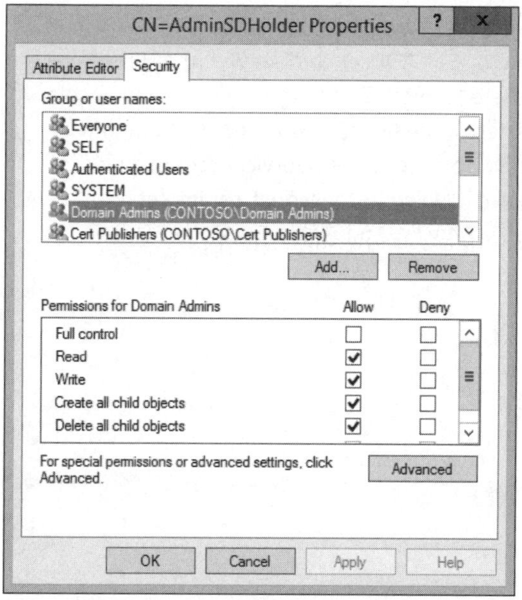

FIGURE 4-31 Configuring permissions on the AdminSDHolder object

Planning for Kerberos delegation

Kerberos constrained delegation is a function in Active Directory that enables a computer, typically a server, to authenticate with a user's credentials. This functionality was introduced in Windows Server 2003 as a way for services to perform authentication on behalf of users. Prior to Windows Server 2012, this action required a high level of trust for the server being delegated because the delegation could not easily be limited to specific actions. Beginning with Windows Server 2012 and Windows Server 2012 R2, service administrators can limit Kerberos constrained delegation to individual front-end services by allowing the domain accounts for those services to authenticate (see Figure 4-32).

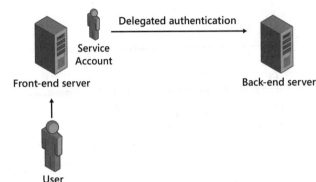

FIGURE 4-32 Kerberos constrained delegation supports limiting delegated authentication to specific services

To view a list of security principals allowed to perform delegated authentication, use the Get-ADComputer, Get-ADServiceAccount, or Get-ADUser cmdlets with the -Properties parameter set to PrincipalsAllowedToDelegateToAccount. To configure a service to enable specific security principals to perform delegated authentication, use New-ADComputer, New-ADServiceAccount, New-ADUser, Set-ADComputer, Set-ADServiceAccount, or Set-ADUser cmdlets with the -PrincipalsAllowedToDelegateToAccount parameter.

In this thought experiment, apply what you've learned about this objective. You can find answers to these questions in the "Answers" section at the end of this chapter.

Your office is responsible for Active Directory implementation for a large enterprise. The company has multiple domains, each serving a regional office dispersed across the country/region.

Up to this point, your corporate strategy regarding Active Directory object permissions has been to allow autonomy at the domain level, with little to no management at the enterprise level. Recent events have led you to limit the access provided to administrators at the domain level.

Each domain has hundreds of users who are to be classified in three separate categories, and administrators should have restrictions on the actions they can perform on each user type:

- Corporate executives will have access to sensitive files and can use encryption on their laptops. Therefore, local administrators should not be able to reset their passwords.

- Local administrators should not be able to manage their own accounts or those of other local administrators.

- All other user objects should be managed wholly by local administrators, including group membership and password resets.

Given this scenario, answer the following questions:

1. How could you meet the requirement of restricting access to user objects based on the type of user?

2. Local administrators should be able to create new objects within their domain, but the number of objects they create should be closely monitored. With what method could you accomplish this goal?

3. A very select group of corporate administrators should be able to manage membership of highly restricted groups throughout the forest, including the Enterprise Admins group. How would you allow access to this group to perform these duties?

4. A local administrator cannot create any new objects in his domain due to the number he has already created. How could you allow this user to continue creating new objects?

Objective summary

- Active Directory objects have ACLs that can be configured to allow permission levels based on administrative requirements.
- Quotas are used to prevent an administrator from creating an excessive number of objects in Active Directory.
- The Delegation of Control Wizard enables you to quickly assign permissions from pre-defined selections or a custom selection.
- The RSAT for Windows 8 and Windows 8.1 are available as a free download.
- High-level administrator groups are protected by having their permissions reset automatically every hour by Active Directory. Permissions on these groups should be modified by configuring the ACL on the AdminSDHolder object using ADSI Edit.
- Kerberos delegation enables a computer to perform authentication on behalf of a user.

Objective review

Answer the following questions to test your knowledge of the information in this objective. You can find the answers to these questions and explanations of why each answer choice is correct or incorrect in the "Answers" section at the end of this chapter.

1. What methods can you use to configure permissions on an object in Active Directory? (Choose all that apply.)

    A. Edit the Security tab in the object's properties

    B. Add the object to the Enterprise Admins group

    C. Use the Delegation of Control Wizard

    D. Edit the AdminSDHolder object

2. Which of the following determines a user's quota when all apply?

    A. Default quota of 100

    B. Group-assigned quota of 200

    C. Group-assigned quota of 1000

    D. User-assigned quota of 500

3. Which command sets the quota for members of the HelpDesk group to 100 objects?

    A. dsadd quota -part dc=contoso,dc=com -qlimit 100
       -acct cn=HelpDesk,ou=Users,dc=contoso,dc=com

    B. dsget group cn=HelpDesk,ou=Users,dc=contoso,dc=com
       -part dc=contoso,dc=com –qlimit –qused

    C. New-ADQuota -Part dc=contoso,dc=com -Quota 100
       -Acct cn=HelpDesk,ou=Users,dc=contoso,dc=com

    D. Set-ADQuota -Part dc=contoso,dc=com -Quota 100
       -Acct cn=HelpDesk,ou=Users,dc=contoso,dc=com

4. What actions might fail due to quota limitations? (Choose all that apply.)

    A. Domain rename

    B. Domain migration

    C. DirSync to Azure AD

    D. Mass user creation

5. What additional step must be taken after installing RSAT for Windows 8.1 to make the admin tools available?

    A. Reboot

    B. Enable the admin tools in Windows features

    C. Run gpupdate /force

    D. Nothing

6. How can you assign permissions to a protected admin group in Active Directory such as Enterprise Admins?

    A. Edit the Security tab in the object's properties

    B. Edit the ACL on the AdminSDHolder object

    C. Use the Delegation Of Control Wizard

    D. Use the Run As Administrator option

7. With what tool do you configure permissions on the AdminSDHolder object?

    A. Active Directory Users and Computers

    B. Active Directory Administrative Center

    C. Delegation of Control Wizard

    D. ADSI Edit

8. Why would you need to create or manage a Kerberos delegation?

    A. To provide administrative privileges to a user in Active Directory

    B. To give access to a Kerberos realm trust

    C. To enable a service to perform authentication on behalf of a user

    D. To authenticate users from UNIX systems

9. What capability in Kerberos constrained delegation is available beginning in Windows Server 2012?

    A. Limiting delegation to individual computers

    B. Limiting delegation to individual services

    C. Configuring delegation with PowerShell cmdlets

    D. Supporting delegation between domains

Answers

This section contains the solutions to the thought experiments and answers to the lesson review questions in this chapter.

Objective 4.1: Thought experiment

1. A two-way forest trust is the quickest way to enable the two corporations to begin sharing resources.

2. For the cities in which both companies have an existing presence, a domain migration enables users, computers, and groups to be brought into the existing domain while maintaining existing permissions.

3. Locations in which an existing domain does not already exist can be most easily incorporated using domain rename to bring the competitor's domain into the corporate forest.

4. Because your corporation uses the Windows Server 2012 forest functional level, you cannot bring in domains using an older domain functional level. One option is to upgrade existing domain controllers and domain functional levels. Alternatively, you can create new domains in the existing forest and then perform a domain migration, bringing over only the Active Directory objects.

Objective 4.1: Review

1. **Correct answers:** A, C

    A. **Correct:** Creating multiple Active Directory forests enables you to segregate administrative responsibilities when required for regulatory or other business reasons.

    B. **Incorrect:** A corporate merger is not reason enough to operate multiple forests, although a multiforest architecture can be used while the two corporations are fully integrated.

    C. **Correct:** When third-party applications modify the Active Directory schema, these changes affect the entire forest. Using multiple forests enables you to limit the scope of these changes.

    D. **Incorrect:** Having multiple corporate locations is easily handled with a single forest.

2. **Correct answer:** A

    A. **Correct:** Forest trusts are transitive and encompass each domain in the two forests.

    B. **Incorrect:** A realm trust is used in conjunction with Kerberos realms.

    C. **Incorrect:** An external trust is nontransitive and creates a trust between only two domains.

    D. **Incorrect:** A shortcut trust is implemented between two domains in the same forest to improve authentication performance.

3. **Correct answer:** C

    A. **Incorrect:** Windows Server 2003 does not support the Active Directory Recycle Bin.

    B. **Incorrect:** The Active Directory Recycle Bin was not introduced in the Windows Server 2008 forest functional level.

    C. **Correct:** Windows Server 2008 R2 forest functional levels were the first to support the Active Directory Recycle Bin.

    D. **Incorrect:** Although Windows Server 2012 forest functional levels support the Active Directory Recycle Bin, they were not the first.

4. **Correct answers:** A, B, C

    A. **Correct:** The Windows Server 2003 forest functional level supports Windows Server 2012 domain controllers, but the Windows Server 2012 domain and forest functional levels require Windows Server 2012 domain controllers.

    B. **Correct:** Windows Server 2008 domain controllers cannot be used in a domain or forest at the Windows Server 2012 functional level.

    C. **Correct:** The Windows Server 2012 domain and forest functional levels do not support domain controllers running Windows Server 2008 R2.

    D. **Incorrect:** Windows Server 2012 domain controllers must be used in Windows Server 2012 forests.

5. **Correct answers:** B, D

    A. **Incorrect:** Windows 8 clients do not support the authentication constraints placed on members of the Protected Users group in a Windows Server 2012 R2 domain.

    B. **Correct:** Windows 8.1 clients support the authentication constraints added in the Windows Server 2012 R2 domain functional level when the user is a member of the Protected Users group.

    C. **Incorrect:** The authentication protections employed for members of the Protected Users group require a Windows Server 2012 R2 domain functional level, which is not supported in a domain with Windows Server 2012 domain controllers.

    D. **Correct:** For the Protected Users group to have its authentication protected, a Windows Server 2012 R2 domain functional level must be reached, requiring Windows Server 2012 R2 domain controllers.

6. **Correct answer:** A

    A. **Correct:** The domain migration tool enables you to move users, computers, and groups between domains. These objects can retain access to resources in the old domain by using SID history.

    B. **Incorrect:** A forest trust enables two forests to share resources, but does not move objects between forests.

    C. **Incorrect:** Although an external trust is used between two domains in different forests, it is used to share resources and not move objects between forests.

    D. **Incorrect:** Domain rename can be used to relocate domains within forests and relocate the objects, but it cannot be used to move Active Directory objects to another domain.

7. **Correct answer:** D

   A. **Incorrect:** A domain upgrade brings your domain functional level up, but it does not change the domain's location in the forest.

   B. **Incorrect:** Domain migrations move objects between domains, not the actual domain.

   C. **Incorrect:** A forest trust enables sharing of resources between forests; it does not change your forest structure.

   D. **Correct:** The domain rename tool enables you to change your forest structure by changing a domain's location in the domain namespace.

8. **Correct answer:** D

   A. **Incorrect:** The Windows Server 2012 forest functional level does not enable authentication to cloud services by itself.

   B. **Incorrect:** Forest trusts enable shared resources and authentication between forests, but do not enable authentication to cloud services.

   C. **Incorrect:** Realm trusts are used to share resources with a Kerberos realm, not cloud services.

   D. **Correct:** A hybrid cloud infrastructure enables you to provide SSO capabilities to cloud services for your users.

9. **Correct answer:** A

   A. **Correct:** Two-factor authentication is supported for Azure AD Free, not only Azure AD Premium.

   B. **Incorrect:** Azure AD Free supports only 500,000 objects.

   C. **Incorrect:** FIM support is not provided in Azure AD Free; only DirSync is supported for synchronizing objects from your on-premises Active Directory forest.

   D. **Incorrect:** Although Azure AD Free is reliable, SLA-backed high availability is supported only in Azure AD Premium.

10. **Correct answers:** B, C

   A. **Incorrect:** Azure AD Free supports SSO.

   B. **Correct:** An STS such as AD FS is required to support SSO to cloud applications such as Office 365.

   C. **Correct:** DirSync is required to synchronize security principals to Azure AD.

   D. **Incorrect:** The Windows Server 2012 forest functional level is not required to support SSO.

Objective 4.2: Thought experiment

1. Domain rename enables you to break down each domain into its own forest root domain.

2. Regional domains within large countries/regions need to be built manually, but objects can be migrated to these domains using the ADMT.

3. There would be a loss of global administration and users would not be able to log on to domains in other countries/regions. Using forest trusts enables cross-forest authentication.

Objective 4.2: Review

1. **Correct answers:** A, C, D

   A. **Correct:** Rendom.exe is the executable that actually performs the domain rename operation.

   B. **Incorrect:** Admt.exe is the ADMT, which is used for domain migrations, not domain rename.

   C. **Correct:** Repadmin.exe enables you to manage replication between domain controllers, which helps the domain rename process.

   D. **Correct:** Gpfixup.exe is used to repair GPOs after a domain rename, changing their domain association from the old name to the new.

2. **Correct answer:** D

   A. **Incorrect:** The rendom /upload command provides the domain rename script to the domain naming master.

   B. **Incorrect:** The rendom /prepare command can be used to check the readiness of domain controllers throughout the forest to run the execute command.

   C. **Incorrect:** The domain rename begins when the rendom /execute command is given.

   D. **Correct:** The repadmin /syncall command enables you to force replication to the domain controllers in your forest.

3. **Correct answers:** B, C

   A. **Incorrect:** The Guid contains the unique identifier for the domain and cannot be changed.

   B. **Correct:** The DNSname determines the FQDN for the domain and should be changed if the domain is to be renamed.

   C. **Correct:** The NetBiosName contains the NetBios name for the domain and can be changed.

   D. **Incorrect:** The DcName does not need to be changed during the domain rename. Domain controllers are renamed after the domain rename process is complete.

4. **Correct answers:** A, D

    A. **Correct:** After a forest structure is changed, redundant shortcut trusts can remain. These shortcut trusts can be safely deleted.

    B. **Incorrect:** User password resets are unnecessary after a domain rename.

    C. **Incorrect:** No migration of objects is required after a domain rename. Existing objects remain in their domain throughout the process.

    D. **Correct:** Domain controllers must be renamed if their FQDNs have changed.

5. **Correct answers:** A, B

    A. **Correct:** Domain preparation occurs as part of the Active Directory Domain Services Configuration Wizard.

    B. **Correct:** The forest preparation step is handled automatically by the Active Directory Domain Services Configuration Wizard.

    C. **Incorrect:** Domain functional level upgrades do not occur during domain controller deployment and must be triggered manually.

    D. **Incorrect:** Forest functional level changes must be handled manually.

6. **Correct answer:** C

    A. **Incorrect:** Shortcut trusts are used exclusively to provide improved authentication performance between two domains in the same forest.

    B. **Incorrect:** Forest trusts enable authentication across forests.

    C. **Correct:** An object's SID history enables it to retain access to resources throughout a domain migration.

    D. **Incorrect:** Password retention enables users to continue to authenticate to the network, but it does not affect their authorization to resources.

7. **Correct answers:** B, D

    A. **Incorrect:** MSAs are copied between domains, not moved.

    B. **Correct:** User accounts are moved in an intraforest domain migration.

    C. **Incorrect:** Computer objects are copied in an intraforest domain migration.

    D. **Correct:** Group objects are moved between domains in an intraforest migration.

8. **Correct answer:** C

    A. **Incorrect:** The admt user option migrates the user object, but does not modify the security on local user profiles.

    B. **Incorrect:** The admt computer command moves computer objects without configuring local user profiles.

    C. **Correct:** Running admt security alters the permissions and configures local user profiles.

    D. **Incorrect:** The admt profile command is invalid.

9. **Correct answer:** B

   A. **Incorrect:** Domain migration is not the best solution for synchronizing objects with a test forest.

   B. **Correct:** FIM provides the flexibility needed to synchronize objects with Active Directory test forests.

   C. **Incorrect:** Domain rename cannot be used to synchronize objects between domains or forests.

   D. **Incorrect:** Active Directory replication synchronizes the Active Directory database between domain controllers and does not copy objects into other domains or forests.

10. **Correct answers:** A, B, D

    A. **Correct:** Inbound synchronization is supported by FIM and enables objects to be brought into the forest from another source.

    B. **Correct:** Outbound synchronization is supported by FIM and can be used to move objects from a production forest to a test forest.

    C. **Incorrect:** User profile migration is a feature of ADMT, not FIM.

    D. **Correct:** FIM enables you to synchronize users based on rule conditions.

Objective 4.3: Thought experiment

1. Creating a GPO with the required configuration, linking it to the domain, and setting the GPO to enforced ensure that the settings in the GPO are applied to all computers within the domain.

2. Using site-linked GPOs is the perfect solution for this problem. Users moving between sites receive the configuration for their current location.

3. Slow-link processing enables you to manage the way GPOs are applied over slow links.

4. Group Policy caching, a new feature in Windows Server 2012 R2, enables your servers to apply the cached copy of the GPO in this scenario.

5. AGPM (with its role-based access control) enables local administrators to create GPOs and also enables you to stage and test the policies prior to implementation.

Objective 4.3: Review

1. **Correct answer:** A

   A. **Correct:** Inheritance blocking prevents GPOs applied at higher levels of the domain from being applied to the OU unless those GPOs are enforced.

   B. **Incorrect:** Enforced GPOs bypass blocked inheritance; they do not block inheritance.

   C. **Incorrect:** Security filtering enables you to restrict a GPO to a list of users, computers, or groups; it does not alter inheritance.

   D. **Incorrect:** WMI filtering is used to target specific computers meeting certain criteria, such as processor type and computer manufacturer.

2. **Correct answer:** B

    A.   **Incorrect:** Inheritance blocking prevents GPOs from higher levels of the domain to be applied to an OU.

    B.   **Correct:** Enforced policies bypass inheritance blocking and receive precedence over other GPOs that might apply to an OU.

    C.   **Incorrect:** Security filtering does not bypass inheritance blocking.

    D.   **Incorrect:** WMI filters are blocked by inheritance blocking.

3. **Correct answer:** C

    A.   **Incorrect:** GPOs applied at the domain level are placed below a GPO applied to the OU or any enforced GPO.

    B.   **Incorrect:** A GPO applied to an OU has a lower precedence than any enforced GPO.

    C.   **Correct:** Enforced GPOs at the domain level have higher precedence over those applied to an OU.

    D.   **Incorrect:** GPOs enforced at the OU level have a lower precedence than those applied above them in the domain.

4. **Correct answer:** B

    A.   **Incorrect:** Enforced GPOs surpass other GPOs that might be applied at a lower level, but not those of the user.

    B.   **Correct:** Loopback processing enables the computer configuration to be applied last, thus ensuring that it receives precedence.

    C.   **Incorrect:** WMI filtering is used to apply a configuration to a computer, but it does not alter the order in which the configurations are applied.

    D.   **Incorrect:** Security filtering does not accomplish the goal of applying the computer configuration, regardless of the user.

5. **Correct answer:** C

    A.   **Incorrect:** Loopback processing prioritizes the computer configuration over the user, but you cannot target computers meeting specific criteria.

    B.   **Incorrect:** Enforced policies do not allow you to target computers in this way.

    C.   **Correct:** WMI filters allow you to target computers with this level of specificity.

    D.   **Incorrect:** Security filtering is not the best fit for this scenario.

6. **Correct answer:** C

    A.   **Incorrect:** Security filters can be used in this scenario, but they are not the best solution.

    B.   **Incorrect:** Enforced policies do not meet this need.

    C.   **Correct:** Site-linked GPOs enable you to target users or computers connecting at a specific Active Directory site.

    D.   **Incorrect:** Loopback processing does not help in this scenario.

7. **Correct answers:** A, C, D

   A. **Correct:** Role-based access control is included in AGPM and allows more control over what individual users can do with GPOs.

   B. **Incorrect:** Group Policy caching is a new feature in Windows Server 2012 R2; it is not tied to AGPM.

   C. **Correct:** Change tracking support in AGPM enables you to manage changes to GPOs and provides improved troubleshooting capability.

   D. **Correct:** Individual GPOs can be rolled back using AGPM, giving you an easy way to quickly resolve problems caused by newly implemented GPOs.

8. **Correct answer:** A

   A. **Correct:** Deployed GPOs can be rolled back because of the AGPM archive.

   B. **Incorrect:** Although change control enables creating, reviewing, and deploying GPOs, GPO rollback is a function of the AGPM archive.

   C. **Incorrect:** Role-based delegation is used to configure what tasks an administrator can perform.

   D. **Incorrect:** The import and export features of AGPM do not affect GPO rollback.

9. **Correct answers:** B, D

   A. **Incorrect:** Site-linked GPOs do not improve performance over slow network connections.

   B. **Correct:** Slow-link processing enables you to configure which aspects of a GPO are processed over slow network connections.

   C. **Incorrect:** Loopback processing is used to give the Computer Configuration precedence over the User Configuration; it does not improve performance over slow links.

   D. **Correct:** Group Policy caching improves performance over slow network connections for GPOs applied in synchronous mode.

10. **Correct answer:** C

    A. **Correct:** Loopback processing does not determine whether cached GPOs are used.

    B. **Incorrect:** Slow-link processing does not enable GPO caching.

    C. **Correct:** GPOs processed in synchronous mode can use cached GPOs to improve performance over slow network connections.

    D. **Incorrect:** Enforced GPOs have no impact on cached GPOs.

Objective 4.4: Thought experiment

1. By placing each user class in its own OU, you can delegate different permissions to each type of user.

2. Active Directory quotas meet this requirement perfectly.

3. Creating a security group containing these corporate administrators and giving them permissions over the AdminSDHolder gives the appropriate permissions over these restricted groups.

4. There are two solutions: You can either increase the user's quota or change the owner of the objects that were created by the user, ideally through an automated method such as a script.

Objective 4.4: Review

1. **Correct answers:** A, C
    A. **Correct:** Editing the Security tab directly enables you to configure Active Directory object permissions.
    B. **Incorrect:** Adding a user to a group does not change the permissions on the object.
    C. **Correct:** The Delegation of Control Wizard provides quick and easy access to set permissions on an object in Active Directory.
    D. **Incorrect:** The AdminSDHolder object is used to manage the permissions only on sensitive administrative objects such as Enterprise Admins.

2. **Correct answer:** C
    A. **Incorrect:** When quotas are assigned to a user through other means, the default quota is not used.
    B. **Incorrect:** When multiple quotas are assigned to a user, the highest quota value is used.
    C. **Correct:** This quota assignment is the highest total of the three assigned to the user, so it is used.
    D. **Incorrect:** When Active Directory quotas are assigned to a user through group membership or directly to the user object, the quota assignation has no bearing on the resulting quota limitations.

3. **Correct answer:** A

   A. **Correct:** The dsadd quota command is used to assign a quota to a security principal, either a user or a security group.

   B. **Incorrect:** The dsget command can be used to determine the quota assigned to a security principal.

   C. **Incorrect:** PowerShell cmdlets for managing Active Directory quotas are not yet available; dsadd quota should be used.

   D. **Incorrect:** PowerShell cmdlets for managing Active Directory quotas are not yet available; dsadd quota should be used.

4. **Correct answers:** B, D

   A. **Incorrect:** Renaming a domain does not create new objects within a domain or change object ownership. Quotas should have no bearing on this action.

   B. **Correct:** Domain migrations create or update large numbers of objects in the target domain. The user performing the migration should not be constrained by quotas.

   C. **Incorrect:** DirSync to Azure AD has no impact on user quotas.

   D. **Correct:** Mass user creation through automation such as PowerShell scripts will encounter problems if quotas are reached.

5. **Correct answer:** D

   A. **Incorrect:** A reboot is not needed to make the admin tools available.

   B. **Incorrect:** The RSAT for Windows 8 and Windows 8.1 do not require you to enable the tools after installation.

   C. **Incorrect:** You do not need to update Group Policy after installing RSAT.

   D. **Correct:** Installing RSAT should be the only step needed to gain access to the tools.

6. **Correct answer:** B

   A. **Incorrect:** Changing the object's ACL directly results in it being overwritten within an hour.

   B. **Correct:** Modifying the ACL on the AdminSDHolder object results in the object's ACL being configured correctly.

   C. **Incorrect:** The Delegation of Control Wizard edits only the ACL of the object, resulting in the ACL reverting to its prior state.

   D. **Incorrect:** The Run As Administrator option does not have any result on the object's ACL.

7. **Correct answer:** D

    A.   **Incorrect:** Active Directory Users And Computers cannot be used to define permissions on the AdminSDHolder object.

    B.   **Incorrect:** You cannot use the Active Directory Administrative Center (ADAC) to configure the ACL of the AdminSDHolder object.

    C.   **Incorrect:** Permissions on the AdminSDHolder object cannot be configured using the Delegation of Control Wizard.

    D.   **Correct:** ADSI Edit should be used to configure permissions on the AdminSDHolder object.

8. **Correct answer:** C

    A.   **Incorrect:** Kerberos delegations do not affect object permissions in Active Directory.

    B.   **Incorrect:** Kerberos delegations are not used in conjunction with realm trusts.

    C.   **Correct:** Delegations enable a computer to authenticate as a user.

    D.   **Incorrect:** Kerberos delegations do not provide authentication to UNIX users.

9. **Correct answer:** B

    A.   **Incorrect:** Kerberos constrained delegation to individual computers has been supported since Windows Server 2003.

    B.   **Correct:** Limiting Kerberos constrained delegation to individual services is a new feature in Windows Server 2012.

    C.   **Incorrect:** Configuring delegation with PowerShell is not a new feature in Windows Server 2012.

    D.   **Incorrect:** Cross-domain Kerberos constrained delegation has been supported since Windows Server 2003.

CHAPTER 5

Design and implement an Active Directory infrastructure (physical)

The previous chapter covered Active Directory's logical structure, which is built using objects such as forests, domains, and organizational units (OUs). Whereas the logical makeup of Active Directory is primarily used to create a management structure for applying Group Policy and delegation of permissions, the physical structure is used to shape and manage replication and authentication traffic.

To authenticate to Active Directory, users must be able to contact a domain controller. SRV records in Domain Name System (DNS) are used to direct network clients to domain controllers for authentication, which is important when there are no domain controllers for the required domain in the user's current site. There are also some complexities introduced when a user from one domain is a member of groups in another domain (this issue of interdomain authentication is discussed later in this chapter). Ideally, every location in your organization would contain at least two domain controllers to provide high availability to a local domain controller, but this scenario is often impossible (for many different reasons).

The other type of Active Directory network traffic is replication. Active Directory replication works in different ways, depending on the scope of the replication. For example, domain controllers within the same site perform replication as objects are modified, and intersite replication occurs in 15-minute intervals to optimize efficiency through compression. Although these intervals can be configured as replication windows, which disables intersite replication during certain time frames, many organizations require intersite replication to occur throughout the day. A large part of designing the site structure in Active Directory involves optimizing intersite replication, ensuring that the replication schedule fits the requirements of the organization and that the paths used by replication traffic are efficient and cost effective.

The physical design of your Active Directory implementation is based on balancing the network traffic required for replication with authentication. This balance is necessary, while still meeting the constraints of cost, physical security, administration capabilities, and corporate policy.

Objectives in this chapter:

- Objective 5.1: Design an Active Directory sites topology
- Objective 5.2: Design a domain controller strategy
- Objective 5.3: Design and implement a branch office infrastructure

Objective 5.1: Design an Active Directory sites topology

The site topology in an Active Directory forest defines the physical locations within your organization and enables you to specify which locations contain domain controllers. Replication and authentication traffic use this structure to determine the most efficient path between domain controllers. By defining the site structure of your organization, Active Directory member computers can automatically connect to the domain controller within the site where they are currently connected. Sites can also be used to enhance printer discovery, telling clients where to find a local printer. (Chapter 4 discusses how sites can be used to link Group Policy Objects to streamline client configuration for location-specific requirements.)

In addition to using sites to define locations in an organization, Active Directory uses site links to define which sites are allowed to pass replication and authentication traffic and the path that this network traffic must take. Site links are a major part of your replication strategy because they are the primary tool for shaping and optimizing intersite traffic throughout your forest.

Both replication and authentication traffic should be considered when you design your physical Active Directory topology. It might be completely acceptable within your organization for intersite replication traffic to occur hours apart, but an intersite authentication requirement can significantly alter the design of your site and site link structure. Conversely, your organization might use intersite authentication only on rare occasions, but if frequent replication is required due to application requirements or centralized administration, you have to take this requirement into account during the design phase of your topology.

> **This objective covers how to:**
> - Plan for domain controller proximity
> - Optimize replication
> - Design site links
> - Identify and resolve Active Directory replication conflicts

Planning for domain controller proximity

In an ideal situation, every site in an Active Directory would have a domain controller with the necessary information to authenticate any user within the forest. Unfortunately, many companies cannot place a domain controller in each corporate location, either due to a lack of physical security, the cost of deploying domain controllers to every location, or mobile workers who do not have a physical office space. Fortunately, Active Directory was built to take on these challenges.

Besides being dispersed throughout an enterprise to optimize authentication performance, domain controllers in large or critical locations should be redundant. Having multiple domain controllers in a single location prevents authentication failures due to a single domain controller being offline. Instead of having multiple domain controllers within each site, ensure that authentication traffic can be routed efficiently to the next best offsite domain controller.

Figure 5-1 illustrates these concepts: Each of the four primary sites has two domain controllers, ensuring availability for authentication, even if one domain controller is unavailable. The two branch sites linked to the primary sites have no domain controllers, so their authentication traffic must be routed to the closest primary site.

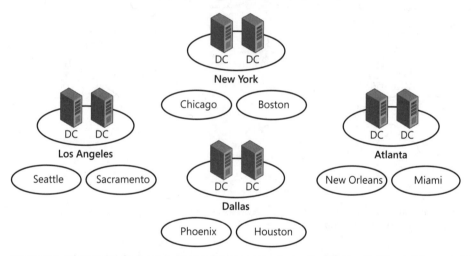

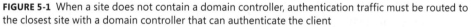

FIGURE 5-1 When a site does not contain a domain controller, authentication traffic must be routed to the closest site with a domain controller that can authenticate the client

In addition to client-domain controller proximity, there are some specific domain controllers in every Active Directory forest that need to be identified and incorporated into your plan for domain controller placement. Specifically, domain controllers that perform operations master roles or act as a global catalog server should be strategically located throughout your enterprise. Operations masters are critical for management aspects of Active Directory: They facilitate changes to the Active Directory schema, change passwords, and issue pools of ID numbers required for object creation. Although some operations master roles are performed by a single domain controller for the entire forest, others are handled by one domain controller in each domain (see Figure 5-2). Global catalog servers can help the balance between replication and authentication traffic by reducing the need for interdomain communication. (Operations master roles are discussed in more detail in Objective 5.2; global catalog servers are discussed in Objective 5.3.)

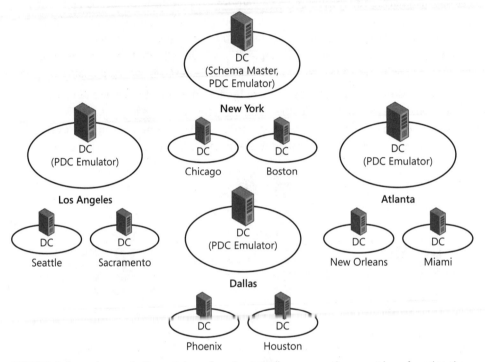

FIGURE 5-2 Even when each site contains a domain controller, some actions must be referred to the domain controller performing an operations master role

Forest root domain controllers enable users to authenticate between different domains in the same forest. Although domain controllers in a forest root domain usually reside in one or more centralized datacenters to optimize cross-domain authentication, sometimes it is necessary to place a forest root domain within specific sites to facilitate authentication between domains. Distributing domain controllers in the forest root throughout the site topology can facilitate authentication between domains or to applications operating in the forest root (see Figure 5-3).

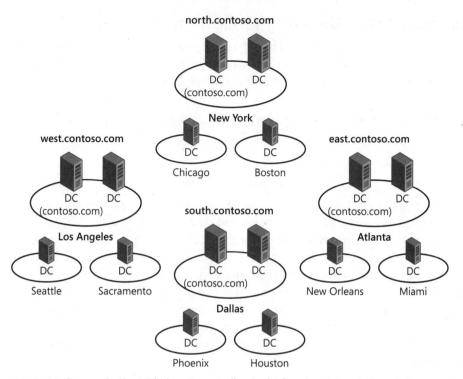

north.contoso.com

DC DC
(contoso.com)

New York

west.contoso.com

DC
Chicago

DC
Boston

east.contoso.com

DC DC
(contoso.com)

DC DC
(contoso.com)

south.contoso.com

Los Angeles

DC
Seattle

DC
Sacramento

DC DC
(contoso.com)

Atlanta

DC
New Orleans

DC
Miami

Dallas

DC
Phoenix

DC
Houston

FIGURE 5-3 Communication with domain controllers in the forest root domain is sometimes required to facilitate cross-domain authentication

Remember that shortcut trusts can also be used to improve authentication to specific domains within the forest. Domain controllers in the forest root can also be heavily relied on by applications that integrate with Active Directory. Keep these factors in mind when you plan the placement of your domain controllers.

Be sure to consider application partitions when you plan domain controller proximity. If you use application partitions to manage replication of DNS or other data in Active Directory, you might want to add a domain controller from each to the application partition so the information stored in the partition is readily available to users.

Many applications integrate with Active Directory for identity and authentication purposes or for various other reasons. Placing a domain controller in close proximity to these application servers can help facilitate communication from the application to the domain controller, potentially improving application performance.

Optimizing Active Directory replication

The goal of Active Directory replication is to limit convergence, which is the amount of time between when an object is changed and when that change has been communicated to all applicable domain controllers. Latency can be the cause of several common problems within an Active Directory forest:

- Authentication failures due to delays in password changes
- Authorization errors due to group membership changes
- Inconsistent application of Group Policy
- Name-resolution failures for Active Directory–integrated DNS zones

Within a single site, replication latency is typically very low because the network connectivity between domain controllers is both fast and stable. Replication within a site occurs whenever an object is updated to prevent user authentication or authorization from being erroneously denied. Logon failures can occur if a user's password is updated on one domain controller and the user tries to authenticate by using another domain controller prior to the change being replicated. Because Active Directory sites typically represent a segment of the corporate network with fast and stable connectivity, replication traffic between domain controllers within a site is transmitted without compression. Although the lack of compression does lead to a negligible increase in bandwidth utilization, it reduces the overhead introduced with the compression and decompression process.

Each site contains an NTDS Site Settings node that contains a replication schedule within the site (see Figure 5-4). Because replication occurs automatically whenever an object is modified within the domain, this schedule is used only if no changes are made within the configured time frame. You should not modify this schedule.

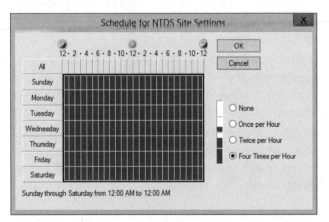

FIGURE 5-4 Replication within a site occurs whenever an object is updated; if no changes are made to objects, the replication occurs based on the site's replication schedule

The replication topology within a site, which is created automatically by the Active Directory Knowledge Consistency Checker (KCC), is ring-shaped. Object changes are replicated around the ring in both directions, limiting the latency (see Figure 5-5).

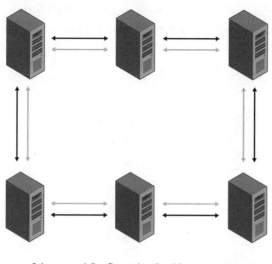

➤ Schema and Configuration Partitions
➤ Domain Partitions

FIGURE 5-5 Within a single site with seven or fewer domain controllers and a single domain, partition replication occurs bidirectionally in a ring until all domain controllers are updated

In sites with more than seven domain controllers in the same domain, the ring can be optimized with a shortcut that splits the ring and reduces the time needed for a replication cycle to complete (see Figure 5-6).

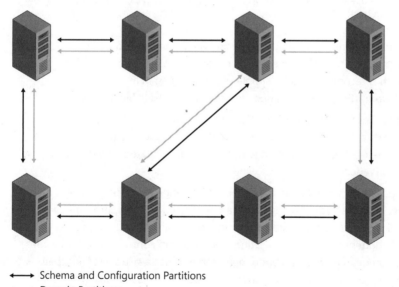

➤ Schema and Configuration Partitions
➤ Domain Partitions

FIGURE 5-6 When a single site contains more than seven domain controllers hosting a single domain, replication is optimized with a shortcut that splits the ring and reduces replication latency

When domain controllers from multiple domains are contained within the same site, the replication topology becomes more complex. Although the common partitions (schema and configuration) are replicated in a ring topology spanning the entire site, separate ring topologies are created for each domain within the site. This configuration, which is automated by the KCC, is shown in Figure 5-7.

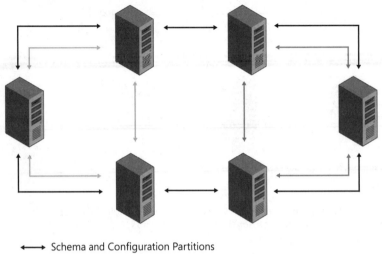

→ Schema and Configuration Partitions
→ Domain A
→ Domain B

FIGURE 5-7 When multiple domains are contained within a single site, a replication ring topology is created for each partition being replicated

Intersite replication is more complex due to the limitations introduced by network connectivity over long ranges. Active Directory can automatically manage intersite replication, which is recommended for simple site topologies. In more complex site topologies, replication traffic can be managed with site links and site link bridges.

Replication across sites is optimized by the KCC, which analyzes site links and site link bridges to perform replication through the path with the lowest cost. Intersite replication occurs in intervals instead of being triggered when objects are updated. The default interval of 180 minutes can be reduced to 15-minute windows.

Changes to objects in Active Directory are collected by bridgehead servers, which manage intersite replication. Multiple bridgehead servers can be located within a site, depending on the domains and other partitions hosted within that site. Active Directory enables you to define preferred bridgehead servers, indicating which domain controllers you want to use to perform replication. If a preferred bridgehead server is not available (or not available to replicate a particular partition), replication for the directory partitions not hosted by an available preferred bridgehead server cannot complete. It is recommended to enable Active Directory to perform a bridgehead server manually to allow for automatic failover if a bridgehead server becomes unreachable.

Figure 5-8 shows a scenario in which a preferred bridgehead server cannot be used to complete replication for a domain partition. Site 1 contains two preferred bridgehead servers, but the domain partition containing the north.contoso.com domain cannot be replicated using either of these servers. In this scenario, the north.contoso.com domain cannot be replicated between the two sites.

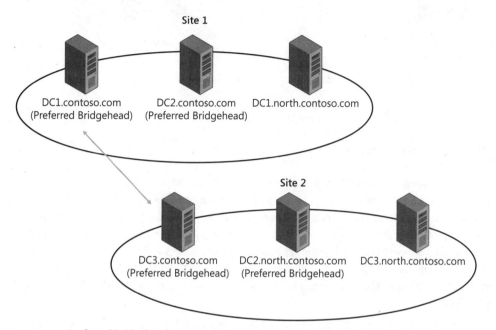

FIGURE 5-8 Preferred bridgehead servers perform replication unless a partition within the site cannot be replicated by using one of these servers

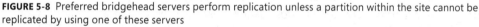

When a replication interval is reached, the replication traffic is compressed and transmitted to a bridgehead server in another site. Because a larger amount of data is being transmitted during each replication cycle for intersite replication, and the network links are typically slower than those within the site, compressing the replication traffic improves efficiency between sites.

Three aspects of intersite replication should always be considered to minimize latency and ensure the most efficient replication strategy. The first aspect is the replication path, which is defined by site links and site link bridges. By default, all site links are bridged, which enables Active Directory to manage these paths for you; but automatic site link bridging can be disabled in the IP transport method properties, which enables you to manage site link bridging manually. The primary goal of using the replication path is to lessen the number of steps required for replication to be completed, thereby limiting replication latency.

Figure 5-9 shows four site links: NY-ATL, NY-LA, DAL-LA, and DAL-ATL. Without bridging, two replication cycles are required before changes from the New York site reach Dallas.

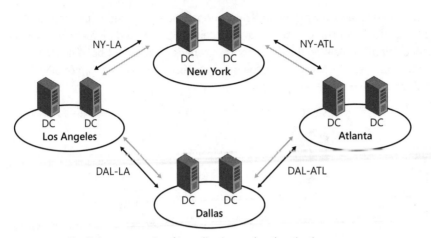

FIGURE 5-9 Site links connect sites for replication and authentication purposes

The second aspect of intersite replication includes the schedule and interval. An Active Directory replication schedule refers to the periods throughout the day when intersite replication is permitted. The replication schedule enables you to control whether you want replication to occur during normal business hours or only during off-peak hours. The replication interval configures how often the replication process occurs within the schedule. If your replication schedule is configured to allow replication throughout the day, and the interval is configured to initiate replication every 15 minutes, replication is triggered 96 times throughout the day.

The third aspect of intersite replication is Active Directory partitions. In an Active Directory forest, several partitions are used to store data (for example, the schema and configuration partitions have a forest-wide replication scope). Each domain in Active Directory is contained within its own partition and is replicated only to domain controllers within that domain. Application directory partitions are replicated to domain controllers that are specifically configured to maintain a copy of that partition.

When you consider all these factors of intersite replication, you see that replication between sites must be configured to limit latency for each Active Directory partition. The path and replication schedule should be managed so that replication requiring multiple steps occurs as quickly as possible. Ensure that domain partitions can be successfully replicated between sites, even if direct links must be created between sites that contain domain controllers from certain domains.

Designing site links

Site links are used to configure replication between two or more Active Directory sites. By configuring the cost associated with a site link, you can manage the way replication traffic travels through your site structure. Replication can be optimized and managed using site links, replication frequency, and the replication schedule. Each of these site links is viable only if at least two sites within a site link contain a domain controller hosting a copy of a partition to be replicated. If each of the branch offices shown in Figure 5-10 hosts its own domain, and no domain controllers from those domains exist outside of the site, the partitions hosting those domains are not replicated to the New York site or to the other branches.

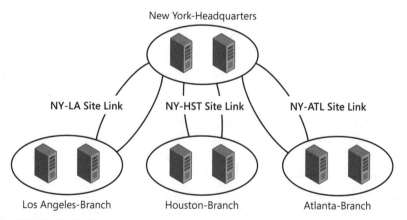

FIGURE 5-10 Site links enable you to shape replication traffic between sites

Site links perform several replication-related tasks. They define which sites can replicate to each other. Each site link contains a cost that is used by the KCC to determine the optimal replication path between sites. Site links also manage the replication schedule and interval, determining which times of day replication traffic is allowed and how frequently replication should be initiated during these windows.

By default, all site links are bridged; they are transitive, and any site can replicate to another site containing a domain controller that hosts a copy of the partition being replicated (assuming that replication schedules coincide). Clearing the Bridge All Site Links check box in the IP or SMTP Inter-Site transports (see Figure 5-11) and configuring site link bridges enables you to manage the sites that can replicate directly.

FIGURE 5-11 Properties of the IP Inter-Site transport, showing the Bridge All Site Links check box

Transitivity between site links through site link bridges or the Bridge All Site Links option can significantly reduce replication latency between sites. Although bridging all site links does relinquish a level of manual control over replication traffic, the shape of replication is managed automatically by the KCC. Manual configuration of site link bridges is recommended only for large deployments with a complex site structure.

Two time factors affect intersite replication. The replication schedule within a site link determines when the link can be used for replication and when replication traffic should be held until the next window. The interval determines how often the replication process should be performed during the replication window.

It is important to understand how site link schedules affect transitivity. When two sites containing a domain controller that hosts a copy of the same partition are connected through bridging, they can communicate with each other through a common site when replication on both links is triggered simultaneously. By using site link bridges, you can reduce the number of hops required for replication traffic, thereby reducing latency. Because bridged replication traffic occurs only when replication is triggered simultaneously for two bridged site links, the maximum replication interval for the two bridged site links is the resulting interval for replication traffic travelling across the bridge.

Figure 5-12 illustrates this concept. The NY-ATL and DAL-ATL site links are bridged and have replication frequencies of 30 minutes and 15 minutes, respectively. Every other time the Dallas and Atlanta sites perform replication, the New York and Atlanta sites perform replication simultaneously. The site link bridge enables replication to travel between New York and Dallas in a single replication session.

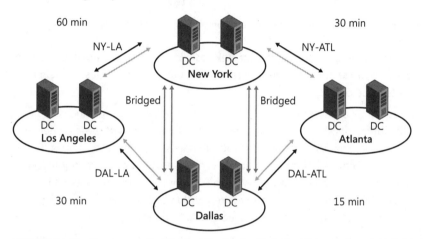

FIGURE 5-12 The frequency of bridged replication traffic is the highest value of the bridged site links

If the shared partner site is unavailable during the replication window, or if no domain controller hosting the partition is available, the two sites can communicate directly. Remember to consider time zone differences when you create replication schedules.

To illustrate these concepts, consider the following scenarios. An organization has three sites: corporate headquarters in New York and branch offices in Los Angeles and Seattle. Site links are created between each branch office and the New York headquarters site.

When the site links are not bridged, changes made in the Los Angeles site require two steps to complete replication to Seattle, regardless of the synchronization schedules (see Figure 5-13). This multistep process also occurs when the two site links are bridged but replication schedules do not coincide.

FIGURE 5-13 Site links without a site link bridge can result in multiple steps

If the site links are bridged, and replication for the two links occurs simultaneously (see Figure 5-14), replication traffic is passed through the common site in a single replication pass. Even if the common replication partner is unavailable or does not contain a domain controller hosting a copy of the partition being replicated, the two branch sites can replicate directly through the site link bridge.

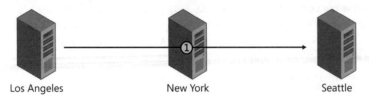

Los Angeles　　　　　　　　New York　　　　　　　　Seattle

FIGURE 5-14 Replication across a site link bridge can be accomplished in a single replication cycle

When site links are bridged, the sum of the site link costs in the replication path is used to calculate the aggregate cost that determines the replication path. Site links must contain a common partner site to be bridged.

Several strategies can be used to perform replication between sites in large and complex topologies. A couple of factors should be considered to determine which of these strategies best fits your organization. The first factor is how your domain structure matches up with your site structure. Some Active Directory partitions, such as the schema and configuration partitions, must be replicated throughout the entire forest. Domain partitions have to be replicated only to sites with domain controllers within that domain. Your site link strategy should be designed specifically to optimize replication for partitions.

Figure 5-15 shows an example of replication scopes for partitions in a forest. The schema and configuration partitions must be replicated throughout the forest, but each domain in the forest has to be replicated only among the three sites represented by that domain. The partitions replicated across the forest are modified with less frequency than domain partitions, which is another factor that you should think about.

Another factor is where changes to Active Directory objects occur (see Figure 5-16). For example, if Active Directory objects are centrally managed, you might need to ensure that replication from the central site occurs quickly to branch sites and be less concerned about replication coming from the branch sites going out to the rest of the forest. As mentioned throughout this chapter, the primary goal is to reduce latency when replicating object changes between sites.

EXAM TIP

Site links and site link bridges form the basis of managing intersite replication traffic in Active Directory. Knowing the process to create and configure these objects and their design is important for the exam.

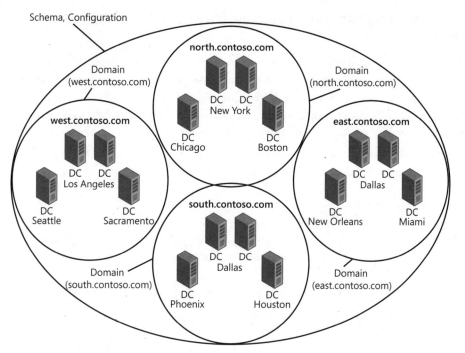

FIGURE 5-15 The replication scope of partitions in Active Directory should be considered when planning a replication strategy

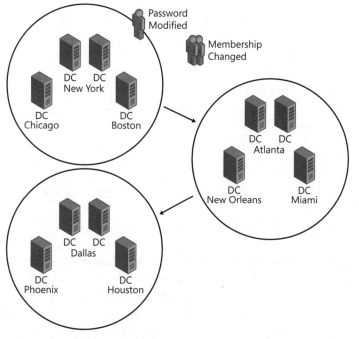

FIGURE 5-16 Administrative actions performed in one site, such as changes to user passwords or group membership, must be replicated before they are reflected in another site

Identifying and resolving Active Directory replication conflicts

In large networks, particularly those spanning wide area network (WAN) links, fluctuations in network connectivity can be expected. Active Directory handles most network problems transparently by resuming replication after connectivity returns, but occasionally troubleshooting is necessary. It is also important to proactively monitor Active Directory replication to optimize the replication process or to identify errors before they become significant problems.

The repadmin command enables you to monitor and test replication. Table 5-1 lists the repadmin commands that can be used to monitor and troubleshoot Active Directory replication.

TABLE 5-1 Repadmin commands

Parameter	Description
/kcc	Initiates recalculation of the incoming replication topology by the KCC on the specified domain controllers ·
/prp	Specifies the Password Replication Policy (PRP) for read-only domain controllers (RODCs)
/queue	Shows inbound replication requests that must be processed by the domain controller to become current with its replication partners
/replicate	Initiates replication of a directory partition between the two specified domain controllers
/replsingleobj	Performs replication of a single object between two domain controllers with a common directory partition
/replsummary	Provides a summary report of domain controllers that fail incoming or outbound replication
/rodepwdrepl	Begins replication of passwords belonging to specified users from a source domain controller to an RODC
/showattr	Shows an object's attributes
/showobjmeta	Displays replication information about an object such as the attribute ID, version number, update sequence numbers (USNs), globally unique identifier (GUID) of the originating server, and date and time stamps
/showrepl	Shows the replication status of the specified domain controller, including when it last attempted inbound replication
/showutdvec	Provides the highest USN that Active Directory has committed on the specified domain controller
/syncall	Synchronizes the domain controller with each of its replication partners

Because of the tight relationship between Active Directory and DNS, many replication errors are actually related to problems in DNS. The dcdiag command-line tool enables you to perform a number of tests related to DNS name resolution and replication. To specifically test replication between DNS servers, you can use the dcdiag /test:replications command. The dcdiag /test:VerifyReplicas command can be used to verify that application directory partitions are properly replicated.

Active Directory replication errors are logged in the Directory Service log of the Event Viewer. Best practice dictates periodically monitoring the Directory Service log for replication errors. The Directory Service log is one of the first places you should look if you experience replication problems.

EXAM TIP

You should be familiar with both the repadmin and dcdiag commands for the exam.

> ## Thought experiment
> ### Planning an Active Directory replication strategy
>
> In this thought experiment, apply what you've learned about this objective. You can find answers to these questions in the "Answers" section at the end of this chapter.
>
> Your consulting firm has been asked to review the physical Active Directory topology of a client and make adjustments to its replication strategy to meet some new requirements. The client company has offices throughout the country, with multiple offices in most states.
>
> 1. Your client wants to limit replication traffic to an hour before and an hour after business hours. Due to time zone differences, the client has not been able to implement this requirement without a high amount of management workload. How could the client implement these changes with minimal effort?
>
> 2. Any changes to the Active Directory domain structure or schema are managed by an administrative team at corporate headquarters. The client wants to ensure that these types of changes occur as efficiently as possible. How could you ensure that the administrative team at corporate headquarters can make changes to the Active Directory domain and schema structure with the greatest efficiency?

Objective summary

- Read-only domain controllers (RODCs) can be used when a domain controller cannot be physically secured.
- The physical placement of domain controllers that perform operations master roles should be carefully planned to improve efficiency in tasks such as password changes and schema modifications.
- Site links and site link bridges enable you to change the shape and schedule of intersite Active Directory replication.
- Replication problems can be diagnosed by using the repadmin and dcdiag command-line tools.

Objective review

Answer the following questions to test your knowledge of the information in this objective. You can find the answers to these questions and explanations of why each answer choice is correct or incorrect in the "Answers" section at the end of this chapter.

1. Which scenario is the best fit for a shortcut trust?

    A. Users are in a site that does not contain a domain controller, which results in a subpar authentication performance.

    B. Cross-domain authentication needs to be improved from one domain to another specific domain.

    C. Authentication requests to the forest root domain need to be optimized.

    D. Replication traffic needs to be prioritized between two specific sites.

2. After configuring site links between three sites (with only one site being contained in both site links), you notice that objects are not being replicated between the two sites that aren't directly connected, even after multiple replication intervals. How could this happen?

    A. The site links are not bridged.

    B. The site links do not have overlapping schedules.

    C. The Bridge All Site Links option is disabled.

    D. The central site does not share the directory partition containing the objects to be replicated.

3. Which option best describes replication within a single site?

    A. Domain controllers from each domain contained within the site form individual ring topologies.

    B. Multiple overlapping bidirectional ring topologies are created, replicating each directory partition contained within the site between the domain controllers hosting a copy of that partition.

    C. All domain controllers in the site perform replication in a bidirectional ring topology.

    D. The replication shape is managed by the KCC, based on the configured site link topology.

4. Users complain that they cannot use their accounts after password resets by the corporate help desk. They state that their accounts become usable after a period of approximately one hour. What might cause this?

    A. Replication latency has resulted in the users' passwords not being written to the domain controller that they are using to authenticate.

    B. The users are attempting to authenticate in a site without a domain controller.

    C. The users are connecting at a site without a domain controller for the domain containing their user object.

    D. The domain controller performing the PDC emulator master role cannot be reached.

5. How can latency in intersite replication be reduced? (Choose all that apply.)

   A. Lessen the number of hops required to complete replication.

   B. Lower the replication interval for site links.

   C. Place a domain controller from each domain in every site.

   D. Place a domain controller from the forest root domain in every site.

6. After selecting two domain controllers as preferred bridgehead servers, you notice that some objects within the site are not being updated properly when changes are made in another site. What might be causing this behavior?

   A. The preferred bridgehead servers are not performing the operations master roles.

   B. A domain controller containing the objects being modified is not available in the local site.

   C. The Active Directory objects have not been modified within the local site.

   D. The preferred bridgehead servers do not host a copy of all directory partitions contained within the site.

7. What conditions must be met for replication to occur across a site link bridge? (Choose all that apply.)

   A. Preferred bridgehead servers must be selected.

   B. A common site between the bridged site links must be available for replication.

   C. A shared directory partition is necessary.

   D. Simultaneous replication intervals must occur.

8. After you configure site links and site link bridges, what other step must you complete to constrain replication traffic to these defined site links and site link bridges?

   A. Clear the Bridge Of All Site Links option in the Inter-Site Transport node.

   B. Reboot the domain controller performing the infrastructure master role.

   C. Delete the DEFAULTIPSITELINK site link.

   D. Ensure that the changes were not made on a read-only domain controller.

9. What command is used to show inbound replication requests?

   A. repadmin /showrepl

   B. repadmin /queue

   C. dcdiag /test:Replications

   D. dcdiag /test:VerifyReplicas

10. Which command can be used to force replication of an object between two domain controllers?

A. repadmin /kcc

B. repadmin /replsingleobj

C. repadmin /replicate

D. repadmin /queue

Objective 5.2: Design a domain controller strategy

A major aspect of designing the physical structure of Active Directory is to ensure that clients and applications can always perform Active Directory tasks such as authentication in the most efficient way. Many of these functions can be performed by any domain controller, but some occur only when the client can communicate with a specific set of domain controllers. These domain controller roles, which are critical to the day-to-day operation of an Active Directory forest, require planning for placement within your enterprise. You should also be able to recognize the symptoms of one of these roles being unavailable to Active Directory.

Each of the tools available to increase performance of a particular action between client and domain controller has side effects or makes other changes to the behavior typically expected from a domain controller. Implementing these solutions in the wrong way can increase replication traffic between sites without offering any benefit for authentication. Understanding the impact of implementing changes to domain controllers helps you properly plan and design a domain controller strategy.

Domain controllers contain the information necessary to access resources throughout your corporate network. Security for domain controllers should start with the physical hardware and continue to the permissions used to control access to Active Directory resources. Some flexibility exists for configuring domain controllers, so you can delegate permissions to subordinate administrators or even deploy domain controllers in locations with limited physical security. You should understand the potential risks of having a domain controller compromised and what steps can be taken to mitigate those risks before and after a compromise occurs.

> **This objective covers how to:**
> - Use the global catalog
> - Optimize operations master roles
> - Plan for read-only domain controller (RODC) placement
> - Understand the partial attribute set
> - Use cloned domain controllers
> - Choose domain controller placement

Using the global catalog

The global catalog contains partial information for all objects within the entire forest. Domain controllers that function as global catalog servers contain full versions of objects within their domain and partial read-only copies of objects from other domains. Global catalog servers provide improved performance when performing searches for Active Directory objects. In these cases, the request to find the Active Directory object can be answered by a global catalog server in the local domain rather than being forwarded outside the domain.

Some circumstances in which the global catalog can be used to improve interaction with Active Directory include these:

- When a user attempts to log on using a User Principal Name (UPN) such as johnsmith@contoso.com, a global catalog server can be used to resolve the UPN.

- When a user who is a member of a universal group from another domain logs on.

- When a user performs a lookup using an Exchange global address list (GAL).

Without a global catalog server, each of these events has to traverse the domain hierarchy and the Active Directory site structure to locate a domain controller capable of performing the required lookup. Figure 5-17 shows the difference between having to traverse the Active Directory structure (User 1) and having a global catalog server available within the local site (User 2).

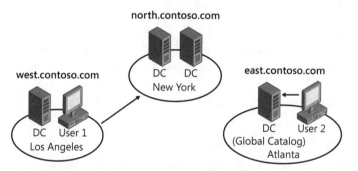

FIGURE 5-17 Deploying a global catalog server can greatly reduce the traffic required to authenticate a user or perform queries for Active Directory objects

A domain controller is configured as a global catalog server within the NTDS Settings properties for the domain controller in Active Directory Sites and Services (see Figure 5-18).

One issue with using global catalog servers is the increased amount of replication required, particularly in large forests with many domains. Replication traffic can be limited by implementing a select number of global catalog servers in each site. Finding a balance between replication and the traffic required to find Active Directory objects can be the most difficult aspect of managing the physical structure of Active Directory.

FIGURE 5-18 The global catalog can be enabled on a domain controller through the NTDS Settings properties for the domain controller

Global catalog servers are of no use in Active Directory forests that consist of a single domain. In a single-domain forest, each domain controller already contains a full writable copy of the entire forest, making the global catalog unnecessary. Large forests with a complex domain structure get the most benefit from deploying global catalog servers, but large forests also exaggerate the increased replication requirements of the partial attribute set.

Optimizing operations master roles

Domain controllers that perform operations master roles, also known as Flexible Single Master Operations (FSMO) roles, manage critical aspects of Active Directory. Three operations roles and two forest-wide operations master roles exist in each domain. Each role and its scope are described in Table 5-2.

TABLE 5-2 Operations master roles in Active Directory

Role	Scope	Description
Schema master	Forest	Maintains the structure of the Active Directory schema, in particular the list of object types and the attributes they contain
Domain naming master	Forest	Contains the domain and forest structure; handles creation and removal of domains in the forest
Primary domain controller (PDC) emulator master	Domain	Performs password changes for the domain and begins replicating the changes to other domain controllers

Role	Scope	Description
Relative ID (RID) master	Domain	Manages ID numbers for the domain, issuing pools to domain controllers to assign to objects as they are created
Infrastructure operations master	Domain	Tracks membership of user principals from other domains for groups within the domain

When an operations master becomes unavailable, different symptoms occur, depending on the role. When the schema master is unavailable, any attempted modifications to the schema fail. Additio n and removal of domains from the forest fail if the domain-naming master is offline. Problems with the RID master result in domain controllers being unable to create new objects after their RID pool is exhausted. Problems with users updating their passwords can be attributed to problems with the PDC emulator master. If the infrastructure master becomes unavailable, problems related to interdomain group membership can occur. Remember that problems related to a missing or unavailable operations master might not be noticed for an extended period of time.

Most actions on Active Directory objects can be accomplished using almost any domain controller. Because certain actions require access to a domain controller performing an operations master role, those servers should be carefully placed to optimize the performance of those actions (they should have network connectivity that is both fast and stable). Depending on the workload involved with handling an operations master role, the domain controllers performing these roles might require additional resources to support the additional workload.

EXAM TIP

You will probably get at least one question on operations master roles in the 70-413 exam. You should know which roles are handled at the forest and domain levels and what each role does for Active Directory.

Planning for read-only domain controller (RODC) placement

Although the primary purpose for RODCs is security (protecting Active Directory from compromised passwords or changes submitted by a rogue domain controller), their use can also have other benefits. Much of the RODC configuration process, such as using the Password Replication Property (PRP) and administrative delegation, is accomplished through the RODC computer object in Active Directory (see Figure 5-19).

The first security benefit of implementing an RODC is that it contains a read-only copy of the Active Directory partitions it hosts, including the domain partition. RODCs are designed to be deployed in environments where the domain controller cannot be properly physically secured. Because the RODC does not perform outgoing replication, there is no potential for a physically compromised domain controller to have objects inserted or modified and then replicated to the rest of the domain. Because all partitions are read-only, RODCs do not perform outgoing replication, so any changes to Active Directory objects are immediately forwarded to a writable domain controller, not replicated from the stored partition. A side benefit of this configuration is that replication traffic is more limited when an RODC is used.

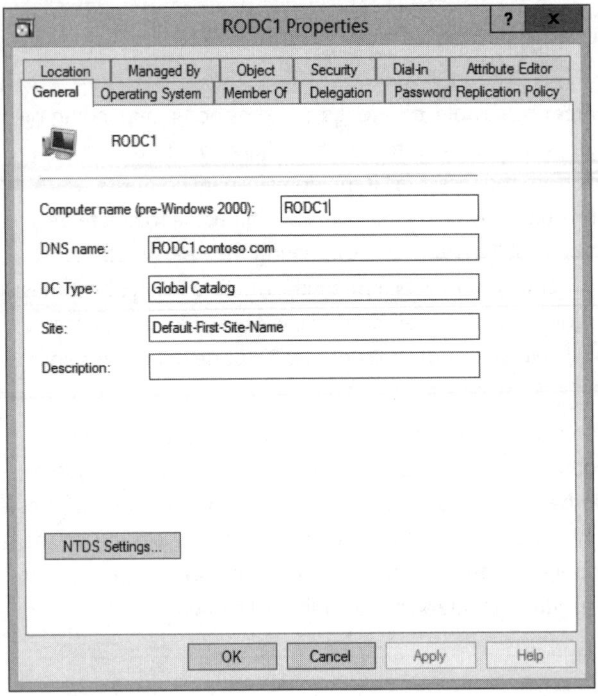

FIGURE 5-19 The properties window for an RODC in Active Directory

Another concern with domain controllers in an insecure location is the potential for passwords or other sensitive information contained within the Active Directory partitions stored on the domain controller to be compromised. RODCs use PRP, which prevents passwords from being cached by default, limiting the capability of malicious users from performing password attacks on a compromised RODC. The Filtered Attribute Set (FAS) can also be configured to manage Active Directory attributes that are replicated to RODCs.

If an RODC is stolen or otherwise compromised, Active Directory immediately remediates the possibility of cached passwords being compromised or the RODC being reintegrated into Active Directory. Deleting the computer object for the RODC triggers a window (shown in Figure 5-20) that asks if you want to reset passwords for user or computer accounts that were cached on the RODC. You can also export a list of the accounts that were cached on the RODC, enabling you to proactively communicate with users who might be affected.

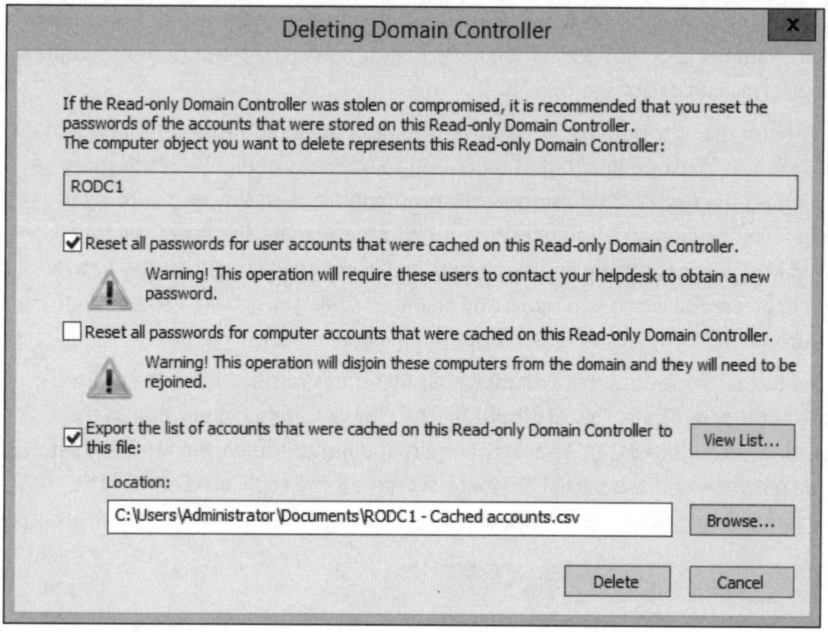

FIGURE 5-20 When deleting the computer object for an RODC, you can reset passwords for accounts cached on the RODC

Domain controller management is typically a job for high-level administrators such as Domain or Enterprise admins. When a domain controller is deployed, any local users and groups are removed, and access to the console is limited to the Domain Admins group. With RODCs, you can delegate control to local administrators to install drivers and updates. Local users can log on to the console of an RODC without having membership in a group that would provide administrative access to objects within Active Directory. Logging on to an RODC with a member of the Domain Admins group is not recommended.

Although loss of connectivity to a writable domain controller does not preclude an RODC from authenticating users, some actions (such as password changes and domain joins) require access to a writable domain controller.

Understanding the partial attribute set

The global catalog contains copies of every object in the domain, but only a subset of the attributes associated with those objects (primarily required attributes or those typically used for searches). You can customize this set of attributes, known as the partial attribute set, to meet the needs of your organization.

Many applications that modify the Active Directory schema also make use of the partial attribute set. For example, Microsoft Exchange Server uses the partial attribute set to contain fields used to perform searches of the GAL.

To configure the partial attribute set, the Active Directory Schema Microsoft Management Console (MMC) snap-in, must be enabled. It relies on the schmmgmt.dll file, which must be registered by running the regsvr32 schmmgmt.dll command from an elevated command prompt. Once enabled, launch an MMC window and add the Active Directory Schema snap-in. Because this management console enables you to make changes directly to the Active Directory schema, be careful when you make any changes. Changes should also be made on the domain controller performing the schema operations master role.

To modify the partial attribute set, navigate to the Attributes folder, locate the desired attribute, and select the Replicate This Attribute To The Global Catalog check box in the attribute properties (see Figure 5-21). After a change is applied to the partial attribute set, both the schema partition and the partial attribute set have to be replicated before the changes are available throughout the enterprise.

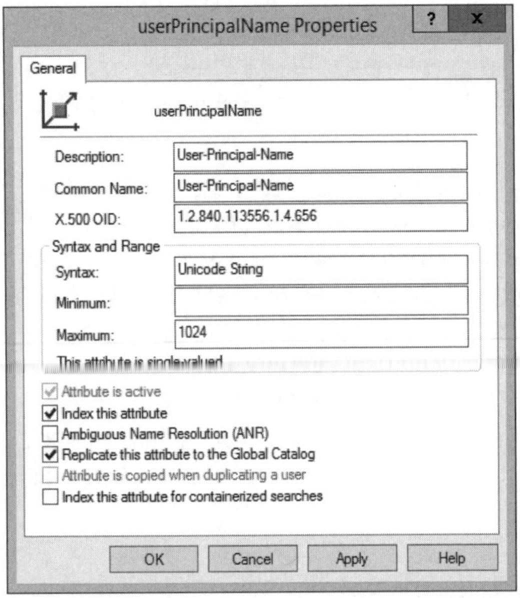

FIGURE 5-21 Attributes can be added to the partial attribute set with the Active Directory Schema snap-in

You can use the Get-ADObject PowerShell cmdlet to retrieve a list of attributes in the partial attribute set by querying the isMemberOfPartialAttributeSet flag, as shown in this example:

```
Get-ADObject -SearchBase "cn=Schema,cn=Configuration,dc=contoso,dc=com" -LDAPFilter "(is
MemberOfPartialAttributeSet=TRUE)"
```

Using cloned domain controllers

Windows Server 2012 introduced improved support for virtual domain controllers. Although they have been supported for some time, there was potential for damaging Active Directory if an old version of a virtual domain controller was introduced to the domain with a snapshot or backup. Windows Server 2012 Hyper-V hosts support a new identifier known as the VM-GenerationID, which is compared to the value in msDS-GenerationID before any changes are made to Active Directory.

The other major change for virtual domain controllers in Windows Server 2012 is the capability to quickly clone virtual machines (VMs) to rapidly deploy multiple domain controllers.

To clone a virtual domain controller, follow these steps:

1. Ensure that the domain controller is a member of the Cloneable Domain Controllers group.

2. Identify and remove any applications or services that do not support cloning, such as the following:

   - Active Directory Certificate Services (AD CS)

   - DHCP

   - Active Directory Lightweight Directory Services (AD LDS)

3. Create a configuration file for the clone operation using the New-ADDCCloneConfigFile cmdlet.

4. After the config file is created, the virtual domain controller is cloned by exporting and then importing the VM.

Applications and services that do not support cloning can be identified with the Get-ADDCCloningExcludedApplicationList cmdlet, which should be run on the virtual domain controller being used as the source. The New-ADDCCloneConfigFile cmdlet enables you to configure options such as computer name, IP address, and DNS information (see Figure 5-22).

After the configuration file is created, the VM can be exported. Upon importing the VM as a copy, which generates a new unique ID, the cloning process takes place on the first startup (as shown in Figure 5-23).

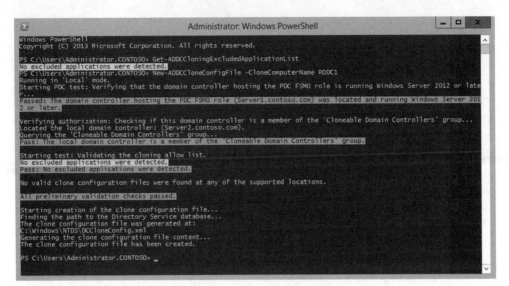

FIGURE 5-22 Creating the configuration file for a cloned domain controller

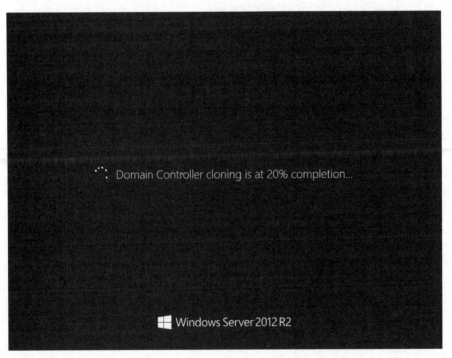

FIGURE 5-23 The domain controller cloning process happens when the cloned VM is first started

EXAM TIP

Virtual domain controllers and domain controller cloning are new and improved in Windows Server 2012 and Windows Server 2012 R2, making them good candidates for the exam. You should know the steps to take to clone a domain controller as well as the new features that make virtual domain controllers a more realistic proposition in Windows Server 2012.

Choosing domain controller placement

Regional domain controllers should be placed strategically to provide optimal authentication performance for domain clients within the physical region. Although domains are not always tied to regions, consider how the two structures compare when you plan domain controller placement. In some site topologies, it might be beneficial to deploy domain controllers from each domain to regional hubs, which streamlines replication to branch offices and provides optimal authentication performance.

Security should be a primary concern for domain controller placement. Ensure that domain controllers are not placed in an area where their physical security can be compromised. RODCs should be considered for locations that lack necessary physical security. When RODCs are used, their replication limitations should be taken into account.

In multidomain forests, global catalog servers can be used to improve authentication performance for users from other domains in the forest not available within the local site. Placement of global catalog servers must balance the need for optimized authentication with the extra cost associated with increased replication traffic. Sites or regions with large numbers of users are typically good candidates for global catalog servers as authentication performance becomes a higher priority.

The administration and management of domain controllers should be a consideration for placement. Although domain controllers can be managed remotely, you might want to ensure that a local management group can perform the necessary management tasks of maintaining local domain controllers.

Objective summary

- Global catalog servers contain partial copies of every object in the Active Directory forest, enabling improved performance in cross-domain authentication and authorization.

- The object attributes included in the global catalog, which are known as the partial attribute set, can be configured using the Active Directory Schema snap-in.

- Domain controllers that perform operations master roles handle specific tasks that require management by a single domain controller.

- The PDC emulator master, RID master, and infrastructure master roles are performed within each domain.

- Schema master and domain-naming master roles are handled at the forest level.

- RODCs, which are helpful in environments with decreased physical security, enable delegation of some administrative tasks.

- Windows Server 2012 improves support for virtual domain controllers, including the safe use of snapshots and the capability to quickly clone virtual domain controllers.

Objective review

Answer the following questions to test your knowledge of the information in this objective. You can find the answers to these questions and explanations of why each answer choice is correct or incorrect in the "Answers" section at the end of this chapter.

1. What domain controller capability can improve cross-domain authentication?

   A. RODC

   B. Domain naming master

   C. Global catalog server

   D. Infrastructure master

2. Which operations master roles are performed at the forest level? (Choose all that apply.)

   A. PDC emulator master

   B. Domain naming master

   C. Infrastructure master

   D. Schema master

3. Which operations master role is responsible for managing password changes at the domain level?

   A. Schema master

   B. Infrastructure master

   C. PDC emulator master

   D. RID master

4. What type of domain controller is best used for scenarios in which the domain controller cannot be physically secured?

   A. Global catalog

   B. Schema master

   C. Infrastructure master

   D. RODC

5. Which features are benefits of an RODC? (Choose all that apply.)

   A. Read-only copy of Active Directory

   B. Improved cross-domain authentication

   C. Capability to limit password caching

   D. Support for local administrator access

6. Which Active Directory feature makes use of the partial attribute set?

   A. RODC

   B. Domain controller cloning

   C. Global catalog

   D. Intersite replication

7. In what ways can the partial attribute set be modified? (Choose two.)

   A. Adding a new domain to the forest

   B. Deploying an application that integrates with Active Directory

   C. Deploying a global catalog server

   D. Manually modifying the schema using the Active Directory Schema snap-in

8. What are the steps to clone a virtual domain controller? (Choose all that apply.)

   A. Add the source domain controller to the Cloneable Domain Controllers group.

   B. Upgrade the domain to the Windows Server 2012 functional level.

   C. Ensure that the source domain controller is not performing an operations master role.

   D. Create a config file using the New-ADDCCloneConfigFile cmdlet.

9. Which of the following services do not support cloning? (Choose all that apply.)

   A. AD CS

   B. DHCP

   C. Active Directory Domain Services (AD DS)

   D. DNS

10. Which operations master role is critical for cloning a virtual domain controller?

   A. Domain naming master

   B. RID master

   C. PDC emulator master

   D. Infrastructure master

Objective 5.3: Design and implement a branch office infrastructure

The most complex aspect of implementing the physical structure of Active Directory can often be incorporating branch offices. In many enterprises, branch offices are small or insecure (or have a limited number of users). The cost associated with supporting a domain controller in numerous sites without large user bases can be prohibitive. Not only do you have to consider the cost of deploying a domain controller but also the costs of the infrastructure to support Active Directory. Branch offices typically require a reliable Internet connection, DNS, and DHCP support, and maintaining these items must be considered in planning. With the additional probability that an organization might have hundreds or thousands of branch offices, implementing and maintaining this infrastructure can become a complex endeavor.

Because of size and location, branch offices are often vulnerable, and deploying domain controllers in an environment in which the security is subpar can be dangerous. For these scenarios, RODCs are recommended because they provide several security mechanisms to protect an Active Directory forest in case of compromise.

Branch offices are often at the farthest point of a site topology, making them particularly susceptible to replication latency and an area of concern for authentication. Due to the limitations associated with placing a domain controller in a branch office, placing more than one domain controller to support multiple domains is usually not possible. Active Directory includes several features that alleviate some of the problems involved with having expansive site structures (some of them are discussed in this section).

Users in branch offices often require access to corporate resources that are located in another site. Any optimization you can provide to branch office users to minimize wait times or maximize availability increases productivity and saves your company money. Through the use of BranchCache, you can optimize WAN connectivity by using client- or server-based storage to retain a locally cached copy of corporate resources in other sites. This section discusses the steps required to implement BranchCache deployments in branch offices and enable content servers to support BranchCache clients.

Improving branch office authentication

In many scenarios, replication and authentication performance with branch offices can be costly due to connectivity requirements, hardware cost, and maintenance. Deploying domain controllers and the infrastructure to support them can also be expensive, particularly when multiple branch offices must be supported. The security of domain controllers in branch offices can be questionable because small offices might not have the physical security capabilities often found in large corporate datacenters.

The features available to meet the needs of branch offices help improve security and authentication performance, but can have a cost in the form of increased network traffic for replication.

Deploying RODCs

The capabilities and benefits offered by RODCs have been discussed in some length. Although the security benefits provided by an RODC are the primary reason for their use, the capability to delegate local administrative rights and reduce replication traffic is another good reason to deploy RODCs in branch offices.

Several requirements exist for RODCs in your enterprise. First, the forest functional level must be Windows Server 2003 or higher. At least one writable domain controller running Windows Server 2008 or higher also must be deployed to the domain before an RODC can be deployed, and this domain controller must also be a DNS server for the domain.

RODCs can be deployed by using either PowerShell or wizard-based deployments. Much of the process is identical to deploying a writable domain controller. Several steps in an RODC deployment deal with the security features that set it apart, such as delegation of management and the PRP.

The first step of deploying an RODC is to prepare the forest using the adprep /rodcprep command, after which the Active Directory Domain Services (AD DS) role can be installed by using either the Add Roles and Features Wizard or the Install-WindowsFeature PowerShell cmdlet. After the role is installed, the RODC can be deployed through the Active Directory Domain Services Configuration Wizard.

To deploy an RODC instead of a writable domain controller, the Read Only Domain Controller (RODC) option must be selected on the Domain Controller Options page (see Figure 5-24).

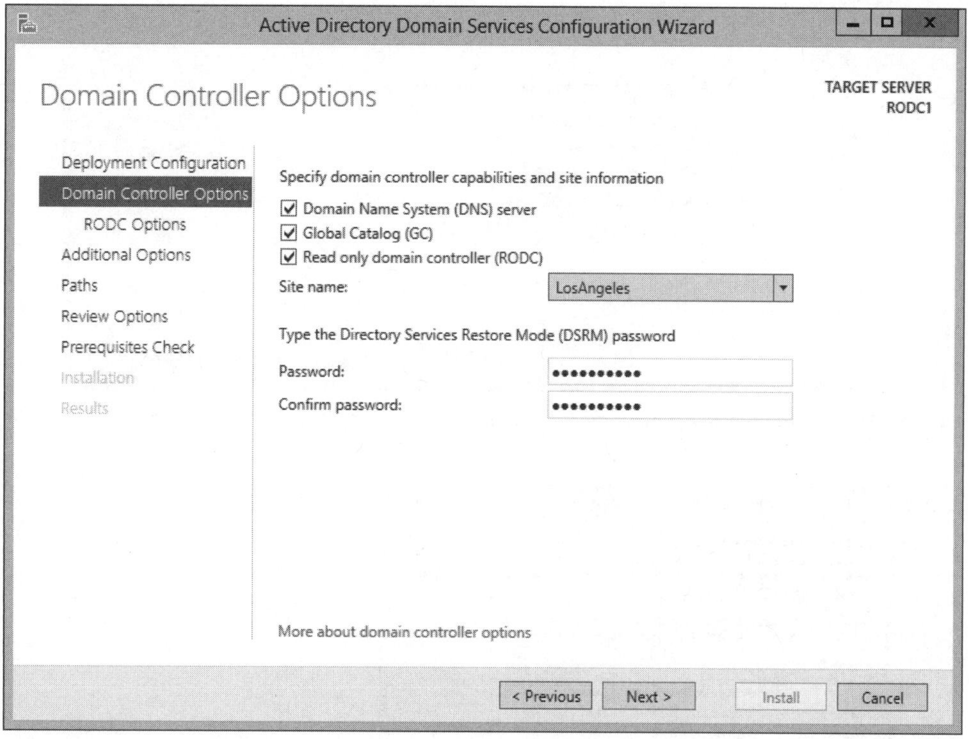

FIGURE 5-24 RODC deployment happens through the Active Directory Domain Services Configuration Wizard by choosing the Read Only Domain Controller (RODC) option

The RODC Options page (see Figure 5-25) enables you to choose a user or group to assign as the local administrator and configure the PRP for the RODC.

Another way to deploy an RODC in your forest is to precreate the computer account for the RODC using the Active Directory Users and Computers Wizard, or PowerShell. A precreated RODC account includes the settings for delegated administration and the PRP, which reduces the configuration required later in the process. During the RODC account-creation process, you have the option to use Advanced mode, which enables you to manually configure the RODC options (PRP configuration is shown in Figure 5-26); otherwise, they are configured automatically.

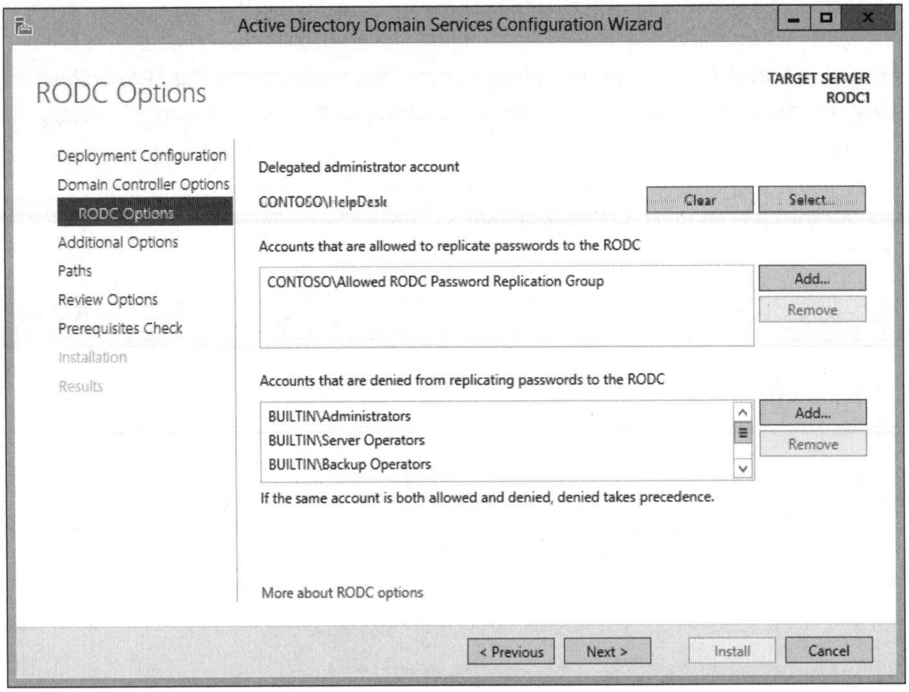

FIGURE 5-25 Deploying an RODC requires configuration of the delegated administrator account and PRP

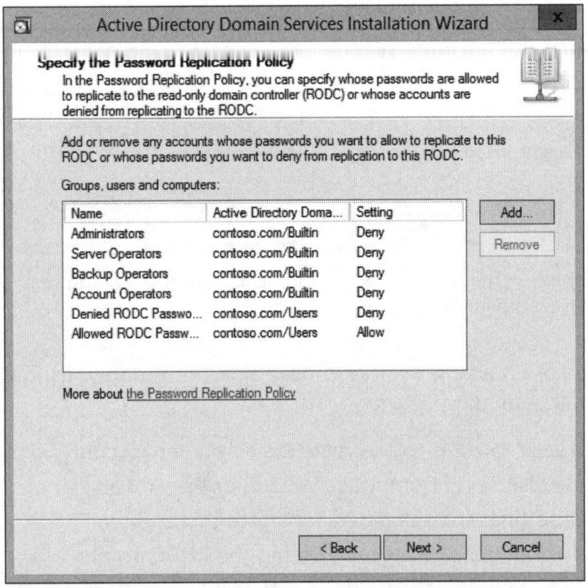

FIGURE 5-26 Precreation of an RODC account enables you to configure the PRP and delegated administration prior to RODC deployment

Upon deployment of an RODC with a precreated account, the Active Directory Domain Services Configuration Wizard indicates that a precreated account exists, giving you the option to use the existing account or to reinstall the domain controller. This behavior is shown in Figure 5-27.

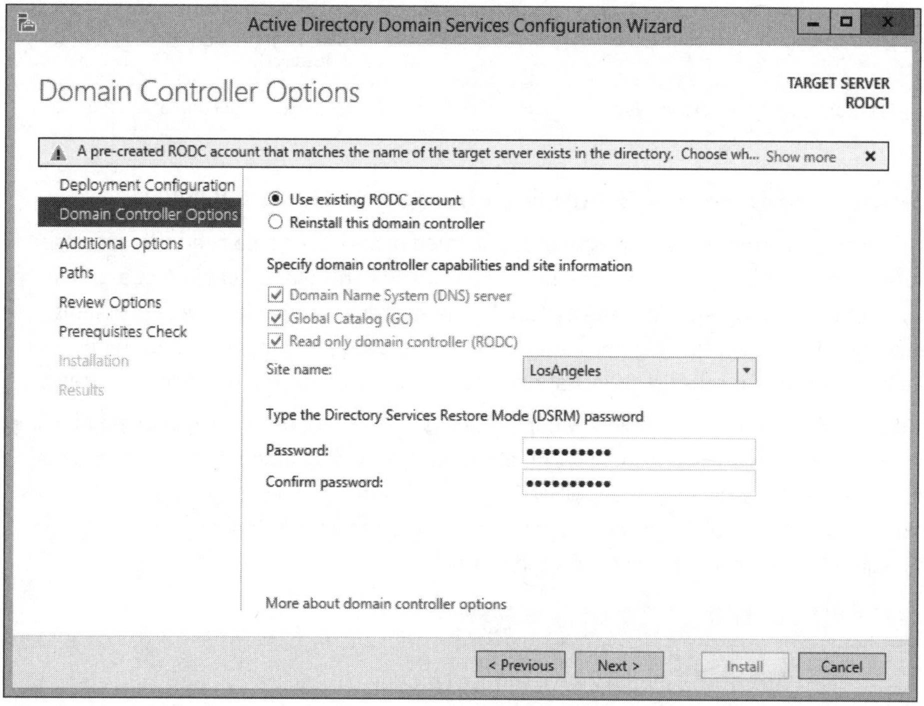

FIGURE 5-27 An RODC with a precreated account enables you to choose between using the existing account and reinstalling the domain controller upon deployment

Each of the steps of deploying an RODC can be completed using PowerShell. The Add-ADDSReadOnlyDomainControllerAccount can be used to precreate the RODC account and accepts the parameters listed in Table 5-3. These parameters can also be passed to the Install-ADDSDomainController cmdlet when the -ReadOnlyReplica parameter is used.

TABLE 5-3 Parameters used for RODC deployment with PowerShell

Parameter	Required	Description
-DomainControllerAccountName	Yes	Specifies the name of the RODC
-DomainName	Yes	Determines which domain the RODC supports
-SiteName	Yes	Places the RODC in the proper site for replication purposes
-AllowPasswordReplicationAccountName	No	One or more users or groups can be specified to manage allow permissions in the Password Replication Policy

Parameter	Required	Description
-Credential	No	Credential object containing the user name and password of a domain administrator; required if the current user does not have permissions to add a domain controller
-DelegatedAdministratorAccountName	No	Sets the user or group permitted to maintain the RODC locally
-DenyPasswordReplicationAccountName	No	Configures the deny portion of the PRP

Implementing Universal Group Membership Caching (UGMC)

When a user is a member of a universal group located in another domain, additional steps in the authentication process (the authenticating domain controller must contact a global catalog server) are required. This process can become a source of performance problems when a site does not contain a global catalog server because performing this authentication over a WAN link might cause authentication delays and even deny the user's logon attempt.

UGMC enables domain controllers within a site to store a user's universal group membership locally upon initial logon. Subsequent logon attempts can then be authenticated without having to contact a global catalog server. UGMC is enabled with Active Directory Sites and Services. Within the NTDS Site Settings properties for a site, you can select the Enable Universal Group Membership Caching check box, as shown in Figure 5-28.

FIGURE 5-28 Enabling UGMC for the site

Using the global catalog

Global catalog servers should usually be deployed when authentication requirements outweigh replication drawbacks (in offices with a large number of users or forests with few domains, for example). Consider using UGMC to optimize authentication in sites large enough for a domain controller but not big enough to support the replication required for a global catalog server.

> **EXAM TIP**
>
> Both UGMC and the global catalog are important for optimizing authentication in Active Directory. At a minimum, you should know how each feature can be helpful and what additional complexity comes from being enabled.

Implementing branch office infrastructure requirements

Regardless of the size of a corporate location or branch office, certain network infrastructure elements must be in place for standard networking and Active Directory authentication. DNS and DHCP are essential, although smaller locations can potentially receive support from DHCP and DNS servers in other sites.

Supporting DNS in the branch office

DNS should be deployed beside each domain controller in the forest—optimally on each domain controller so that Active Directory–integrated zones can be used. Even RODCs can be used as DNS servers, although they maintain only a read-only copy of the DNS zones. The DNS in a branch office should be configured in caching mode with forwarders configured to reference domain controllers that host the corporate root domain. This configuration provides optimal performance while enabling any DNS queries necessary for Active Directory to be resolved properly.

Supporting DHCP in the branch office

Because DHCP is such a necessary part of any network, some sort of DHCP in your branch offices is critical. Branch offices should ideally have redundant DHCP support through DHCP failover or split scopes, even if the secondary server is located off-site. DHCP can be a powerful tool for configuring network clients with the appropriate DNS server, thereby directing Active Directory member computers to domain controllers.

Deploying BranchCache

BranchCache is a technology that provides network optimization for remote locations by caching network resources on computers in the local network, thus reducing the amount of traffic required over slow and expensive WAN links. Windows Server 2012 and Windows 8 support two modes for BranchCache: hosted cache mode and distributed cache mode.

Hosted cache mode uses Windows Server–based storage to contain the cache, whereas distributed cache mode stores the cache on Windows clients on the network.

Figure 5-29 illustrates the use of distributed cache mode to optimize WAN traffic to a content server in a remote site.

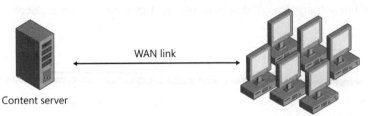

Content server

WAN link

Branch office clients

FIGURE 5-29 BranchCache in distributed cache mode is normally used when there is no available server-based storage within the local site

Not all WAN traffic is cached using BranchCache-only traffic originating from BranchCache-enabled content servers such as a Windows Server 2012 file server, an Internet Information Services (IIS)–based web server, and Windows Server Update Services (WSUS).

EXAM TIP

Although BranchCache will probably not be tested heavily in the exam, you should expect one or two questions. You should know the difference between the two modes and what pieces must be in place for BranchCache to be implemented and used effectively.

Securing branch office deployments

Numerous challenges often prevent branch offices from meeting the security standards of your corporate datacenter. Physical security, maintenance schedules, and even the way users protect their passwords can be challenges without the plans and processes often associated with corporate IT environments.

Windows Server 2012 offers solutions to many aspects of securing information contained in Active Directory and prevents sensitive information about Active Directory objects from being read or modified by users without the proper permissions.

Implementing confidential attributes

Some attributes on Active Directory can be sensitive in your organization. Active Directory enables you to control what attributes are visible to users by defining this sensitive information as confidential attributes.

Confidential attributes are configured by defining the searchFlags value for an attribute by using Active Directory Service Interfaces (ADSI) Edit. Changing the searchFlags value from 0x0 (the default of 0) to 0x80 (128) marks the attribute as confidential (see Figure 5-30).

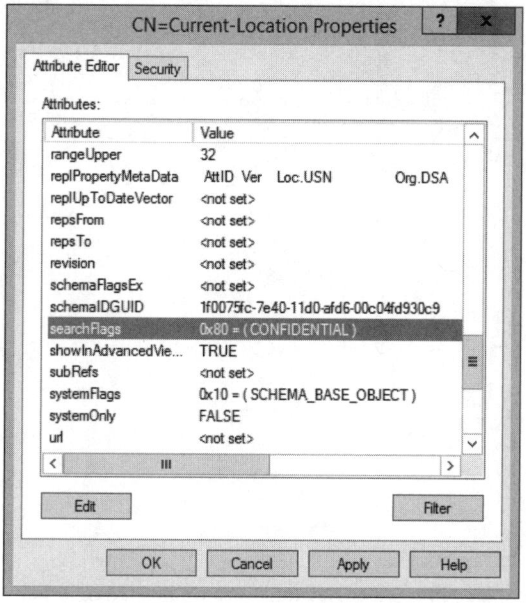

FIGURE 5-30 Setting the searchFlags value enables you to mark attributes as confidential

Delegating administration

Unlike writable domain controllers, RODCs enable you to delegate administrative access to the server without also granting access to the Active Directory domain. This enables you to permit local users within a branch to perform basic administration tasks such as performing software updates and installing drivers without compromising Active Directory.

You can delegate permission to an RODC on the Managed By tab of the RODC computer object in Active Directory, as shown in Figure 5-31. A user or group can be selected to provide local administrator rights to the RODC.

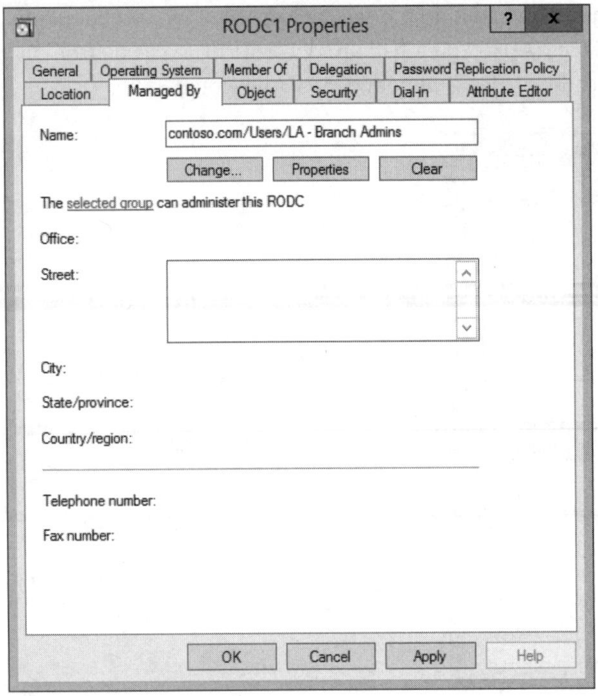

FIGURE 5-31 The Managed By tab of an RODC enables you to delegate administrative privileges to the domain controller

> ***NOTE*** **DELEGATING RODC ADMINISTRATION**
>
> **Because RODCs enable you to define only a single security principal for delegated administration, you should create a group specifically for that purpose. Other groups or users can be given membership to this group as needed to support your RODC.**

Modifying the filtered attributes set

The filtered attribute set contains a list of object attributes that should not be replicated to an RODC. Because the primary reason for an RODC deployment is to lessen the risk involved with placing a domain controller in an insecure environment, the filtered attribute set should be used to prevent sensitive information from being replicated to RODCs.

As with confidential attributes, the filtered attribute set uses the searchFlags field in ADSI Edit to mark which attributes should not be replicated to RODCs. Setting the searchFlags value to 0x200 (512) adds the attribute to the filtered attribute set and prevents replication to RODCs.

Configuring Password Replication Policy

You can configure PRPs for RODCs. By adding users or groups to the Password Replication Policy tab of the RODC computer object in Active Directory, you determine and manage the users allowed to have their passwords cached by a particular RODC (see Figure 5-32). In the Advanced Password Replication Policy window, you can view the resultant policy of a PRP, enabling you to determine the results of a policy that might affect users' membership in multiple groups.

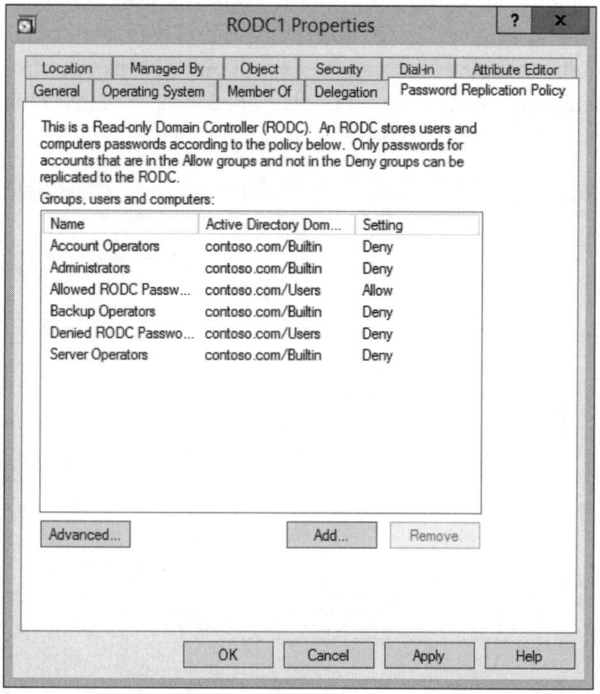

FIGURE 5-32 An RODC PRP is configured through the RODC computer object in Active Directory

The PRP for an RODC can also be managed using the PowerShell cmdlets listed in Table 5-4.

TABLE 5-4 Parameters used for deploying an RODC with PowerShell

Cmdlet	Description
Add-ADDomainControllerPasswordReplicationPolicy	Allows the addition of security principals to the PRP for an RODC
Get-ADDomainControllerPasswordReplicationPolicy	Retrieves the current PRP for the specified RODC
Remove-ADDomainControllerPasswordReplicationPolicy	Removes security principals from a PRP

Each of these cmdlets accepts the -Identity parameter, which is used to specify the RODC containing the PRP being managed. The allow and deny policies can be managed using the -AllowedList and -DeniedList parameters.

Configuring hash publication

To enable BranchCache support in your file servers, you must configure hash publication using Group Policy or local security policy.

BranchCache hash publication is configured in Group Policy under Computer Configuration, Policies, Administrative Templates, Network, Lanman Server, Hash Publication For BranchCache. When enabled, the setting enables you to configure automatic hash publication for all Branch-Cache-enabled shares, disallow hash publication on all shared folders, or allow hash publication for all shared folders (see Figure 5-33).

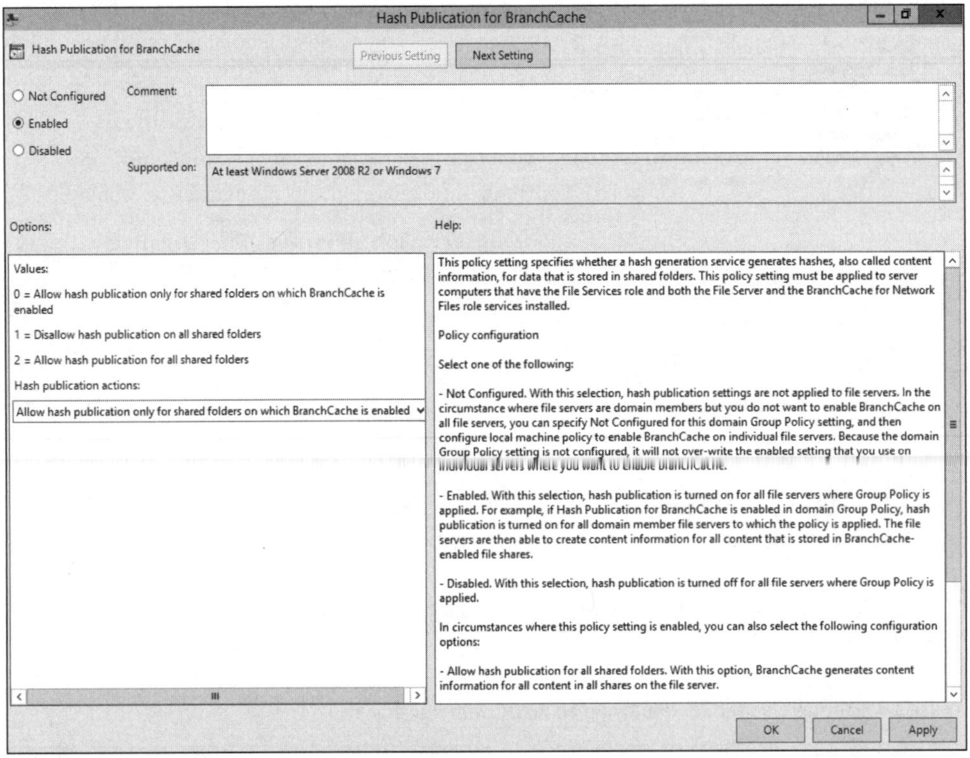

FIGURE 5-33 Hash publication can be enabled through Group Policy for all shared folders or only those that are BranchCache-enabled

Thought experiment

Implementing a branch office deployment

In this thought experiment, apply what you've learned about this objective. You can find answers to these questions in the "Answers" section at the end of this chapter.

You have been brought in by a large corporation to assist in implementing branch office deployments across the country. Answer the following questions regarding how you would meet corporate requirements for branch office deployments:

1. The corporate IT department is worried about deploying domain controllers in each branch, specifically because of lack of physical security and the risk of a compromised domain controller (which might result in the entire corporate network being compromised). What can you use to minimize the risk of deploying a domain controller in a branch office?

2. The IT department likes the idea of using RODCs in each branch office, but still has concerns about some specific user categories that should not have passwords saved to RODCs. What tool is available to prevent passwords from specific sets of users from being replicated to an RODC?

3. Corporate IT does not have the manpower to manage system updates, software installs, and driver updates on servers deployed in branch offices. This situation is problematic for domain controllers because only members of the Domain Admins group can log on to the console. Is there a way to enable local users to install software and updates on a branch office domain controller?

4. To keep costs down, network connectivity at each branch office is a relatively slow link. The IT department is worried about authentication performance, particularly for users with membership in universal groups from other domains. Configuring each branch office domain controller as a global catalog server would cause a significant uptick in replication traffic that might cause additional problems due to the slow network connectivity. What can you suggest to improve logon performance for branch office users?

5. In the past, the slow WAN link at each branch office used to access corporate file shares and SharePoint sites has resulted in reduced productivity. What capabilities are available to improve performance for corporate resources such as these in the branch offices?

Objective summary

- Both UGMC and the global catalog can be used to reduce authentication time for users with membership in universal groups in other domains.
- BranchCache allows for WAN optimization through the use of a local cache. Both hosted cache and distributed cache are supported by using server-based or client-based storage, respectively.
- Confidential attributes can be configured to prevent certain Active Directory object attributes from being visible to all users.
- Both the filtered attributes set and PRP enable you to manage the information that can be replicated to RODCs.
- BranchCache requires support from content servers to cache network resources. File servers must be BranchCache-enabled, and hash publication must be configured for file shares.

Objective review

Answer the following questions to test your knowledge of the information in this objective. You can find the answers to these questions and explanations of why each answer choice is correct or incorrect in the "Answers" section at the end of this chapter.

1. What tool increases authentication performance in a multidomain forest without requiring replication of the partial attribute set?

   A. BranchCache

   B. UGMC

   C. Confidential attributes

   D. Global catalog

2. Which configuration options pertain specifically to RODC replication? (Choose all that apply.)

   A. UGMC

   B. Confidential attributes

   C. Filtered attribute set

   D. PRP

3. What method enables you to define the PRP and delegated administration for an RODC prior to deployment?

   A. Group Policy

   B. Precreating the RODC account

   C. Install-ADDSDomainController PowerShell cmdlet

   D. Local security policy

4. What command enables you to deploy an RODC using a precreated account?

   A. Add-ADDSReadOnlyDomainControllerAccount -DomainControllerAccountName

   B. Install-ADDSDomainController -UseExistingAccount

   C. Install-ADDSReadOnlyDomainControllerAccount -DomainControllerAccountName

   D. Add-ADDSDomainController -UseExistingAccount

5. What cmdlet enables you to add an entry to the PRP of an RODC?

   A. Add-ADDomainControllerPasswordReplicationPolicy

   B. Set-ADDomainControllerPasswordReplicationPolicy

   C. Get-ADDomainControllerPasswordReplicationPolicy

   D. Remove-ADDomainControllerPasswordReplicationPolicy

6. What value must be set in the searchFlags field to configure confidential attributes?

   A. 0x0

   B. 0x80

   C. 0x128

   D. 0x200

7. Which BranchCache option uses client-based storage to cache network resources?

   A. Hosted cache mode

   B. Global catalog

   C. Hash publication for BranchCache

   D. Distributed cache mode

8. For which of the following resources does a branch office benefit from a BranchCache deployment? (Choose all that apply.)

   A. SharePoint at corporate headquarters

   B. File server at the branch office

   C. File server at corporate headquarters

   D. Public cloud–based web applications

9. What step must be taken to enable BranchCache support for a content server?

   A. Enable BranchCache in hosted cache mode.

   B. Install the BranchCache server feature.

   C. Install Windows Server 2012 R2.

   D. Configure hash publication.

10. How can a user be given administrative access to an RODC but not to Active Directory?

    A. Select the user in the Managed By tab of the RODC computer object.

    B. Add the user to the PRP for the RODC.

    C. Add the user to the Domain Admins group.

    D. Add the user to the RODC local Administrators group.

Answers

This section contains the solutions to the thought experiments and answers to the lesson review questions in this chapter.

Objective 5.1: Thought experiment

1. Configuring site links that include the sites for a specific time zone and then configuring the replication schedule for these site links enable you to configure replication based on office hours.

2. Changes to the schema should be made in the same location as the domain controller performing the schema operations master role.

Objective 5.1: Review

1. **Correct answer:** B

    A. **Incorrect:** Shortcut trusts, which are used between two domains within a forest, have no impact on sites, particularly those without a domain controller.

    B. **Correct:** Shortcut trusts are used to facilitate authentication requests from one domain to another. Rather than having to traverse the forest hierarchy, authentication requests can be referred directly to the appropriate domain controllers.

    C. **Incorrect:** No improvements occur when attempting to create a shortcut trust to the forest root domain.

    D. **Incorrect:** Shortcut trusts have no impact on replication. Site links would be used in this scenario.

2. **Correct answer:** D

    A. **Incorrect:** Even if the two site links are not bridged, replication should still reach the site after two replication intervals.

    B. **Incorrect:** Overlapping replication schedules are beneficial only if multiple site links are contained in a site link bridge.

    C. **Incorrect:** Even with manual management of site link bridges, replication can reach across multiple site links.

    D. **Correct:** If replication to one site is dependent on another, each directory partition should be represented in the site acting as the intermediary.

3. **Correct answer:** B

   A. **Incorrect:** Domain controllers for each domain form ring topologies to replicate the domain partition, but they must also replicate the other directory partitions such as the schema and configuration partitions.

   B. **Correct:** Replication within a single site uses a ring topology for each directory partition whether it is a domain, application directory, schema, or configuration partition.

   C. **Incorrect:** All domain controllers are included in a ring only for partitions shared between every partition in the site.

   D. **Incorrect:** Site links have no bearing on the replication topology within a site.

4. **Correct answer:** A

   A. **Correct:** When an object is modified on a domain controller in one site, the changes must be replicated to be reflected on other domain controllers. With intersite replication, this process can take some time. This replication latency can occasionally cause authentication or authorization issues.

   B. **Incorrect:** Even in a site without a domain controller authentication, traffic should be routed to the next closest domain controller for authentication.

   C. **Incorrect:** If a site does not contain a domain controller for the user's domain, the authentication request should be routed to a domain controller capable of authenticating the user.

   D. **Incorrect:** The PDC emulator master is responsible for handling the initial password change. The replication process then takes over and must communicate the new password throughout the forest.

5. **Correct answers:** A, B

   A. **Correct:** Reducing the number of steps in the replication process, either through new site links or site link bridges, should help reduce replication latency.

   B. **Correct:** Although more frequent replication helps reduce latency, it can increase the workload on bridgehead servers' network utilization over WAN links.

   C. **Incorrect:** Placing domain controllers from every domain at each site increases replication traffic and provides no improvement in replication latency.

   D. **Incorrect:** Deploying a domain controller from the forest root domain within each site increases replication traffic and does not reduce replication latency.

6. **Correct answer:** D

   A. **Incorrect:** Operations master roles have no impact on which domain controllers perform as bridgehead servers and are not required to be performed by bridgehead servers.

   B. **Incorrect:** If a domain controller for the domain is not available, authentication or authorization requests are passed on to another site.

   C. **Incorrect:** When objects are modified in another site, the changes should be replicated to other sites.

   D. **Correct:** If the preferred bridgehead servers do not host a copy of all directory partitions within the site, the domain controllers containing other domain partitions cannot receive updates from other sites.

7. **Correct answers:** C, D

   A. **Correct:** Replication through a site link bridge can occur without preferred bridgehead servers being selected.

   B. **Incorrect:** Even if a site common to two bridged site links is unavailable, the two remaining sites can perform replication.

   C. **Incorrect:** Sites that perform replication through a site link bridge must share a directory partition.

   D. **Incorrect:** Replication across a site link bridge can occur only if both site links have a simultaneous replication period.

8. **Correct answer:** A

   A. **Correct:** Selecting the Bridge All Site Links check box results in replication being unconstrained between all sites in the forest.

   B. **Incorrect:** Rebooting the infrastructure master has no effect on replication.

   C. **Incorrect:** Deleting the DEFAULTIPSITELINK site link does not limit replication traffic to only the defined site links.

   D. **Incorrect:** Changes made on an RODC are simply forwarded to a writable domain controller.

9. **Correct answer:** B

   A. **Incorrect:** The /showrepl switch for repadmin shows the replication status for a domain controller, but does not show inbound requests.

   B. **Correct:** The /queue switch for repadmin shows inbound replication requests for a domain controller.

   C. **Incorrect:** The dcdiag /test:replications command runs the replications test for DNS servers.

   D. **Incorrect:** The dcdiag /test:VerifyReplicas command checks the replication status of directory partitions.

10. Correct answer: B

   A.   Incorrect: The /kcc parameter forces the KCC to recalculate replication paths.

   B.   Correct: The /replsingleobj option enables you to specify an object and two domain controllers, replicating the object between the source and target domain controllers.

   C.   Incorrect: Full replication between two domain controllers can be triggered with the /replicate option.

   D.   Incorrect: The incoming replication queue for a domain controller can be viewed by using the /queue parameter.

Objective 5.2: Thought experiment

1.   Applications that integrate closely with Active Directory sometimes make changes to the Active Directory schema. Changes to the schema are handled by the domain controller performing the schema master role. Placing these applications in the location that hosts the schema master is usually recommended.

2.   When a user with a membership in universal groups from other domains authenticates, the other domain must be contacted unless a global catalog server exists within the user's domain.

3.   The partial attribute set replicates to global catalog servers throughout the forest. Managing the attributes contained in the partial attribute set enables you to prevent replication of these attributes to global catalog servers.

4.   RODCs are the first step of providing protection in areas with concerns over physical security. Both the read-only nature of RODCs and the PRP help ensure limited risk from a compromised RODC.

Objective 5.2: Review

1.   **Correct answer:** C

   A.   Incorrect: RODCs furnish no inherent benefits for cross-domain authentication.

   B.   Incorrect: Although the domain controller performing the domain naming master role does not improve cross-domain authentication performance, it is used when changes are made to the domain structure (such as adding or removing domains).

   C.   Correct: Global catalog servers use the partial attribute set to improve authentication performance.

   D.   Incorrect: The infrastructure master role tracks the membership of users outside the domain in groups within the domain. Authentication performance for users within the domain does not improve based on proximity to the infrastructure master.

2. **Correct answers:** B, D

    A. Incorrect: The PDC emulator master role is performed at the domain level and handles password changes for the domain.

    B. Correct: The domain naming master role is performed by a domain controller at the forest level to maintain a writable copy of the structure of domains within the forest.

    C. Incorrect: Infrastructure masters are located within each domain to maintain a record of security principals from other domains with membership in universal groups in the local domain.

    D. Correct: Schema changes are written to the schema master, which is a role performed at the forest level.

3. **Correct answer:** C

    A. Incorrect: The schema master handles changes to the Active Directory schema.

    B. Incorrect: Infrastructure master servers track security principals from other domains that are members of groups in the local domain.

    C. Correct: The PDC emulator master handles password changes within its domain.

    D. Incorrect: RID masters maintain RID pools for each domain, ensuring that each object in an Active Directory forest has a unique ID.

4. **Correct answer:** D

    A. Incorrect: Global catalog servers contain the partial attribute set for the forest and do not provide any security benefits.

    B. Incorrect: The schema master handles changes to the Active Directory schema.

    C. Incorrect: No security benefits are gained by assigning the infrastructure master role to a server.

    D. Correct: RODCs have several security benefits for locations with physical security limitations.

5. **Correct answers:** A, C, D

    A. Correct: A compromised RODC does not allow changes to Active Directory objects to be written back to Active Directory.

    B. Incorrect: RODCs do not improve authentication performance.

    C. Correct: The PRP for an RODC enables you to limit password caching to the RODC.

    D. Correct: An RODC can be managed by a local administrator without also providing full access to Active Directory objects.

6. **Correct answer:** C

   A. **Incorrect:** RODCs make use of the filtered attributes set, not the partial attribute set. Both are configured with the searchFlags attribute in ADSI Edit.

   B. **Incorrect:** Domain controller cloning is not associated with the partial attribute set.

   C. **Correct:** Global catalog servers contain copies of attributes from every object in the domain; these attributes are determined by the partial attribute set.

   D. **Incorrect:** Attributes are replicated between sites regardless of the partial attribute set.

7. **Correct answers:** B, D

   A. **Incorrect:** Adding a new domain to a forest does not alter the schema or the partial attribute set.

   B. **Correct:** Some applications that integrate with Active Directory, such as Microsoft Exchange Server, use the partial attribute set to make certain attributes readily available throughout the forest.

   C. **Incorrect:** Deploying a global catalog server does not modify the partial attribute set.

   D. **Correct:** You can modify the partial attribute set manually by using the Active Directory Schema snap-in.

8. **Correct answers:** A, D

   A. **Correct:** The source domain controller must be added to the Cloneable Domain Controllers group.

   B. **Incorrect:** The forest does not have to be at the Windows Server 2012 functional level to support cloned domain controllers.

   C. **Incorrect:** Although it makes sense not to clone a domain controller performing an operations master role, it is not a requirement.

   D. **Correct:** Creating the config file is one of the last steps of cloning a domain controller.

9. **Correct answers:** A, B

   A. **Correct:** AD CS does not support cloning. Attempting to clone a virtual domain controller that is also performing the AD CS role results in failure.

   B. **Correct:** The DHCP server role cannot be cloned.

   C. **Incorrect:** The AD DS role supports cloning and is required to clone a virtual domain controller.

   D. **Incorrect:** The DNS role supports cloning.

10. **Correct answer:** C

   A. **Correct:** The domain naming master is not necessary for cloning a virtual domain controller.

   B. **Incorrect:** A RID master is not used when cloning a virtual domain controller.

   C. **Correct:** The PDC emulator master is responsible for password changes, and the virtual domain controller cloning process requires the PDC emulator master to be available.

   D. **Incorrect:** The virtual domain controller cloning process does not require the infrastructure master server.

Objective 5.3: Thought experiment

1. RODCs help protect Active Directory from the risks involved with a compromised domain controller.

2. Configuring the PRP for an RODC helps protect users with elevated privileges or sensitive accounts from having their passwords stored on the domain controller.

3. RODCs support the assignment of local administrative privileges for this scenario.

4. UGMC, which can be configured for the site, improves authentication performance for users with membership in universal groups from other domains.

5. BranchCache can help optimize access to resources on corporate servers by creating a cache in the local site, either on a central server (hosted cache mode) or spread across clients (distributed cache mode).

Objective 5.3: Review

1. **Correct answer:** B

   A. **Incorrect:** BranchCache is used to optimize access to corporate resources across slow WAN connections.

   B. **Correct:** UGMC enables rapid authentication for users with membership in universal groups from other domains without the replication overhead associated with global catalog servers.

   C. **Incorrect:** Confidential attributes prevent users from viewing sensitive attributes on Active Directory objects without the necessary permissions.

   D. **Incorrect:** Although global catalog servers optimize authentication performance, there are significant replication costs.

2. **Correct answers:** C, D

   A. **Incorrect:** UGMC is not specific to RODCs; it is an option for any site with a domain controller.

   B. **Incorrect:** Confidential attributes affect any domain controller, not just RODCs.

   C. **Correct:** The filtered attribute set determines what attributes can be replicated to RODCs.

   D. **Correct:** An RODC PRP determines which users can have their passwords replicated to the RODC.

3. **Correct answer:** B

   A. **Incorrect:** Group Policy does not allow you to configure the PRP and delegated administration for an RODC. These aspects of RODC configuration are usually specific to the site in which the RODC is deployed. Group Policy is best used for configuring multiple machines across one or more domains.

   B. **Correct:** When you precreate the computer account for an RODC, you can use Advanced mode, which enables you to configure the PRP and the user or group delegated for administration.

   C. **Incorrect:** Although the Install-ADDSDomainController cmdlet enables you to configure both the PRP and delegated administration, it occurs during deployment of the RODC, not before.

   D. **Incorrect:** The local security policy of an RODC is not the proper place to configure the PRP and delegated administration, especially prior to deployment.

4. **Correct answer:** B

   A. **Incorrect:** Although the Add-ADDSReadOnlyDomainControllerAccount with the -DomainControllerAccountName parameter enables you to precreate an RODC account, it does not actually deploy the RODC.

   B. **Correct:** The Install-ADDSDomainController with the -UseExistingAccount parameter enables you to use a precreated RODC account to deploy an RODC.

   C. **Incorrect:** Install-ADDSReadOnlyDomainControllerAccount is not a valid PowerShell cmdlet.

   D. **Incorrect:** Add-ADDSDomainController is not a valid PowerShell cmdlet.

5. **Correct answer:** A

   A. Correct: Add-ADDomainControllerPasswordReplicationPolicy enables you to add security principals to the PRP for an RODC from either an allow or deny standpoint.

   B. Incorrect: Set-ADDomainControllerPasswordReplicationPolicy is not a valid PowerShell cmdlet.

   C. Incorrect: Get-ADDomainControllerPasswordReplicationPolicy enables you to retrieve the existing PRP from an RODC.

   D. Incorrect: Remove-ADDomainControllerPasswordReplicationPolicy removes security principals from an RODC PRP.

6. **Correct answer:** B

   A. Incorrect: The default searchFlags value is 0x0.

   B. Correct: A confidential attribute can be configured by setting the searchFlags field to 0x80.

   C. Incorrect: The 0x80 value equates to 128, but 0x128 is incorrect.

   D. Incorrect: A searchFlags value of 0x200 is used for filtered attributes, not confidential attributes.

7. **Correct answer:** D

   A. Incorrect: Hosted cache mode uses server-based storage to host the cache.

   B. Incorrect: Global catalog servers are not used for BranchCache.

   C. Incorrect: Hash publication is part of the process to configure file servers to support BranchCache.

   D. Correct: Distributed cache mode enables you to use client storage to contain BranchCache.

8. **Correct answers:** A, C

   A. Correct: SharePoint sites hosted using IIS do support BranchCache optimization. Optimizing traffic across the WAN connection is the goal of BranchCache.

   B. Incorrect: Although Windows Server–based file servers offer BranchCache support, no benefit is gained by caching what is already a local resource.

   C. Correct: Windows Server–based file servers support BranchCache and are a common use-case for BranchCache optimization when located in another site.

   D. Incorrect: Public web applications cannot be cached using BranchCache.

9. **Correct answer:** D

   A. **Incorrect:** The BranchCache deployment mode does not determine whether a content server supports BranchCache.

   B. **Incorrect:** BranchCache is not installed as a server feature on a content server.

   C. **Incorrect:** BranchCache support is not a new feature in Windows Server 2012 R2.

   D. **Correct:** Hash publication must be enabled for clients to use BranchCache when accessing resources from a content server.

10. **Correct answer:** A

   A. **Correct:** Adding users and/or groups to the Managed By tab of the RODC gives them local administrator permissions to the domain controller.

   B. **Incorrect:** The RODC PRP has no effect on which users have administrative privileges on the server.

   C. **Incorrect:** Although the Domain Admins group would give users administrator permissions to the RODC, it would also give them access to the objects within Active Directory.

   D. **Incorrect:** When a server is promoted to a domain controller, its local users and groups are removed.

Index

Symbols

T

U

V

network protocols, 132
protocol implications, 134

W

WAIK (Windows Automated Installation Kit), 6
WDSUTIL command-line utility, 25
WDS (Windows Deployment Services), 18–20
Web Application Proxy, 151–156
    access for internal/external clients, 155–156
    authentication and authorization, 152–154
    certificates, 155
    configuring for clustering, 164
    multifactor access control, 155
    multifactor authentication, 154
    planning for applications, 151–152
    SSO (Single Sign-On), 155
    using devices, 154
    Workplace Join, 153–154
Web Application Proxy Configuration Wizard, 152, 164
web-based enrollment, certificate-based
        authentication, 131
Web Platform installer, 16
wildcard certificates, 155
Windows ADK Quick Start guide, help file, 3
Windows Assessment and Deployment Kit (ADK), 9–10
Windows Automated Installation Kit (WAIK), 6
Windows Deployment Services (WDS), 18–20
Windows Internet Name Service (WINS), 95
Windows Management Instrumentation (WMI)
        filters, 228
Windows PowerShell
    deploying servers to public/private cloud, 26
    Microsoft Azure, 16–17
Windows Security Health Validator, 173
Windows Server Migration Tools (WSMT), 29
Windows Update Standalone Installer file, 243
WINS (Windows Internet Name Service), 95
wizards
    Active Directory Domain Services
        Configuration, 217, 293
    Add An Entry Point, 162
    Add Network Service, 115
    Add Node, 67
    Add Prestaged Device, 23
    Certificate Export, 15
    Configure Failover, 68

    Configure NAP, 172, 175
    Connection Manager Administration Kit, 136
    Create Capability Profile, 39–40
    Create Cluster, 67
    Create IP Pool, 42
    Create Multicast Transmission, 18
    Create Run As Account, 37
    Delegation of Control, 241–242
    Delegation Of Control, 238–239
    Enable Load Balancing, 162
    Enable Multisite Deployment, 162
    Getting Started, 143, 163
    Import Operating System, 8
    New Deployment Share, 6–7
    New Guest OS Profile, 38–39
    New Hardware Profile, 39–40
    New iSCSI Virtual Disk, 51
    New Physical Computer Profile, 41
    New Scope, 72
    New Share, 53–54
    New Trust, 217
    New Zone Delegation, 96
    Provision IPAM, 103–104
    Remote Access Server Setup, 141–142, 147–148
    Remote Access Setup, 163
    Security Translation, 220
    Validate Configuration, 67
    Web Application Proxy Configuration, 152, 164
    Zone Signing, 87
WMI (Windows Management Instrumentation)
        filters, 228
workflows, 222
Workplace Join, 153–154
WSMT (Windows Server Migration Tools), 29

Z

zone delegation, DNS, 96–97
zone hierarchy, DNS, 96–98
zone signing, DNSSEC, 86–87
zone signing key (ZSK), 86, 88–89
Zone Signing Wizard, 87
ZSK (zone signing key), 86, 88–89

About the authors

PAUL FERRILL has a BS and MS in Electrical Engineering and has been writing in the computer trade press for over 25 years. He serves as CTO for Avionics Test and Analysis Corporation, a woman-owned small business specializing in providing engineering expertise to help solve complex data analysis problems. He's written hundreds of articles over the years for publications like Datamation, Federal Computer Week, Information Week, InfoWorld, Network Computing, Network World, PC Magazine and is the author of two books.

TIM FERRILL is a system administrator and writer living in Southern California with his wife, Jodi, and their five kids. Over the years Tim has written for a number of publications such as WPCentral.com, MaximumPC, and InfoWorld. Tim's love of technology encompasses Windows Server, Windows Phone, scripting, web and graphic design, and gadgets of all shapes and sizes. Tim holds several industry certifications, including the MCSE on Windows Server 2003, the MCITP: Enterprise Administrator on Windows Server 2008, and a Security+ from CompTIA.